READER'S DIGEST

Complete Guide to Drawing & Painting

Reader's Digest

PUBLISHED BY THE READER'S DIGEST ASSOCIATION LIMITED
LONDON NEW YORK MONTREAL SYDNEY CAPE TOWN

A READER'S DIGEST BOOK

Published by The Reader's Digest Association Limited
11 Westferry Circus
Canary Wharf
London E14 4HE

www.readersdigest.co.uk

Front cover: artworks by (left) Penelope Anstice; (top right) Louise Hill;
(centre right) Susan Pontefract; (bottom right) Richard Smith
Back cover: artwork by Derek Daniels
Front and back cover photography: Eaglemoss/Nigel Robertson

ISBN 978 0 276 42689 6

This book was designed, edited and produced by Eaglemoss Publications Ltd,
based on the partwork *The Art of Drawing &Painting*

Printed and bound in China
Phoenix Offset

410-023 UP0000-2

Contents

Introduction

I'm a firm believer that anyone can learn to draw or paint. But you can't expect simply to pick up a pencil or paintbrush and start to draw like Leonardo da Vinci or paint like Van Gogh. All the great artists had to work at their craft, and you'll have to do the same.

The first step is to learn the fundamentals of drawing and painting. Just as you have to learn vocabulary, spelling, and grammar in order to speak or write a language, so too in art you have to learn to handle the tools of the trade and to develop certain skills in order to produce a good picture.

Learning to draw, getting perspective right, knowing how to mix colours, and much, much more – these things are the spelling and syntax of art. *Complete Guide to Drawing and Painting* sets out to show you all the basic skills and techniques you will need.

The book is divided into a number of chapters that deal with the important disciplines of art. We begin with drawing, which needs a good deal of practice – ideally every day! You'll also learn about colour and composition – these are important no matter which media you work in. Certain techniques, however, are specific to a particular medium, so drawing implements, watercolours, oils, acrylics, and soft pastels are all covered separately.

You'll learn new methods that you can use at once to improve your work, and discover shortcuts to accurate picture-making. Find out how to make objects appear to advance or recede, and learn new ways to add texture to your paintings – scratching into the paper, scraping paint off, or layering it on.

The techniques in this book are the artist's tools. You can use them in your own way, developing your own styles and systems of working. Remember, reading this book is only a starting point. With practice you'll master these techniques, unlock the creativity within you, and learn to express your ideas and feelings through your art. So pick up your materials and get going. Good luck, and above all, enjoy yourself!

Stan Smith

Stan Smith

CHAPTER ONE

LEARNING TO DRAW

LIGHT AND TONE

To start you off on the road to drawing three-dimensional forms convincingly, Stan Smith introduces you to light and tone.

▲ This special drawing course is devised by Stan Smith, an established artist with wide teaching experience.

His paintings are regularly exhibited throughout Europe, often as one-man shows.

I know it sounds perfectly obvious, but without light you can't see a thing. Think of someone going into a totally dark room. Naturally you blunder around, bumping into the furniture. But as soon as you turn on the light, you can see everything in detail: perhaps a pine chest of drawers, a round waste paper bin or a lumpy armchair. One glance gives you a vast amount of information about shapes, forms, textures and distances. What enables you to interpret all this information are the many shades of light and dark – the tones, in fact. In the real world there are scores of tones, from white at one extreme, through a large number of mid tones (which can be seen as a range of greys), to black at the other extreme. At first, it's difficult to see tone since colours, patterns, shadows, and different light sources confuse things. But if you screw up your eyes and concentrate, you'll find that the lights and darks are exaggerated and easier to identify. (It helps if you look at a black and white photograph, where all the information is expressed only in terms of tone.)

> **"** *Study your subject through half-closed eyes before starting to draw.* **"**

Set 1	Set 2

USING TONE FOR 3-D
You can see the dramatic effect tone has from these two sets of shapes. The first set looks flat. But as soon as they are shaded, you can see them as solid, three-dimensional forms.

◄ Learning to describe form by using lights and darks as well as this takes practice.

'CLASPED HANDS' BY IAN SIDAWAY

A tonal strip

The minimum number of tones you need to achieve a three-dimensional effect on paper is just three – white, black and mid grey. These make for a strongly contrasting image. Five tones give more subtle effects. And the more tones you build in (up to 9 or 10, say), the more three-dimensional it becomes.

By seeing – and then interpreting – the tones carefully you can begin to depict solid forms convincingly in your paintings and drawings.

To help you see how tone works, make a tonal strip like the one I've drawn here. Draw five squares on a sheet of white paper, then, using a soft 4B pencil, colour the last one black. Working back along the squares, shade each one a lighter shade of grey until you reach the final square – which should be left white. (You may find it a lot easier to put a mid grey in the centre, then work lighter and darker tones on each side.)

4HB 2HB HB H B 2B 3B 4B

▲ Before you start drawing, it helps to try out a few marks on a scrap of paper. Choose several different strengths of pencil – here I've picked a good range, from 4B (very soft) to 4HB (very hard). Draw a few lines using the pencil point and the side of the pencil; do the same with shading, pressing lightly and then more firmly.

I think you'll find it helpful to refer to this range of marks when you begin a picture.

2B

HB

H

▲ Smudging is a very useful little technique. Make some pencil marks, then soften and blend them by rubbing gently with your finger. This gets rid of hard lines and gives greater subtlety of tone and texture. Keep the scrap of paper handy in case you want to check some marks later on.

1

2

TRY THIS FOR TONE
Seeing tone clearly takes practice, so I find this little experiment helps. Put a white jug or cup in a darkened room, then light it from the side with a single light source – a desk lamp, for example (**1**). You can see that the jug has a very bright side nearest the lamp and a very dark side furthest from it. Notice too, in particular, how the light travels across the curving side of the jug, creating a gradual transition between the strongest lights and the darkest darks.

Now try the experiment again, this time folding a small piece of white card and standing it up so that one flat surface is at right angles to the light, with the angle of the fold facing you (**2**). Again, you can see one bright surface and one dark surface – but this time the transition between the light area and the dark area is abrupt, creating a crisp 'edge' along the fold. Look for these transitions in your subject while you are drawing.

Drawing in tone – bowl of eggs

This simple still life group of some eggs in a little pottery bowl helps you to see and draw tones (five have been used here). It also makes the most of the lovely range of greys you can get with just three different pencils – hard, soft and one in between.

Eggs are a good subject: they're small enough to put on a surface near your drawing where you can study them closely, and you can draw them almost life size. Their smooth surface and curv-

ing shape show how a range of lights and darks make things look three-dimensional.

Set up your group in good natural light – by a window for example, but not in direct sunlight. If you use artificial light, a single table lamp provides good areas of contrasted light and dark tones. But keep the main overhead light on as well or the bright light shining from your lamp will be too harsh and cast severe shadows. This makes it difficult to see the tonal gradations.

◀ **1** The colour photo shows that the sides of the eggs facing the main light source are light in tone while the sides facing away from the light are darker. (The black and white photo, shown below left, helps you see the main tones without the distraction of colour.)

It's best to work in natural daylight, but it will change while you work as clouds and sun alternate outside. Don't worry. Simply draw what you see and if the light changes, alter your drawing as needed.

Tip

Sit comfortably

Sit where you can see both the eggs and the paper without moving your head. You want your eyes to move easily between subject and drawing, checking one against the other. Spend more time looking at the subject than the drawing.

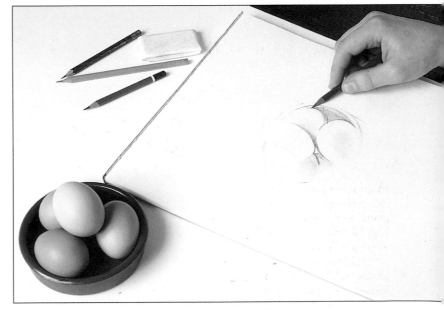

▶ **2** I worked directly into a pad which provided a firm surface, but you could fix your paper to a board with drawing pins or masking tape. Start near the middle of the sheet of paper.

Looking at the group, sketch in the eggs and bowl with the point of the H pencil. Don't press too hard – you only want a light mark. Let your eye travel around the subject, comparing shapes.

Screw up your eyes, look for the dark tones between the eggs and shade these in with the side of the HB pencil. For gently graduated tones, blend the pencil marks with your finger. Don't rub too hard. Refer to your tonal strip (previous page) to help you identify the five main tones.

◄ **3** Continue working in the same way, developing the entire surface of the drawing. Let your eyes skip across to the subject and back, all the time assessing the relative lightness or darkness of each area.

For this drawing, I chose just three pencils: an HB for the middle tones, an H which is much harder and gives a lighter, crisper mark; and a 4B which is softer and darker.

◄ **4** Put in the mid tones on the top surface of the eggs with the HB pencil, then smooth them down with your finger. Soften the middle tones towards the light areas and make them heavier towards the darker areas.

I used the paper itself to provide the bright white highlight areas on the rim of the dish and where the eggs catch the light. Develop the dish using a mid tone. Although the dish is darker in colour than the eggs, notice that it is not the darkest tone – you find that in step 2, between the eggs and outside at the base of the dish.

◄ **5** Continue to intensify the depth of tone in the base of the dish, using the soft 4B pencil (don't press too hard with this pencil or you'll get a line that's much too dark).

► **6** In my final drawing the graduated tones I've used create solid-looking eggs that sit convincingly in the bowl.

LOOKING AT LINE

Stan Smith demonstrates how you can use the freshness and directness of line only to describe form.

In the previous demonstration drawing, I used shaded tonal areas to describe form. You will see that patches of tone can create the illusion of a solid – in that particular case, a bowl of eggs. This time I'm going to show you a different technique – using line only.

Whether you are drawing with pencil, charcoal or ink, you can use line to capture not only light, tone and shadow but texture as well. This means that a convincing line drawing is usually more sophisticated than it looks. Don't be put off by this, though – line has a great range of beautiful qualities. And with a bit of practice you'll soon learn to harness them.

> *Line is so versatile – you can do a fine, tight, closely observed description or simply put a line around an idea – like a cartoonist.*

put your hand flat on a piece of paper and draw round it. But in order to make a drawing of a solid, you have to describe the contours of surfaces too. A good line drawing should lead the eye in and around the object. To do this you need to make the lines work really hard. An HB pencil can produce a great range of lines of different quality: rich, dense, shiny, black lines, delicate grey ones, thick lines, thin lines, elegant, flowing, rhythmic lines, and broken, stuttering ones. First I'll show you how to achieve some of these qualities and then I'll use some of them in a simple still life drawing.

The qualities of line

Think of line and you'll probably think of outline – the kind of result you get when you

▼ The artist has used a variety of lines in this simple ink drawing. Fairly thick, considered curves describe the outline of the plate in the front. Much lighter, quickly drawn straight lines stand as the prongs of the forks, while thick rhythmical lines capture the decorative edge of the napkin.

A little cross-hatching adds some light and shade, but the forms themselves are drawn in contour and outline.

'TABLE SETTING' BY JOHN CRAWFORD-FRASER, INK ON PAPER, 15 X 15CM

OUTLINES AND CONTOUR LINES

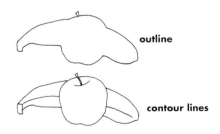

outline

contour lines

When you are drawing with line it's essential to understand the difference between outlines and contour lines. You can see the difference if you look at the two little drawings above. In the top one the apple and banana are drawn in outline only, giving a mere silhouette of the two objects, with no details at all. In the bottom one, contour lines describe outlines as well as the basic forms of the two objects – including the dimple and stalk in the top of the apple.

Irises in a Coca-Cola bottle

The quality of the line you produce depends very much on the support. A soft pencil on a heavily textured paper appears soft, whereas the same grade of pencil on smooth paper appears quite hard. Good quality cartridge paper is ideal for most drawing. If you want a slightly more textured surface, try working on to a piece of NOT watercolour paper.

The hardness of the pencil is an essential factor and you must never be afraid to change to a different grade during a drawing if it will help you. You can vary the tone of a line either by using a harder or softer pencil or by varying the pressure. So, for example, you might take an H or 2H and press very lightly to give a pale grey. More pressure might give you a line no darker than a mid grey. Whereas if you used a 3B and applied light pressure you'd start where you left off – with a mid grey – pressing harder to build up to a rich, dense black. In fact, an HB is often a good general-purpose grade to start with.

To some extent, the scale of the drawing should determine the drawing medium. The bigger the surface, the larger, bolder and darker your lines need to be. A surface bigger than about 51 x 76cm is starting to get too big for anything other than very soft pencil. A surface of 20.5 x 30.5cm or 20.5 x 38cm is manageable, giving you control with rather a wristy feel.

Commonsense should always prevail. Try to keep your drawing clean. If you are going to work over the whole of the drawing, be careful not to get graphite on the heel of your hand and then smear it over the surface you are working on. If you have to lean on your drawing, slip a piece of clean paper under your hand. When you've finished your drawing you should fix it or at least protect it by covering it with a piece of thin paper.

YOU WILL NEED

- ☐ A sheet of good quality A3 cartridge paper
- ☐ Two pencils – HB and 2B
- ☐ A craft knife to sharpen your pencils
- ☐ Putty rubber; fixative

Different qualities with an HB

1. A thin, continuous line of consistent tone made with a sharp point and an even pressure.

2. A line varying in thickness and intensity, made with a sharp point by changing the pressure.

3. A thick line varying in tone across its width, made with the side of the point.

4. A fluid line made by keeping the pencil flowing as smoothly as possible.

5. A discontinuous, stuttering line made up from short, quickly made marks.

6. A shaggy line made by drawing from the wrist and moving the pencil back and forth.

◄ **The set-up** So many everyday objects become enchanting when interpreted through the eyes of the artist. Here I've chosen a very simple motif to work from – two irises in a Coke bottle.

It's the combination of the natural and man-made that makes this subject interesting. The symmetry and brittleness of the glass bottle contrasts with the natural, living forms of the flower heads and stems.

Notice how the light plays on the bottle and how the glass modifies the shapes within.

▼**1** Starting with your HB pencil, simply draw the bottle. Look carefully at its circular cross-section. When seen in perspective this becomes oval and it's important to get these ovals right – particularly at the base and the neck. Notice how the fluid quality of the lines suits the smooth texture of the glass. Don't overdo the name on the bottle – just suggest the lettering, or else it will dominate the drawing.

◀**2** I've put part of the stalks in with a fairly blunt pencil using a confident, flowing line – stronger in tone than those of the bottle in order to give a sense of the colour and growth. By drawing away from the elipse you can get them shooting naturally from the neck.

Keep working over the whole of the drawing. At this stage I've left the stems outside the bottle and, using the same pencil, started to strengthen the stems inside – to give a sense of continuity.

▶**3** You can stay entirely with line if you wish, but here I used the tip of my finger to soften the pencil. The idea was to bring an overall tone to the body of the bottle. But don't obliterate the line entirely. Try to retain a sense of solidity at the same time as capturing the bottle's transparency.

A clean, dark fluid curve in the base, and shadows on the table help to make the bottle look as though it is resting on something.

Tip

Bread rubber
After carefully blending areas of tone with your finger tip, you can use a putty rubber to take out some of the smudging to give lighter tones and highlights. But if you haven't got a putty rubber, a piece of clean, white sliced bread kneaded into a little ball serves equally well.

▲**4** Now draw the flowerheads with the 2B pencil. Freer use of a soft, sharp pencil helps you keep a crisp, fresh feel. This is where you can really change the tone and thickness of a line so it appears to move in and out of the paper. Look at the curve on the left hand edge of the middle petal. The nearest part is stressed to bring it forward, while the 'back' is less emphatic.

▲**5** Remember that though the petals are curled flat surfaces they still have form. Try to capture this by using all the qualities of line at your disposal.

I've sharpened the pencil again so that I can get a really thin, concentrated line flowing from the point – almost like ink! Compare this with the much thicker but softer line in the petal above.

▲ **6** Use a kneaded putty rubber or bread to wipe out some of the rubbed areas of tone on the body of the bottle where the light is shining through. Here I am working into the rubbed tone with a kneaded rubber.

I've also rubbed out an area in the shadow on the table where the light manages to penetrate between the stems. Don't use the rubber as an eraser in the normal sense – to rectify mistakes. Try to stay with the marks you have made and modify them as you go along. This way you'll learn far quicker.

◄ **7** The bottle has an elegant, almost classical, shape and you can see these same curves in the stem of the left hand iris. A horizontal line helps to push the bottle forward – into space.

The finished image shows a wide range of marks made with both blunt and sharp pencils. It looks simple, but there is actually quite a lot going on when you look closely.

DRAWING FROM THE SHOULDER

Drawing is as much a physical as a mental activity. Here Stan Smith explains how to make your shoulder work for you.

I said on page 14 that the scale of your drawing should help you choose the medium you draw in. So if you are working on a surface larger than 51x 76cm, a soft medium – such as charcoal, or, at the very least, a 3B or a 4B pencil – would be a reasonable choice. Another factor allied to the

> *You don't get anything simpler than this – I'm sure it is the way the cave men drew. It's a good way of freeing yourself up.*

scale and the medium is the type of drawing movements you make.

In general, sweeping gestures from the shoulder allow you to make generous marks, well suited to large scale work. The more confined

▲ Work on an easel if you have one or simply tape a large sheet of paper to the wall. If you've chosen a small subject – such as an artichoke – I suggest you hold it at arm's length to get a good overview.

YOU WILL NEED

☐ An A2 sheet of good quality cartridge paper

☐ A large drawing board, easel or wall space

☐ Thick sticks of soft willow charcoal

☐ Bulldog clips, tape

☐ Putty rubber

☐ Fixative

◀ Adopt a stance rather like that of a darts player. With your feet planted firmly, use your whole arm to capture the rhythms in your subject. Remember to look for the light, tones and shadow.

movements of your wrist enable you to describe precise marks of the kind called for in detailed, small scale drawings. So, for example, you'd find it natural to draw on a sheet of A4 (210 x 297mm) paper using an HB pencil, ball point pen or dip pen, using mainly wrist and elbow movements. But you should feel equally at home working on a sheet of A2 (420 x 594mm) paper with a stick of soft, thick charcoal, Conté crayon or oil pastel using shoulder and elbow movements.

In fact the wrist, elbow and shoulder don't operate entirely independently, and any drawing, whatever its scale, requires some input from all three. But you can certainly put emphasis on drawing from either the shoulder or the wrist. As you'll see, the results are entirely different.

Here an artichoke makes an attractive subject, but you could choose any convenient object. If, like the artichoke, it is fairly small, you'll have to make a larger interpretation. (I've drawn the artichoke about five times life size so the scale is appropriate for drawing from the shoulder.)

As always, look carefully at your subject but don't fuss about detail. Explore and enjoy the range of movement your shoulder allows and use it to give a straightforward account of what you see.

SOLVE IT

Thick or thin?

Sweeping gestures made from the shoulder tend to put quite a bit of pressure on the charcoal. If you use a hard, thin stick it will probably break. So for working on this scale I recommend a soft, drenching black charcoal of a good thickness – at least 5mm diameter, say. This way you can even use a fairly longish stick if you wish – making full use of its length as an extension of your arm.

▶ This is the finished charcoal drawing (top). I've made use of vigorous downward movements of my whole arm to describe the artichoke's scales. A little smudging helps to convey its globular form. You can still maintain great sensitivity when working from the shoulder. Notice that where the light strikes – on the left – I've made the marks less dense, while on the right side they're richer.

A smaller, pencil drawing made within the compass of the wrist and elbow (inset) has a much tighter feel (bottom right).

LOOKING AT NEGATIVE SHAPES

Stan Smith explains what negative shapes are, why they're essential to composition and how you can use them to draw more accurately.

Spaces between the forms – the solid parts – of the subject of your drawing can create some very strong and interesting shapes. These are called 'negative shapes'. They are important because they contribute to the composition – playing just as great a role as the positives (the solids), in fact. And they enable you to check the accuracy of your drawing. Make the best use you can of negatives. When composing a still life, don't concentrate merely on the objects. Give due regard to the spaces between them. You can change the spaces by moving the objects away from one another, closer together or by turning them around. Don't forget that altering your viewpoint changes the shapes too. So a slow, observant stroll around your subject might reveal some attractive negatives

66 ***The positives make the negatives and the negatives make the positives.*** *99*

(useful for landscapes, where you can't move hills and trees).

Think negative to run a quick visual double-check. For example, imagine a drawing of three oranges trapping a triangular space between them. The oranges look fine, but what about the shape between? If it's too small, too large or the wrong shape, then one or more of the drawn oranges isn't quite right. A moment's careful study enables you to spot faults and correct them. If all the positives and negatives are right, then your drawing must be accurate.

DID YOU KNOW?

Tree shapes
Most trees are rich in negatives, their branches overlapping to create a wealth of shapes. The Dutch artist Piet Mondrian knew this and used the tree as a theme in his paintings. You can see his use of negative shapes in his expressionistic rendering of 'The red tree' (1908-10) and even more so in the more abstract 'Grey tree' and 'Apple tree in flower' (1912).

▶ Try to spot the negative shapes in this portrait (right). You might like to check them on the thumbnail sketch (above).

Negatives are a good guide in figure drawing. Shapes such as the division between the legs or, as here, those trapped in the crook of an elbow can help you get the limbs and posture right.

'MRS JASON HICKLIN' BY HENRY HAGGAR, CHARCOAL ON PAPER, 35 X 35CM

Bicycle bits

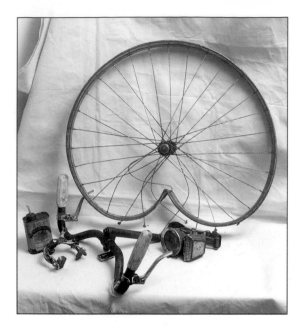

▶ **The set-up** Sometimes the old rather than the new provides the most interesting subject and often you don't have to look far to find it. The cobwebbed corner of an outhouse yielded these rusty cycle parts. (Notice that the broken wheel holds a very fine negative shape already.)

Arrange your group, paying careful attention to the shapes trapped between the objects. Walk around it, watching the shapes change as you go. Choose a viewpoint from which the negatives look strong and interesting in their own right. Shadows sometimes subdivide the negatives, so take those into account too.

▶ **1** Look at the set-up. The composition has two main components – the wheel and the cluster of items below and to the left. Draw the rim of the wheel with a generous sweep of the arm. Then, working loosely and lightly from the wrist, draw the cluster of objects.

Make sure everything fits on the paper. If it doesn't, scale down slightly – as I did. Check to see that the negatives trapped by your group and the edges of the paper work properly.

▲ **2** Once you are satisfied with your group and the shapes around it, start to consolidate things.

Look at the set-up and you'll notice that there aren't any really heavy masses. The slender forms are almost linear and divide the light background into abstract shapes.

Capture these with the careful use of line. Start by strengthening the hard rim of the wheel with a firm grey line. Try to retain the rhythm and symmetry of this elegant form by using the full sweep of your arm again.

◀ **3** Do the same for the handlebars, lamp, oil can and brake assembly in the foreground. Where forms have more mass, use the tip of your finger to smudge the line and give a range of greys. Leave untouched the very lightest areas – such as the the nearest brake lever and the rim around the face of the lamp.

Indicate just a few of the spokes. You can get a good equivalent to the straight, slender ones by turning the charcoal on its side and making a thin incisive line – as I'm doing here.

◄**4** By now, most of the negatives should be obvious: the one below the wheel but above the handlebars; the triangle trapped within the nearside curve of the handlebars; the shape between the nearest handle grip and its brake lever and the face of the lamp; that enclosed by the brake calipers; and the ones to the right of the oil can and under the handlebars. Then there are the larger spaces within the wheel and around the whole group.

▼**5** Your drawing isn't meant to be a technical one, so try to preserve the looseness as it develops, never completing one area before moving on to another.

You can see in the foreground here that although the drawing is still fairly loose, I've tried to convey a sense of texture – the ribbed handle grips as opposed to the smooth bars – and even a sense of colour by using lighter tones on the grips.

▼**6** The wheel serves as the focal point and carries connotations of motion and rhythm. Look at the wheel in the set-up and you'll see that some of the spokes are straight and orderly, while others flail from the crumpled rim. Try to capture this precisely in your drawing.

Before you draw the spokes, count them. This helps you space them correctly and, though you might not want an exact copy, it should prevent you from making the kind of blunder that shows five fingers and a thumb on one hand!

◀ **7** Here the shadows can work for or against you. In one respect they help by seating the objects firmly on the horizontal plane, but they can muddle the composition, bisecting some of the good negative spaces. If they are interfering in your drawing, try playing them down or, for the purpose of this exercise, leave them out entirely.

▼ **8** I completed the drawing using the side of the charcoal to skim some shadow inside the wheel.

The smoothness of the paper has helped me to keep a wide range of tones from the white of the paper itself, through greys to a rich black – something that's difficult if the paper is rough because the greys tend to jump too dark.

The negative shapes play a particularly important part in this spacious composition, but you'll benefit by thinking negative in every drawing or painting you do.

Tip

Oil slick

There's an easy way to get a good impression of the design on the oil can. Use the tip of your charcoal to touch in a brief outline of the design, then add a few scribbles to stand for any writing.

Soften the charcoal with the tip of your little finger. By rubbing it to the right tone you can even convey a sense of different colours on the can.

MAKING MEASURED DRAWINGS

The sight of an artist standing in front of his model, holding a pencil at arm's length and squinting at it might be a familiar one. But what's he supposed to be doing? Stan Smith tells you.

Your pencil makes a convenient instrument for taking precise measurements from your subject and transferring them to your paper. This method is particularly useful when drawing complex subjects – such as the rooftop scene I've chosen for the exercise – but you can use it for figure drawings and still life work too.

In this exercise, measuring helps in two ways. First, it prevents your eye from being deceived by the effect of perspective on scale. For example,

> *"This is a good way of getting absolute reassurance that the proportions in your drawing are correct."*

the tower on the horizon is taller than the chimney stack in the foreground. But on the two-dimensional surface of a photograph the height of the tower is less than the chimney stack. (You can check this with a ruler.) This should hold true for your drawing too, but it's just the sort of anomaly that's easily overlooked. Measuring can alert you to it.

Secondly, by taking a few preliminary measurements, you can pinpoint key features that'll keep your drawing on course as it develops. So, for example, you shouldn't find later on that you've room for only three rooftops where there ought to be four.

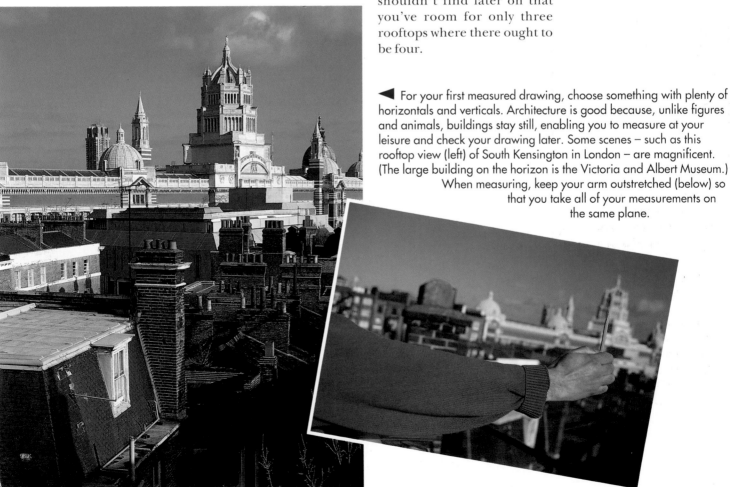

◄ For your first measured drawing, choose something with plenty of horizontals and verticals. Architecture is good because, unlike figures and animals, buildings stay still, enabling you to measure at your leisure and check your drawing later. Some scenes – such as this rooftop view (left) of South Kensington in London – are magnificent. (The large building on the horizon is the Victoria and Albert Museum.) When measuring, keep your arm outstretched (below) so that you take all of your measurements on the same plane.

YOU WILL NEED

☐ A new HB pencil

☐ A sheet of A3 cartridge paper

☐ Drawing board and pins or tape

☐ Coloured pencils

South Kensington rooftops

Try your hand at measuring horizontals and verticals. Distance yourself sufficiently from your subject so you can work on the received scale – that is to say, so you can put marks down directly without having to scale up or down to fit them on the paper. (Scale is something we'll look at later but at this stage it's a good idea to keep things as simple as possible.)

Where you need an angle – the slope of a roof, for example – pinpoint each end of the line by taking horizontal and vertical measurements and then join the points together (see Tip, page 26).

Taking measurements from your subject

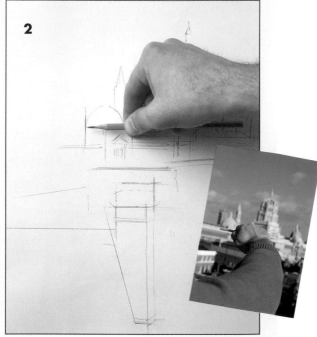

Look for a convenient dimension – one you can use more than once. I'm going to use the height of the chimney stack as my yardstick (**inset**). Hold your pencil at arm's length so it falls alongside the stack. Line up your pencil tip with the top and slide your thumbnail down your pencil until it coincides with the base. Keeping your nail in place, transfer this measurement to your drawing (**1**). Measure horizontally in the same way by turning your pencil through 90°. (**inset** and **2**).

Work across your drawing, repeating key measurements. Here (**3**) I'm laying the height of the stack on top of itself. This takes me almost to the top of the tower. I've used the width of the stack (**inset** and **4**) as a key dimension for the horizontals. (Notice that this is equal to the width of the dome. One-to-one relationships like these provide short-cuts to accuracy.)

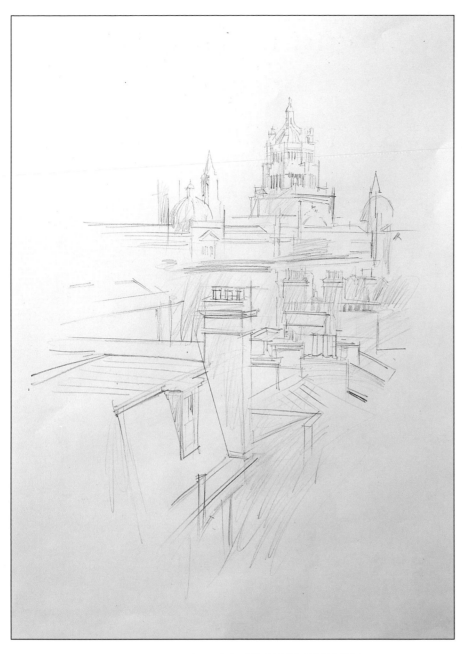

◀ **1** With the exception of eccentricities such as the leaning tower of Pisa and the slightly twisted spire on Chesterfield Cathedral, most buildings stand vertical – upright. Make sure the verticals in your drawing are vertical! If you think it'll help, use a ruler – it's quite acceptable as long as you remember you're making a creative interpretation and not an architect's mechanical drawing.

▲ **2** Once you are satisfied you've got the basic proportions right, you can develop your drawing with coloured pencils if you wish. But don't think of it as 'colouring in'. Redraw, measure and edit where necessary, playing down features of less importance.

  Here I'm mixing colour optically – scribbling with the pencil so that strokes of different colour lie beside one another.

◀ **3** The effect of aerial perspective and strong sunlight means the foreground is contrasty and warm in colour, while the background appears hazy and the colours cooler.

  The chimney stack is a warm red-brown, the shadow in the middleground a fairly warm purple, while the sky is a pale tone of cool blue, against which the white tower sings out. The shadow on the side of the tower is a stronger tone of the same blue as the sky.

Tip

Extending a line
Many of the pencil lines in my drawing stick out beyond the buildings. This is deliberate. By extending some of the lines in your drawing you'll find it's easier to pinpoint the ends of angled lines. In fact you might find you need to add verticals and horizontals that don't exist. (The verticals are known as 'plumblines'.) Both are useful aids to construction.

◄ **4** Here I'm putting a dense purple shadow in the foreground to encourage your eye to linger a while before moving on.

Pencil marks made in random directions promote a lively feel but if you want to describe a plane then let your marks conform to the direction of the plane. Notice how the ochre marks on the side of the chimney show that it's built up in layers and that the plane lies at right angles to the front of the stack.

▲ **5** Here I'm using the equivalent of a burnt umber to chisel out some recesses in the foreground. Had they been in the middleground or background then, due to the censoring effect of haze (which is particularly strong in a city), they probably wouldn't be significant and I'd have left them out. In the foreground, though, you expect accents and it's important not to disappoint.

◄ **6** You'll notice that I haven't drawn the whole scene. I've left out the area of deep shadow you can see on the right in the foreground of the opening photo. Instead, a smooth curve leads your eye up the right side of the drawing to the towers in the background.

If you've got the tones and colours right, then foreground, middleground and background should all stay put. In other words, the middleground shouldn't argue with the foreground.

DRAWING FROM THE WRIST

The saying goes that 'small is beautiful'. Here, Stan Smith finds a use for those left-over pencil stubs and shows you how to make an intimate study of a small natural subject.

I've mentioned the importance of matching your drawing movements to the medium you are using and to the scale at which you are working. On pages 17–18, I used large, sweeping gestures from the shoulder to make a bold charcoal drawing on a sheet of A2 paper. The treatment was sympathetic to the subject: a large bronze sculpture. This time I've chosen a small subject – an intimate group comprising two shells and a starfish – and I'm going to make a small drawing. Look for a similar subject so you can try this exercise for yourself.

Working full-size, your drawing should fit easily on a sheet of A3 paper (at a squeeze, it might even fit on a sheet of A4). For a drawing of this size, your range of drawing movement needs to be more confined. The answer lies in your wrist.

Movements made within the compass of your wrist are naturally small, which means that you can make small, controlled marks. While these might be too fussy and tentative for a large drawing, they're perfect for small, detailed studies. Subjects of natural history spring to mind – flowers, birds, skulls, rocks, fossils, shells and starfish, for example – but any small object of interest would lend itself to this kind of 'wristy' approach.

Choose a compatible medium. Pencil, dip pen and ink, ballpoint or fibre-tip are all well suited. But for this exercise I recommend pencil: not a new pencil, though, which might be rather too long and cumbersome in the hand, but a short one – a stub.

The advantage of a short pencil is that you can hold it so the point falls directly under your palm, and, in this way use the compass of your wrist to describe tight curves and circles. Give it a try. If you haven't got a pencil stub, cut a couple of inches off a new pencil, thus creating a second pencil at no extra cost!

> *If you've worked over all of your drawing, it should finish itself – often when you least expect it!*

These delightful studies of flowerheads display great sensitivity and a masterful handling of line and shading. Even on the smallest scale, it's important to try to get some rhythm into your drawing.

Wrist movements (combined with a bit of elbow) are perfectly suited to small, detailed studies like these. They afford just the right degree of freedom for describing small curves with fluidity. Look at the petals and leaves here – you can see the rhythms at work.

'STUDY OF SWEET VIOLETS' BY LEONARDO DA VINCI, INK ON PAPER, 183 X 203MM

Shells and starfish

▲ **The set-up** With lots of detail and texture to explore, this group – comprising the shell of a land snail (bottom left), starfish and sea shell – makes an excellent subject. In fact, any of these would have served on its own. The creased paper on which they rest catches the light, dividing the surface into good shapes.

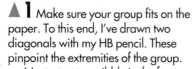

▲ **1** Make sure your group fits on the paper. To this end, I've drawn two diagonals with my HB pencil. These pinpoint the extremities of the group.

Next, start to scribble in the forms, drawing sensitively and looking for the negative shapes between them.

Tip

Stump-wise
Don't throw away those pencil stubs that seem to accumulate in your drawers and jam jars.

Save them for your next wrist drawing. As long as you don't overdo it, they can be useful for putting detail into large drawings too.

◄ **2** The spiral shell is from a Haitian snail, and its beautiful, curled form is perfect for a wrist drawing. I've moved my pencil aside to show you my marks, but if you keep your pencil under your palm, and locate it over the centre of the shell, you should be able to draw it using a single circular motion of your wrist. Make sure your spiral goes in the right direction. Like around 95% of all snails, this one has a right-hand spiral.

▶ **3** Use the full range of marks at your disposal, holding the pencil upright to make fine, tracing lines – such as those in the spiral – or, as I'm doing here, angling the tip slightly to give a thicker, softer line. Try blending some of these soft lines to make patches of subtle tone.

▲ 4 Although the lighting is fairly strong, the subject is so delicate and pale in colour that many of the tones in my drawing are light or mid greys. To get these, rub the shaded areas with the tip of your little finger, so the pencil strokes blend together. At this stage, it's best to understate things. Later, you can make your drawing more contrasty by using a softer pencil to introduce darker tones.

▲ 5 At this stage, everything is still in a state of flux. Notice that the snail's shell is tilted forward slightly, so you can see more of the back than the front. To capture this, I've drawn the spiral closer to the front of the shell. And by wrapping contours around the shell and blending them together, I've tried to describe its cylindrical form.

◀ 6 After some heavy blending using my thumb, I'm working back into the rubbed areas with an eraser. The idea is not to mimic the creases in the paper but to give an equivalent – a shorthand that captures the energy of these angular lines. You'll notice that I've wiped into the snail shell too, to give the highlight. Look carefully at your own subject and try to see where you can use an eraser.

▶ 7 Draw with your eyes **and** mind open. Ask yourself: why is this shaped the way it is? The conch shell once housed an animal. A predator, it lived in the Indian Ocean feeding on clams – into which it drilled holes. Its offensive appearance was meant to deter large crabs.

This hostile world is a far cry from the mantelpiece on which it ended up. Nevertheless, I'm using the 3B pencil to make my shell look spiky and fearsome!

SOLVE IT

Thick and thin

It can be very hard on your paper if you use extra pressure to make your pencil lines darker, and such lines are also hard to remove. Instead, keep a selection of different pencils handy. Start with an ordinary HB pencil, then emphasise dark areas with softer pencils, like the 3B used here. Likewise, mix sharp and blunt pencils to vary the thicknesses of the outlines. This also helps to give your picture more variety.

▶ **8** The snail shell is hard, but, unlike the conch, it's smooth and shiny. Instead of the abrupt marks you used for the conch, try to get a more fluid feel. I made the line at the front too emphatic, so I'm softening it with an eraser.

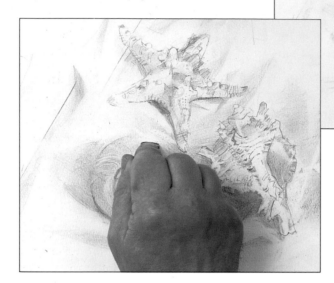

◀ **9** Look at the set-up and you'll see that the lightest tones on the shells are often close to those in the background; edges are lost and one thing appears to melt into another. Here I'm using the eraser to knock back the top of the snail shell so that it blends into the background.

▼ **10** Don't be afraid to use the great variety of marks that pencil affords. The starfish – an omnivorous scavenger from the ocean floor – has a hard, abrasive appearance. To this end, I've raised the four nodules in its centre with careful scribblings, and then added the abrupt marks, such as the zigzag on the right leg. In the centre of the snail shell you'll see a broken line that looks like stitching. These marks help to make the drawing lively.

INTRODUCING FIGURE DRAWING

The human figure provides the artist with what is perhaps the most exciting challenge of all. But where do you start? Stan Smith lends a guiding hand.

You might find the thought of drawing people rather daunting. This is not surprising. Whether clothed or not, the human form is complex. Furthermore, because we see people around us every day, we can usually tell when a figure is drawn badly – even if we can't say what's wrong with the drawing. However, I want to show you a way of conceptualising the figure that makes it as simple to draw as a bowl of eggs. The argument behind this approach is as follows.

You want to create the illusion of a solid figure in space. You know how to use light, tone, reflected light and shadow to do this for simple

geometric forms – such as cylinders. So, if you can reduce the figure to simple geometric equivalents, then, by observation, and armed with a little knowledge of proportion, you should be able to draw a solid figure.

You'll see from my drawings that the figure does indeed reduce to a series of interrelating cubes, spheres, cylinders and cones. Mannequins like these can help you to understand and draw human figures. You can use them to resolve problems associated with a particular pose before you start a more representational drawing, or use them in their own right as the basis for a drawing. With a solid underlying structure in place, you can flesh out your mannequin, into a nude, or, by wrapping a costume around the forms, make a clothed figure.

�◄ ▲ The idea of reducing the figure to geometric forms is not a new one. As early as the 16th century, the German artist Albrecht Dürer was experimenting with drawing the figure (left) and features of the head (above) as a series of cubes in his 'stereometric' man.

FIGURE STUDIES BY ALBRECHT DÜRER, INK ON PAPER

Constructing the figure

In **1** you can see how, in general, the neck, torso, pelvic region, arms and legs reduce to tubes. The pelvis tilts forward. The head sits on a column – a cylinder – and this also tilts forward so the forehead and chin protrude. The head is heavy, so the neck has to be thick enough to support it – though not usually a great bull neck.

In **2** differences emphasise the forms. The torso is a tube – flattened slightly at the top to take the neck and narrowing towards the waist. The pelvis is still a tube but it spreads to take the joints of the thighs. Remember that the body is symmetrical about the central division (drawn down the middle of the trunk). In **3** you can see that the arms hang so that the tips of the fingers come about halfway down the thighs. (The hands, fingers, feet and toes can be reduced to

▼ You can achieve a good equivalent to the figure using basic geometric forms (1 and 2, below). In Western art it's conventional for the light to come from above and from one direction. Here (2) I've drawn the figure as though there were a single light source above and to the left.

1

2

geometric equivalents in the same way as the major parts of the body. We'll study them in detail later.)

The figure in **4** is standing in the classic three-quarters pose – turned slightly from the profile towards the observer. Notice how the far half – beyond the central division – appears smaller than the front half when seen in perspective.

It's easiest to start with static figures. But geometrical equivalents are very useful for summarising figures in motion (**5**).

▶ Correct proportions are essential to good figure drawing. If you make the arms too short, for example, the figure doesn't look convincing. If you make them too long they become gorilla-like.

Theoretical knowledge can help but there's no substitute for observation. You can get an idea of where an elbow comes in relation to the whole arm, say, by running a check on yourself in the mirror.

3

◀ The figure is symmetrical about the central division. Seen in perspective, three-quarters on, the far half appears smaller. The raised arm appears to travel into the space behind the figure. This is again achieved by making the cylinders conform to the rules of perspective. To this end the farther arm is actually made shorter than the nearer arm (it is foreshortened), although you read it as being the same length.

The fingers are tubes radiating from the flattened box of the palm. The thumb works in opposition to the fingers so the hand can grip. The feet can be thought of as arched platforms. They're quite small but, because there are two of them and they can be positioned separately, the body's weight can be distributed in a variety of ways.

4

5

▲ This figure is seen in motion – as if it were high-stepping or kicking a ball. Notice how the limbs tend to move in opposition to one another for balance – the right leg and left arm, for example. The limbs are able to move because of the skeleton's joints, the contraction of the muscles providing the force.

Knowledge of the skeleton and its musculature gives a deeper understanding of the human form but is best taken on board as and when you need it.

▲ The nose is the most prominent feature. Think of it as constructed from a cylinder penetrating a sphere – at the end – with quarter spheres attaching on each side for the nostrils.

► The aim of constructing the figure from geometric forms is to make it appear three-dimensional. So always think of the head as a solid object in space.

Constructing a head and features

At this stage, when it comes to drawing the head, think not of a person's face and its expressions – smiling, frowning, laughing, crying, for example – but of a solid mass in space. This way you should avoid falling into the trap of drawing a superficial mask with added hair. (We'll look at expressions and likenesses later.) Having said this, always have a go at drawing the features – don't leave a blank mask.

Notice that, like the body, the features are dispersed evenly about a central division. The head is symmetrical – and the distance between the eyes is about the width of an eye. Studying heads in photographs – newspapers and magazines, for example – or your own in the mirror, can be very helpful.

► Of course, the features don't sit on the surface like those of a cartoon character. They are integrated into the surface – as though they had been chiselled out of a solid block of wood.

▼ The cranium is a spherical structure that protects the brain and forms a large part of the total mass. The features are dispersed symmetrically about a central division – just as the limbs are.

▼ The rules of perspective apply to the features in just the same way as they do to the body. The far half appears smaller and the distance between the eyes – of one eye's width – is foreshortened.

▼ Light coming from above forms pools of shadow in the eye sockets, and under the nose, upper lip, lower lip and chin. They form a kind of code for a face which is instantly recognisable.

PLUMBLINES AND HORIZONTALS

Stan Smith dips into the toy chest and comes up with another method for accurate drawing. Here he explains how to draw as if you were looking through an imaginary grid.

'BALLET DANCER IN POSITION' BY EDGAR DEGAS, 1872, SOFT BLACK GRAPHITE WITH BLACK CRAYON AND WHITE CHALK ON PINK PAPER, SQUARED, 410 X 284MM (COURTESY OF THE FOGG ART MUSEUM, HARVARD UNIVERSITY, BEQUEST OF META AND PAUL J. SACHS)

One useful aid to accuracy is to draw as if you were looking through a sheet of glass with a squared grid on it. This helps you notice vertical and horizontal lines and relationships. For example, say you are looking at a house from a fixed viewpoint. The corners of the building and the sides of the windows are vertical. The ridge of the roof and the windowsills are horizontal. All these lines might appear in your finished drawing.

However, if you were looking through a grid you'd notice other things. You'd see that a vertical through the chimney pot coincides

> ❝ *Imagine you are looking through a sheet of glass with a grid on it.* ❞

with the plant pot on the lawn and that a horizontal through the plant pot also travels through the garden gnome. You'd see that if you extended the vertical edge of the window, it would pass through the milk bottle on the doorstep and that the broken guttering is hanging at an angle of precisely 45°. You might even notice that the house is exactly five front doors high. In other words, imaginary as they are, these verticals and horizontals help you to relate one feature to another. With practice you'll be able to visualise lines like these, pick out the significant ones and use them as construction aids in your own drawings.

▶ This drawing has probably been 'squared up' prior to making a painting – a procedure we'll look at later – but you can see just how certain features coincide. A vertical through the dancer's left shoulder falls plumb through her left elbow and hand and down the sole of her right foot. Her hands are positioned so that a string held between her fingertips would be perfectly horizontal.

The toy chest

▲ **The set-up** Choose a subject with some straight lines and regular curves. This makes the job of recording edges, pinpointing intersections and estimating angles far easier. These toys comprise mostly geometric forms and they're more suitable for this exercise than, say, a bunch of flowers. I made a quick drawing on some graph paper. You can think of the squares as being like an imaginary grid. Look along the lines and notice which features coincide. (Try the vertical through the drum.)

◄ **1** Your starting point depends on your subject and viewpoint. But in general look for one helpful vertical and one horizontal. I dropped a plumbline from the top right corner of the blackboard down to the tip of the foremost teddy's right ear. I've positioned it right of centre on my paper, so the drawing should fit. But just to make sure, I used my pencil to measure horizontally (see page 24) from the vertical to the outer rim of the bucket at the extreme left.

► **2** To get the angle of the left side of the blackboard, draw in the vertical first. Look at the set-up and you'll see that a plumbline dropped from the top left corner of the board hangs through the left side of the drum. The leg of the board cuts the drum just right of centre. I know where the top of the board comes because I've already measured it. So it's an easy matter to join up the two points.

▲ **3** Look for coincidences – where the length of one object or gap is equal to the length of another, or twice its length or half its height, say. Relationships like these provide short cuts to accuracy. Here the height of the front of the chest is roughly equal to the height of the drum.

▲ **4** Often shadows are as important as the objects that cast them. For example, the shadow behind the drum runs across the floor and up the side of the chest. It describes these surfaces and links them together. Other shadows help to create the atmosphere of an attic corner.

▲ **5** The little triangular gap, bounded by the drum, chest and shadow of the leg of the board, serves to anchor my viewpoint. Negative shapes like this should remain constant as you draw. If they appear to have changed, your head isn't in the same position as it was when you started.

Tip

Deconstruction
It might take a few goes to wrestle a line into place. Once you've succeeded, don't rub out the 'wrong' ones straight away – they remind you of

the route you've taken. If you remove them too soon you might lose your way. In fact, a few construction lines in the finished drawing can often add to the effect.

▲ **6** I'm rubbing back into the areas where I had outlined and shaded the shadows, using my fingertip to make soft, uniform greys. This helps to kick up the contrasts and make the whole thing look more solid. It's a good idea to clean up your drawing first, though.

▲ **7** After rubbing the blackboard to make a soft grey, I tried to indicate the house by drawing into it with a putty rubber. The rubber proved too clumsy so I decided to leave the board blank, content to use a dark tone to convey an impression of its colour.

▶ **8** I'd usually recommend giving foreground objects attention early on. But there are exceptions. Here the building bricks are much simpler than the toy chest. So it makes sense to get the chest right and then add the bricks. I've positioned them by dropping plumblines from the central group (inset). As a result of perspective, the bricks right in the foreground appear larger than the one close to the chest. Notice how I've taken care to make the bricks' shadows consistent with those in the rest of the group.

▶ **9** If you've used your vertical and horizontal guidelines to good effect, and drawn and measured accurately, then all the objects should fall into place. Here the toys fit comfortably into the chest without being cramped or appearing too isolated. The building bricks, drum, bucket and chest appear to sit on the same plane. A grid dropped over my drawing (below) shows that it's pretty close to my original sketch.

CHECKS FOR ACCURACY

A place for everything and everything in its place – Stan Smith pulls out all the stops to help you draw more accurately.

Whether you are making an objective architectural study, a factual account of a court-room scene or trying to draw a freehand circle for an abstract composition, your work will benefit from accurate and sensible drawing. Here I recap on the methods I've mentioned so far and suggest some new ones.

As a general guide, concentrate on proportions and spatial relations early in a drawing. You can address such

> **66** *If whatever you are drawing has a function, bear this in mind.* **99**

things as detail, colour and texture later but no amount of cosmetic fudging compensates for poorly assessed masses and spaces.

Draw logically – if you are drawing a cheese grater, for example, make the grater in your picture look as though it would cut cheese. In other words, if whatever you are drawing has a function, bear this in mind.

▶ Use tick marks to position key features. Don't worry if they show at the end – construction marks tell you something about how a picture was made. Here, red and black ticks are an integral part of this artist's painting.

'ORANGE TREE 1' BY WILLIAM COLDSTREAM, OIL ON CANVAS, 914 X 711MM, COURTESY OF THE TATE GALLERY, LONDON

Use mechanical drawing aids such as rulers and set-squares if you really need to but remember that in themselves they do not guarantee accuracy.

In any case, technical skill is no substitute for vision and originality. If accuracy is all you are after, you might be better off with a photograph. Ask yourself just how accurate you need to be and set your limits within the scope of what you are trying to achieve.

Nine checks

When making any objective drawing use measurements, horizontal and vertical (plumb) lines, negative shapes, logic, space and time to help you.

Measured drawing (see pages 23–26) is a good method for keeping your drawing on track. Use a pencil held at *arm's length* to take measurements and transfer these to your paper. Look for a convenient unit of measurement. For example, if you are making a figure drawing, the length of the head – measured from the crown to the chin – would be a better choice than a finger (too small) or leg (too large). The length of the arm might be three and a half heads, say. Always take your measurements from precisely the same spot.

Horizontal and vertical (plumb) lines (see pages 35–38) drawn through and beyond key features help you to relate these features precisely. To draw a line at an angle, pin-point both ends using horizontals and verticals and

◢▶ To take a measurement, hold your pencil against the feature (here the chimney stack). Then slide your thumb along the pencil to record it. Transfer this measurement to your drawing (right). Here the height of the stack serves as a vertical unit of measurement for other parts of the roofscape.

▲ The width of the stack (above left) serves as a useful horizontal unit – the width of the stack and diameter of the small dome are equal (above right). Measuring helps prevent your eye from being deceived by changes in scale due to perspective. For example, the Victoria & Albert Museum is monumental, the chimney stack comparatively small. The Museum's large tower appears only slightly larger than the height of the chimney stack in the foreground – as it should.

EXACT NEGATIVES

Not only do the negative shapes between objects serve an important role in composition, they're a good guide to accuracy too.

Look at the little shape between the lower eggs here. If I make it too small, too large or the wrong shape in my drawing, then I know that I've got one or more of the eggs wrong. Similarly, the shape between the eggs and the side of the bowl helps me to draw the ellipse accurately.

then join the points together. It's a method that works in tandem with measured drawing.

Negative spaces (see pages 19–22) serve as a means to double-check the positive shapes in a drawing. If the negatives aren't right then neither are the positives!

Turn your drawing on its head to get a new viewpoint. This helps you to spot faults that your eye has become accustomed to. Don't limit yourself by merely looking – you can achieve interesting results by actually drawing with your paper upside down!

Reverse the image by viewing it through the paper to spot faults. This method is particularly useful for drawing symmetrical shapes – such as an ellipse at the top of a jar. By reversing it, any errors suddenly appear in a direction opposite to that to which you have become accustomed – so

◀ These Venetian masks make an intriguing and dramatic subject. Even though they are masks rather than real faces, it's still important to draw them carefully, observing the rules of perspective. Although I ended up using very wet paint extremely loosely to make a colourful picture, I underpinned it with a pretty steady charcoal drawing.

▲ A plumbline dropped from the centre of the beak of the mask in the centre falls down the left side of the oval-faced mask below. A horizontal line drawn from the bottom of the eye of the centre mask will cut across the tip of the nose of the mask to its right. These coincidences helped me to position the masks in correct relation to one another.

A LOGICAL CONSTRUCTION

Whether you are drawing a motorbike or a figure, you should be at least aware of what's going on under 'the skin'. This doesn't mean it's necessary to train as an engineer to make a good drawing of a bike or as a surgeon to draw a good figure, but it does mean you should draw sensibly, putting parts in the correct relationship to each other – making the bike look rideable and the figure solid and capable of supporting its own weight.

the fault should consequently seem to jump out and hit you!

A mirror image produces a similar result. Prop your drawing in a corner of the room, walk to the other side and view it through a small mirror. Apart from spotting faults (verticals not being quite upright, for example) – you should get a fresh and unbiased impression of your composition.

Let logic be your ally and, where necessary, count the features in your subject – the number of chimney pots, windows or columns in a building, say, or the number of supports holding up a bridge. Certainly, you should always avoid the sort of mistake that puts five fingers and a thumb on a hand!

Stand back from your drawing and view it from a distance from time to time – it's surprising how obvious faults become when you do this.

Return to your drawing after an hour and you can often see precisely what's wrong with it and put it right immediately.

TAKE A FRESH LOOK

Symmetrical curved figures such as circles and ellipses can be tricky. You might not even notice there's anything wrong. What's required is a fresh look. Take the cylinder here, for example.

Turn the drawing upside down and you see that the ellipse at the bottom (was the top) isn't symmetrical and that the sides of the cylinder are skewed to the right and do not lie parallel.

Looking through the paper gives you another perspective. Now the whole figure skews over to the left. If you can recognise your mistakes then you're halfway to putting them right.

▼ If you are working on an opaque painting or making a faint drawing on a thick sheet of paper, you won't be able to see your image through the support. In this case, simply use a mirror to view it in reverse.

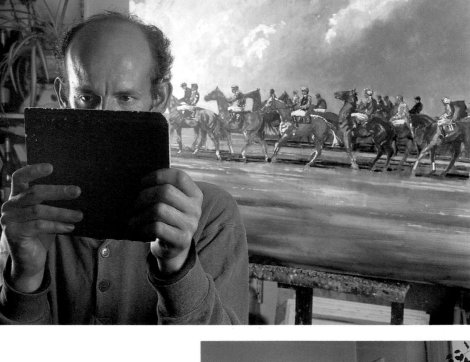

▶ A mirror image gives you an entirely new look at your picture. Not only does it allow you to spot that the verticals (say) aren't upright but it presents the composition in a fresh light and, in the case of a good self-portrait, enables you to see yourself as other people see you! Try propping your drawing up in one corner of the room and looking at its reflection in another.

CHAPTER TWO

UNDERSTANDING
COLOUR

INTRODUCING COLOUR

Every painting has colour as one of its main ingredients and the challenge for any artist is how to handle it successfully.

We all have a colour sense which is uniquely our own and is reflected by the colours in our home, the colours we like to wear, and so on.

These subjective likes and dislikes trigger an immediate response in you when you look at the colours in a painting, and of course when you choose your own colour schemes.

Composing with colour

Everything has a colour – even if it is only black or white – and the challenge for all artists is how best to interpret the colours around them with the paints on their palette.

Colour is an important part of any composition. This is not just because of the emotional qualities of colour – it is also because of the powerful physical effect colours can have. Composing successfully with colour requires a good grasp of why – and how – colours can affect one another.

Colours are often described as being either 'warm' or 'cool'. The warms are yellow, red and orange while the cools are blue, violet and green. (Remember that the terms 'warm' and 'cool' are relative – there are warm blues and

cool reds.) The idea of colour temperature is based on an emotional response rather than a physical reality, but is invaluable to the artist. Warm colours appear to advance towards the viewer while cool colours recede. You can exploit this – and create an illusion of space in a picture – by putting cool colours in the background and warm ones in the foreground.

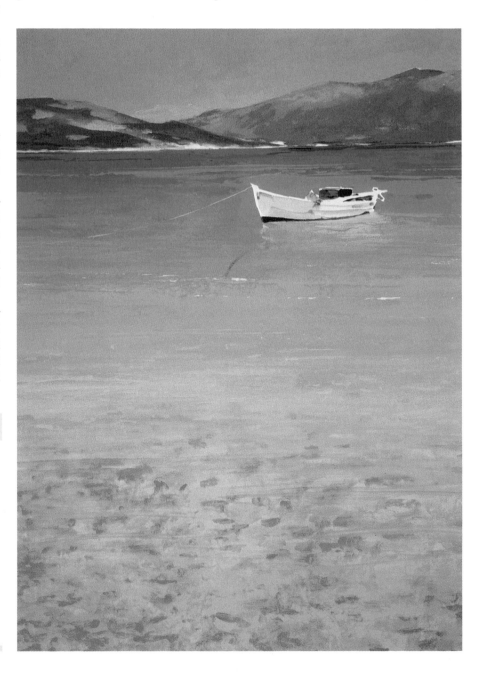

▼Masterly use of warm and cool colours is the key to the sense of depth in this painting.

'CLEAR WATER – GREECE' BY DONALD HAMILTON FRASER RA. OIL ON PAPER, 21 X 15IN

The language of colour

Every colour has three qualities: hue, tone and intensity, and the everyday word 'colour' combines these three qualities.

Hue is a colour's name – red, yellow or blue, for example. A colour's lightness or darkness is referred to as **tone**. Adding black to a hue makes it change gradually towards dark; adding white changes it gradually towards light.

The gradations towards dark are called **shades**, the gradations to light are called **tints**. Both shades and tints describe tone.

Intensity refers to the brightness or brilliance of a colour. A hue of strong intensity seems vivid, while a hue of low intensity appears dull. Dull, in this sense, doesn't mean dreary – it is simply the opposite of bright.

Note

Later chapters look in detail at the different ways of using colour – composing with colour, colourmixing, and exploiting its qualities to get the atmosphere you want. There will also be more details on the colour wheel and how the position of individual segments indicate the way those colours interact.

The colour wheel

One of the most useful devices for understanding colour is the colour wheel – a circular diagram designed to show not only how colours can be mixed to create others but also how they are related to each other.

The three key colours on the wheel are the **primaries**: red, yellow and blue. These are important because they are 'pure' colours. This means that they cannot be mixed from any other colour combination.

Between the primaries on the wheel, you find orange, green and violet. These are called the **secondaries** because each one is made by mixing two primaries. Red and yellow produce orange; yellow and blue give green; red and blue create violet. By mixing any primary with an equal amount of the secondary next to it, you create another group – the **tertiaries**. Blue

and green, for example, make blue-green.

Technically it is perfectly possible to mix an infinite range of colours from the three, pure primaries by blending them in varying amounts. But this isn't really practical for artists because it takes far too much time.

▼ This basic colour wheel shows the primary and secondary colours. Primary red, yellow and blue are separated from one another by the secondaries – orange, green and violet. The colours in one half of the wheel – red, orange and yellow – are 'warm'. 'Cool' green, blue and violet make up the other half.

▲ In this detail from the previous page, the tiny touches of almost pure red, blue and yellow – the three primaries – instantly draw your eye. In the same way, the yellow hull (left) carries your eye into the heart of the picture.

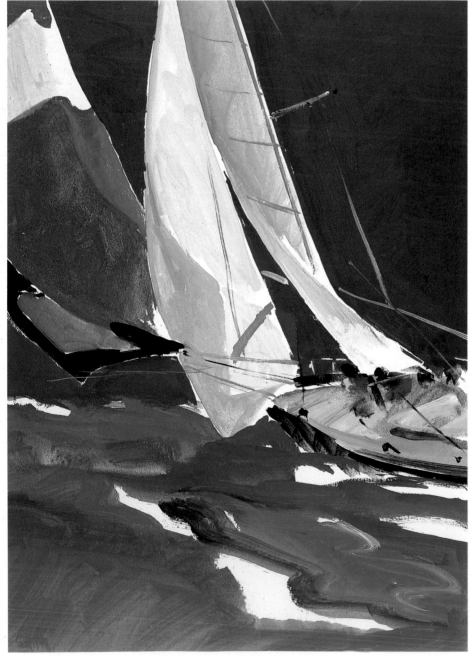

◄ Action and excitement explode from this painting. The vibrant colours in the top half of the picture produce great energy and tension – enhanced by the surprising crimson of the sky.

'SPINNAKER' BY DONALD HAMILTON FRASER RA. OIL ON PAPER, 19 X 14IN

COMPLEMENTARY PAIRS

You rarely see colours in isolation in a painting. The important thing is how they interact. Some have such a close relationship they can be grouped together – in complementary pairs.

▼ Large flat areas of complementary violet and yellow, and smaller areas of red and green, give this painting tremendous visual excitement.

'VAHINE NO TE VI' BY PAUL GAUGUIN, OIL ON CANVAS, 70 X 45CM

Complementary colours are pairs of colours linked in a fundamental way. Laid side by side a pair of complementaries has the most powerful and intense effect on each other, the one heightening and intensifying the other. Reds look redder – they positively sizzle – placed next to their complement green, and blue seems more vivid and vibrant with orange nearby. Using such pairs next to each other can inject great zest and vitality to a painting.

The term 'complementary' comes from what happens when you add together any such pair of colours. They result in what is called a complement – meaning, in this sense, something complete. In theory, what they produce is black – but in practice, because no colour is ever absolutely pure, it's actually more like grey or brown. When you come to mix

OPPOSITES ATTRACT

You can tell at a glance which colours are complementary by taking a look at the basic six-segment colour wheel (left). Here you'll find them arranged directly opposite each other. This shows you that red is the complement of green, yellow is the complement of violet, and blue that of orange.

The colour wheel is made up of the three primary colours (red, yellow and blue), with the three secondaries alternating in between. The primaries are the most important colours for the artist. In theory, you can mix any colour from them – the three secondaries, for instance. These are made by mixing two primaries together: orange is made from equal quantities of red and yellow; green is mixed from yellow and blue; and violet is a combination of blue and red.

A quick way to remember this colour wheel sequence is to think of a rainbow and recall the saying: **R**ichard **O**f **Y**ork **G**ave **B**attle **I**n **V**ain. Knock out the 'In' and you have clockwise – **R**ed, **O**range, **Y**ellow, **G**reen, **B**lue, and **V**iolet.

SEE FOR YOURSELF – THE AFTER-IMAGE EFFECT

You can take advantage of the way the human eye works to see the complementaries of the four colours shown here.

Stare fixedly for about a minute at the dot in the centre of the coloured squares above. Then switch your gaze to the dot in the grey square below. In each quarter you'll see the complementary of the colour in the corresponding section of the first square. In place of the red in the top right hand square, for instance, there'll be green, then clockwise you'll see orange, red and blue.

This is called *successive* contrast – *after* looking at the original colours for a while, your eye automatically sees their complementaries.

complementary pairs in varying proportions you can produce a marvellous range of neutral colours which give depth, and subtlety to your painting.

Learn a few simple rules on the way complementaries interact and you are equipped to make maximum use of colour in your own work – and to see how artists past and present handle it in their individual ways.

▶ Here, placing the red hat in a background of complementary green instantly draws the viewer's attention – it's the focal point of this painting.

'STILL LIFE, WOODEN TOY' BY DONALD HAMILTON FRASER RA, OIL ON CANVAS, 28 X 36IN

HOW PRIMARIES AND SECONDARIES COMPLEMENT EACH OTHER

The relationship between primaries, secondaries and complementaries is best shown by the double colour wheel below. Here the primaries are in the central wheel, and the secondaries in the outer one. Notice that the complementaries are still opposite each other.

What this double wheel also shows you is that the complementary of a primary is a secondary made up from the other two primaries. For example, the complementary of red (a primary) is green (a secondary mixed from the other primaries yellow and blue).

Looking at it the other way round: the complementary of a secondary is the primary which isn't included in its mixture. So the secondary orange, for instance, which is made up of the primaries red and yellow, is the complementary of the remaining primary blue.

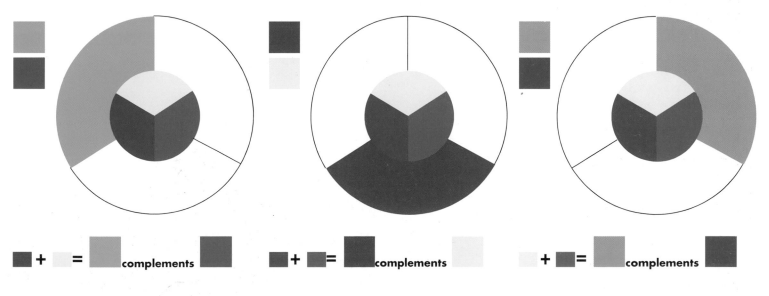

complements

complements

complements

**give a red
apple a green
shadow**

Putting theory into practice

With the theory of complementary colours securely under
your belt, you can now look at one of its many uses.

Shadows are all too often treated as unimportant areas
of a picture, just needing to be covered with the same grey
paint all over. No wonder they can turn out looking flat
and dull. To produce lively shadows, the rules are simple.
Paint them the complementary colour of the object. So,
for an orange, paint a blue shadow; for a red apple, a green
shadow; and for a banana, a violet one. (You don't have to
pick the brightest colours for this – muted ones work
perfectly well.)

**paint a blue shadow
for an orange**

**do the banana's
shadow in violet**

▶ Take a leaf out of this
artist's copybook when
composing a still life. Set
against the blue background
the orange positively vibrates.

'ORANGE AND BLUE STILL LIFE' BY CAROLINE
MILLS, WATERCOLOUR ON 300LB
BOCKINGFORD PAPER, 76 X 56CM

USING COMPLEMENTARIES

As you have already seen, complementary colours are very closely linked. But their powerful influence on each other isn't always obvious. Side by side they enhance each other, but when mixed together they produce muted, subtle effects.

Love it or loathe it, the effect of the blue and orange in the picture on the right is certainly eyecatching. And no wonder – when the artist, Ernst Ludwig Kirchner, chose to put this complementary pair next to each other he was using the maximum colour contrast available to any artist. This contrast is so effective because of a process known as simultaneous contrast, which is all to do with the way the human eye works.

When you look at a colour your eye actually sees its complementary as a 'shadow' right next to it – although you're not aware of this. So when you look at blue you're also seeing orange. What happens when that complementary is really there (as in the Kirchner painting) is that both colours look brighter and more intense: effectively you're seeing two layers – the paint itself and, on top of that, the shadow from its complementary next door. You can prove this for yourself by doing the test with the blue squares below.

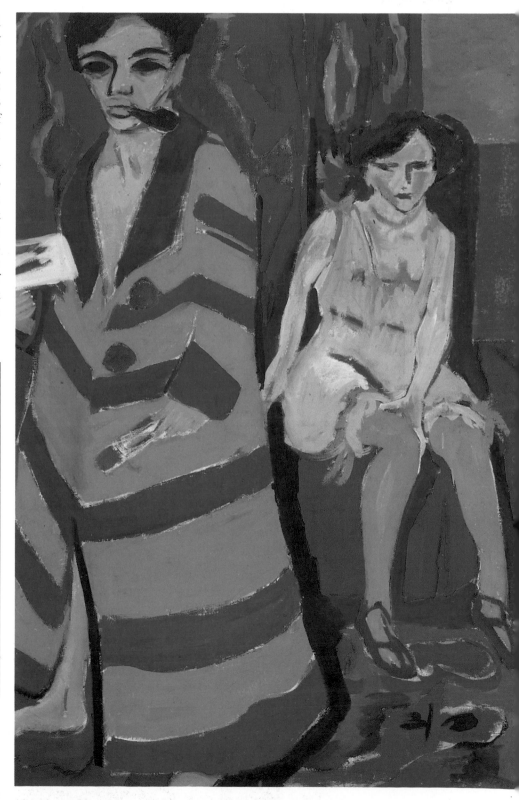

▼ Sizzling complementary relationships are exploited throughout this painting, especially in the dressing gown. But notice too how red is set off by green.

'SELF-PORTRAIT WITH MODEL' BY ERNST LUDWIG KIRCHNER, C1913, OIL ON CANVAS, 59 X 39⅜IN, KUNSTHALLE, HAMBURG

SEEING TWO BLUES?

Look carefully at the two blue squares in the centre – are they or aren't they the same colour?

They are in fact identical, but the one on the left looks bluer because it's surrounded by orange, its complementary – the two colours influence each other. As you look at the blue square on the left, you take in the orange next to it. Because of the way your eye works, you also see a 'shadow' of complementary blue all around the orange, which intensifies the blue. This doesn't occur with the other square since violet and blue aren't complementary.

Putting theory into practice

You can make full use of simultaneous contrast to add zest to your painting. Introduce touches of red or reddish brown into areas of green foliage or grass and you make them look more lively. Place a pair of complementaries strategically and you can draw the eye to a focal point. And if you dab a single touch of complementary red in a field of green it sings out.

The other side of the coin

Simultaneous contrast is not the only influence complementary pairs have on each other. Mix them together and they have quite a different effect – they neutralise each other, producing a whole range of greys. These are no ordinary greys, however – muted and subtle, they're more interesting and useful than the rather steely greys derived from black and white.

Take complementary red and green, for example. By mixing these in varying quantities you achieve dirty red and greyish green, earthy colours which resemble sienna and ochre. Add white to each of the mixtures, and you create a series of beautiful, delicately coloured greys.

These neutral greys are extremely effective and a delight to use, providing a marvellous foil for brighter, more vibrant colours. They have an inherent harmony and are never strident.

Putting theory into practice – again

A simple rule to draw from all this is that when a colour looks too dominant in your painting, you can knock it back by adding a little of its complementary. So you can knock back a glaring red with green.

What's more, with muted and earth colours you can take every bit as much advantage of the complementary influences. Try pairing a red ochre with a cerulean blue (which is greenish) for instance, or a

▲ This picture is a symphony of complementary contrasts. Patches of reddish brown in the grass (enlarged in inset) make the grass look greener and livelier. And the cool blue of the sky and the warm ochre of the grass reflect in the woman's frock.

'WOMAN WITH PARASOL, TURNED TO THE LEFT' BY CLAUDE MONET, 1886, OIL ON CANVAS, MUSÉE D'ORSAY, PARIS

AMAZING GREYS

ultramarine

cadmium orange

Winsor red

viridian

Winsor violet

cadmium yellow deep

ivory black

Chinese white

Payne's gray

Mix complementary pairs together and you produce wonderful neutral greys, more subtle than the rather steely versions made from mixing black with white or those that come ready mixed in pans or tubes.

▼ No paintbox gives you the luscious palette of pearly neutrals seen in this picture – they are achieved by mixing. What's more, some of the loveliest neutrals are made from complementary pairs.

'THE TULIP' BY FRED CUMING, 1993, OIL ON BOARD, 32 X 24IN, (COURTESY OF BRIAN SINFIELD GALLERY, BURFORD, GLOS)

muddied yellow-green with a mauve-grey. You can see this effect in action by turning back a couple of pages and looking at the vibrating complementary pair in the top right-hand corner of the Kirchner painting.

Optical colour mixing

A group of 19th century painters – the Pointillists – made use complementary influences for quite different purposes. They wanted to create colour that captured the luminosity of light. To do this they laid down dots of two (often complementary) or more colours with minimal regular spaces in between.

Seen from a distance these spots are automatically blended by the eye to make a new colour, which is much more brilliant and vibrant than the equivalent colour produced by mixing pigments. This process is called optical colour mixing – and you can try it for yourself.

► Dots of colour create an image which seems to scintillate above the picture plane. Here there are no very dark tones. Instead form is modelled by playing off warm and cool colours – blues and lilacs in the shadows and warm yellows and oranges where the form catches the light. In the straw hat of the title, dots of complementary blue and orange, and yellow and violet add a particularly luminous quality.

'THE STRAW HAT' BY THEO VAN RYSSELBERGHE, (COURTESY OF WHITFORD & HUGHES, LONDON)

TERTIARY COLOURS

So far we've looked at a six-colour wheel, made up of primaries and secondaries. It's now time to expand the range with another group – the tertiaries.

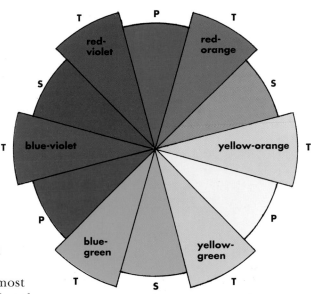

P = Primary; S = Secondary; T = Tertiary

To create a tertiary all you do is mix a primary with an equal quantity of one of the secondaries next to it on the six-colour wheel. If you combine red with its neighbour to the right – orange – you get red-orange; and if you combine red with its neighbour to the left – violet – you get red-violet.

By adjusting the proportions of the primary and secondary you can create a whole range of interesting 'intermediate' colours – for example, a red-orange that is more red than orange, or a red-violet that is more violet than red (in which case, you'll probably call it *violet-red*).

When you've mixed each primary and each secondary you get a 12-colour wheel, with a tertiary between each primary and secondary. All these – including the tertiaries – can be described as 'pure' because they're all mixed from just two primaries.

The primaries are the most visually stable of all colours, but the gradations between them are less so. That's because the secondaries and tertiaries are made

▼A colourful yet subtle effect is created here by the palette of tertiaries – bluey greens, greeny blues, and the russets and burnt oranges of the Chinese lanterns.

'STILL LIFE WITH POTS AND CHINESE LANTERNS' BY SARAH SPACKMAN, 18 X 20IN, OIL ON CANVAS

▲ The 12-colour wheel of three primaries, three secondaries and six tertiaries is the most useful one for getting to know colour since most people can visualise all 12 colours accurately.

PUT A NAME TO THESE

Try putting a name to the swatches of colour below. Some of them are easy, some of them not so easy. Now, which are the tertiaries?

Identifying tertiaries is easy. When you're in two minds whether it's blue or green, say, the chances are it's a tertiary. And as soon as you refer to nature – with colours like jade and lime green – it's more than likely you are naming a tertiary. These are all tertiaries, apart from the top blue and bottom yellow.

▶ Here tertiary blue-greens and turquoises sing out, set off by the neutral tones of the white bed linens and the muted colours of the walls. Touches of russet and orange provide a warm contrast.

'FIONA IN THE TURKISH GOWN' BY JOHN WARD CBE, RA,. OIL ON CANVAS, 36 X 50IN

up of two primaries and the mixture tends towards just one of them. In many ways, though, these intermediate hues are more subtle, expressive and dynamic than the primaries. This is why artists so often work with them, saving the primaries for specific and limited applications.

Now we'll look at the tertiaries in turn, two colours at a time.

The blue-greens and yellow-greens

This family of colours has several interesting characteristics. First, there are a lot of them. Second, there is great debate about exactly where the border between blue and green lies.

Most colour confusion is in this area; and even people who consider themselves to have acute colour perception disagree about whether a colour is more blue than green. From this we can draw one of the rules of colour – it's fickle, and context is always influential in the way it's perceived. A colour you'll swear is definitely turquoise you might well have to re-assess on seeing a turquoise that is entirely different.

The semi-precious stone turquoise does indeed lend its name to a particularly intense version of the greenish blues. Aquamarine also gives its name to this colour range, as does emerald. There are also the cerulean blues of an azure sky and the jade of the Mediterranean.

Then there are the iridescent blue-greens of a peacock's tail and a mallard's neck feathers, and the lovely soft blue of a duck's egg. From these are derived colours like celadon (a greyish green taken from the glazes used on Chinese pottery), *eau de nil* (from the River Nile) and pistachio.

Turning to the yellow-green side of the range, you find the sharp, acid greens of lime green and apple green, and the bright shades of beech leaves and new grass in spring.

The yellow-oranges and the red-oranges

This range gives us some delicious fruit colours – cheerful and sunny. Think of peaches, apricots and tangerines. Also included are warm earth colours like terracotta and brick red.

Again, they are difficult to identify in isolation – a colour that looks pinkish in one context can look yellow against a reddish background. And one man's peach may be another man's apricot.

The red-violets and blue-violets

In nature these are fruit and flower colours – plum, grape and damson, violet, heather and lavender. There are also earthy shades like puce.

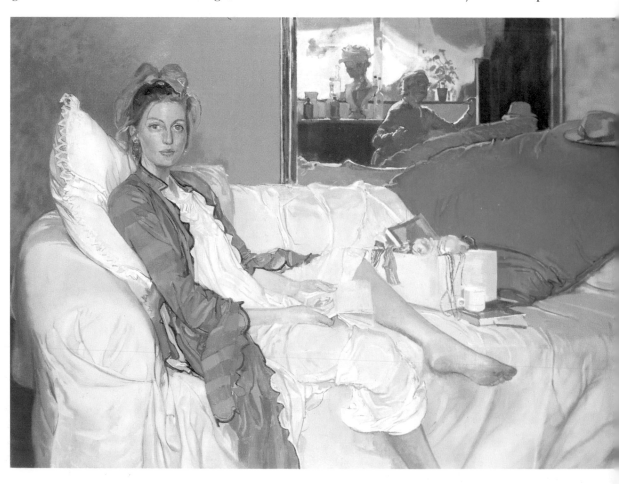

WARM AND COOL COLOURS

All colours have a temperature, whether it's warm, cool or somewhere in between. This is no arbitrary description, however. There's general agreement about which are which.

From the beginning of this chapter you'll be familiar with the idea of the six-colour wheel dividing in half. One side of it contains the warm colours – red, yellow and orange – and the other the cool – blue, violet and green.

For us these two sets of colours have familiar associations. Reds, yellows and oranges conjure up sunlight and fire, while the blues and blue-greens we connect with snow and ice, sea, sky and moonlight.

But the theory of colour temperature isn't quite so black and white! Within the warm half and the cool half of the colour wheel there are degrees of warmness and coolness.

Warm 'cools' and cool 'warms'

Take the reds, for example. In the nine-colour wheel shown on the right there's both a hot red and a cool red. The hot red is cadmium red because it has a bias towards *warm* orange. By comparison alizarin crimson is relatively cool because it's next to *cool/in-between* violet on the colour wheel.

It's the same story with the yellows. Cadmium yellow pale is warm because it veers towards *warm* orange. And lemon yellow is cool, located as it is next to *cool* green on the wheel.

Secondary colours, too, are warm or cool. Green is cool as it comes from a mix of *cool* yellow and *cool* blue. Orange meanwhile is warm (derived from *warm* red and *warm* yellow).

The effect of adjacent colours

A colour may appear all the warmer or cooler depending on what it's next to. This is particularly true of violet, which is an in-between colour anyway (mixed from *cool* blue and *warm* red). Next to a warm colour such as red it appears cool, while next to a cool colour such as blue it appears warm. Similarly, if you saw a patch of alizarin crimson in a painting of cool blues and greens, you'd probably describe it as 'hot'.

Using colour temperature

It would be wrong to dismiss colour temperature as just another fancy theory. In the hands of the artist, it becomes an indispensable tool. That's because in general terms warm colours *advance* (come toward you) and cool colours *recede* (sit back). You can capitalise on this to describe three-dimensional form (see overleaf).

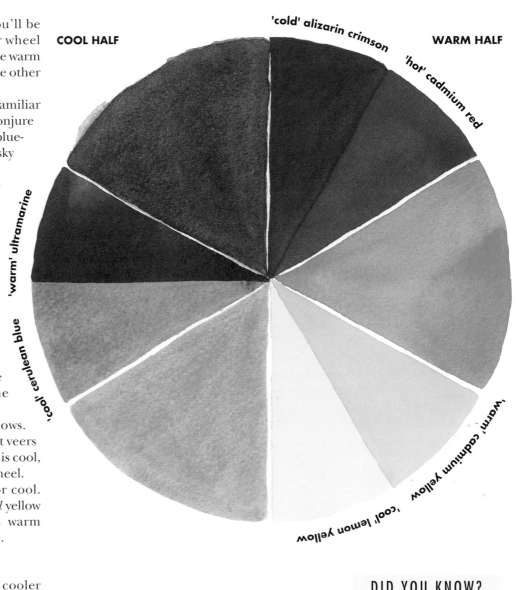

COOL HALF

'cold' alizarin crimson

WARM HALF

'hot' cadmium red

'warm' ultramarine

'cool' cerulean blue

'warm' cadmium yellow

'cool' lemon yellow

DID YOU KNOW?

Physical effects
Colour temperature isn't all in the mind. In a controlled experiment, people set the central heating thermostat in a blue room 4°C higher than one in a red room.

SEE FOR YOURSELF

You can see for yourself how warm colours advance and cool colours recede by looking at the two squares below. The warm red one seems to come towards you while the cool blue one seems to sit back.

Most of us are familiar with this idea anyway from interior design – to make a room feel warm and cosy we paint the walls red. Decorate them light blue and the room is transformed into a cool and airy space.

► The roundness of these two oranges is beautifully conveyed by the skilful use of warm and cool watercolours. There are obvious areas that travel forward – the oranges and reds – and other areas that travel back – the blues and greens – where the forms tuck under.

◄ Half-close your eyes and even the simpler use of warm and cool colours in this collage conveys a wealth of information about three-dimensional forms. Notice how blue/green stands in for the cooler shades of orange around the dimple at the top of the left-hand fruit.

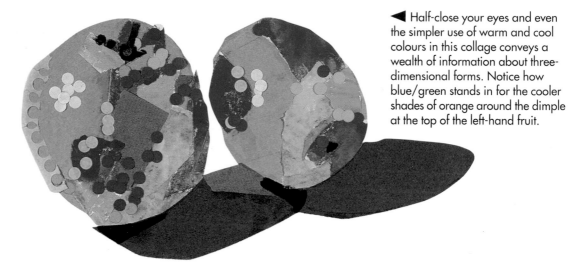

► The limited palette of warm and cool colours here describes form while giving the girl's flesh a luminous quality.

Notice the yellowy tones on the subject's right shoulder (they also warm her right buttock), and the pink flush where the weight of her body meets the mattress and where the arm and torso meet. In the small of the girl's back bluish lilac tones describe the way the forms flatten out. And in the foreground, folds of golden fabric pull that area right up to the picture plane.

'RECLINING NUDE' BY VICTOR PASMORE, OIL ON CANVAS, 305 X 406MM, 1942

STARTING TO MIX COLOURS

So far so good for the theory of colour. Now the fun really starts and you can get down to the nitty gritty of mixing your own colours from a palette of six paints.

There comes a point in most things when reading is no substitute for doing. This is certainly true of colour theory. So when you come to the end of this chapter, get out your paper and paints and try colour mixing for yourself!

Where practice and theory part

As you've been reading the colour chapters so far, the chances are you've stopped to ask yourself the following question: why, if the three primaries can be mixed to produce all other colours, can't I make do with a tube of red, yellow and blue,

plus a tube each of black and white?

The answer, quite simply, is that there is no such thing as a 'pure' pigment primary. Approximating to each primary there may be as many as 16 tube colours, and these all have one thing in common – a bias towards one of the adjacent secondaries. Take the reds, for example: the tube colour cadmium red has a bias towards orange, while another, alizarin crimson, tends towards violet.

All this is highlighted when it comes to mixing the three secondaries – violet, orange and green.

◀ In this abstract landscape much of the colour is almost pure pigment, used straight from the tube. But the artist has done some mixing, both on the palette and on the canvas.

The colours he used are ultramarine, spectrum red, cadmium orange and Winsor green – a particularly sharp transparent green that you can't produce by mixing.

'LANDSCAPE' BY JOHN BARNICOAT, 76 X 76CM, OIL ON CANVAS, 1993

Mixing pure secondaries and muted secondaries from 'six' primaries

From the six-segment colour wheel you've seen that you need three primaries to mix three secondaries. So much for the theory, now for the practice.

In fact you need two versions of each primary – one that has a bias to the secondary on one side of it on the colour wheel and one that has a bias to the secondary on the other side. With red, for example, you need one that tends towards orange (to make

orange) and another that tends towards violet (to make violet). With only one red, you'd have one secondary that was correct and one that was wrong.

The same is true for the other two primaries. So you need a violet blue and a greenish blue, and an orange yellow and a greenish yellow.

Pure secondaries For pure secondaries you need two primaries that tend towards the secondary in

Pure secondaries and muted secondaries

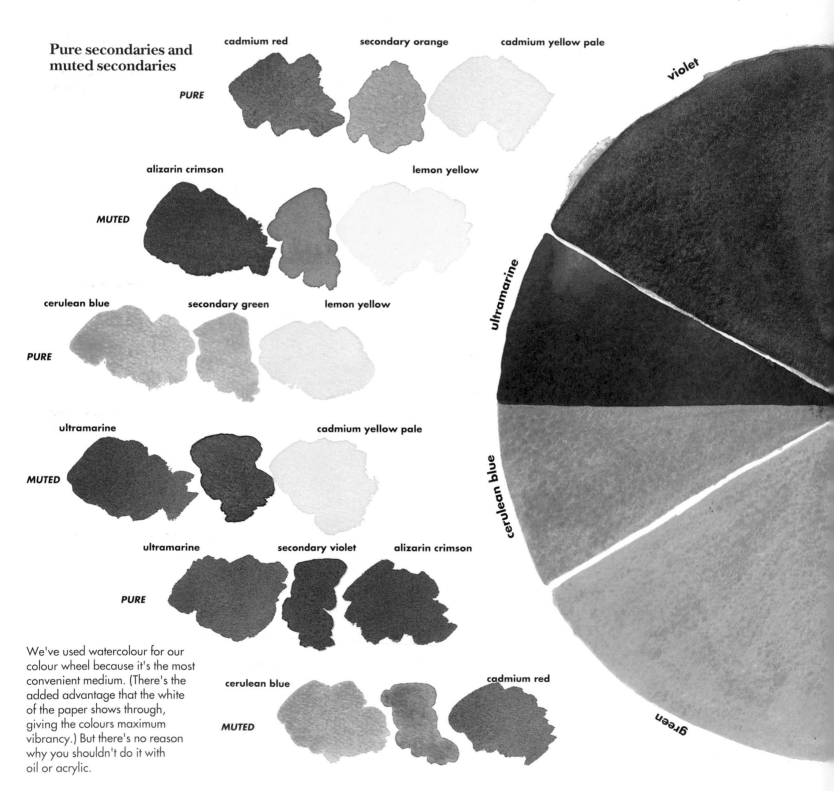

cadmium red   secondary orange   cadmium yellow pale

PURE

alizarin crimson   lemon yellow

MUTED

cerulean blue   secondary green   lemon yellow

PURE

ultramarine   cadmium yellow pale

MUTED

ultramarine   secondary violet   alizarin crimson

PURE

cerulean blue   cadmium red

MUTED

We've used watercolour for our colour wheel because it's the most convenient medium. (There's the added advantage that the white of the paper shows through, giving the colours maximum vibrancy.) But there's no reason why you shouldn't do it with oil or acrylic.

violet

ultramarine

cerulean blue

green

between them. So an *orange* red (cadmium red) and an *orange* yellow (cadmium yellow pale) produce a strong orange that approaches secondary orange.

Muted secondaries Mix together a red and a yellow that are farther apart on the colour wheel and the story is rather different. A violet red (alizarin crimson) and a greenish yellow (lemon yellow) give a sort of burnt orange. That's because alizarin crimson

and lemon yellow approach a complementary relationship – you've already seen how complementary pairs mixed together neutralise each other (see pages 51–54).

Secondaries like burnt orange are described as muted, neutral or dirtied. Don't be put off by the names – these colours are useful and attractive. It's just that they are not pure secondaries.

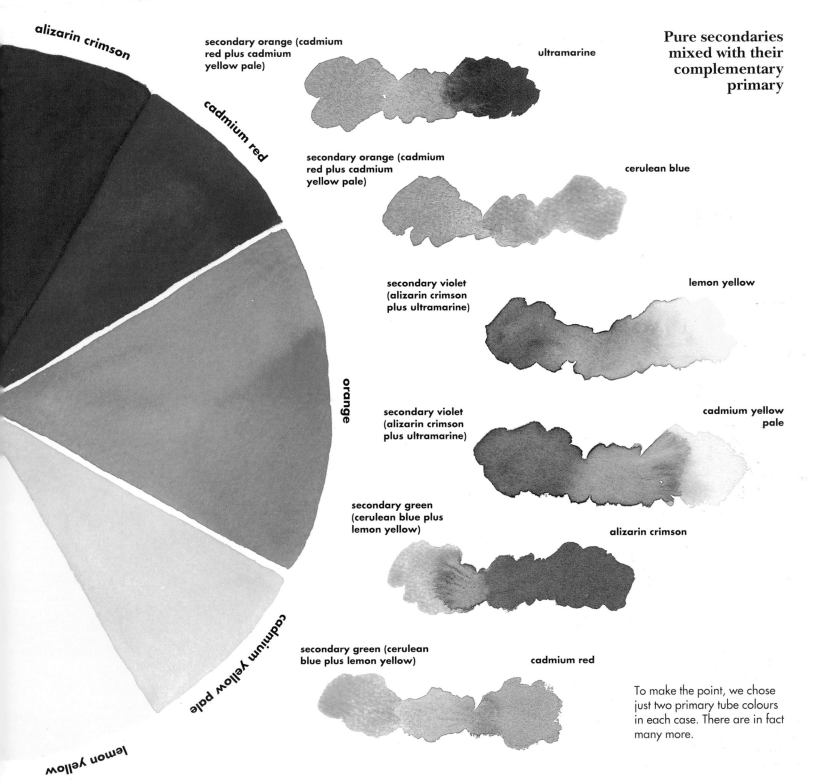

Pure secondaries mixed with their complementary primary

alizarin crimson

secondary orange (cadmium red plus cadmium yellow pale)

ultramarine

cadmium red

secondary orange (cadmium red plus cadmium yellow pale)

cerulean blue

secondary violet (alizarin crimson plus ultramarine)

lemon yellow

orange

secondary violet (alizarin crimson plus ultramarine)

cadmium yellow pale

secondary green (cerulean blue plus lemon yellow)

alizarin crimson

cadmium yellow pale

secondary green (cerulean blue plus lemon yellow)

cadmium red

lemon yellow

To make the point, we chose just two primary tube colours in each case. There are in fact many more.

Doing it for yourself

If all this sounds rather complicated, be reassured – it is much easier to grasp when you've done it for yourself. And as you do it, you'll be acquiring an understanding of how colour mixes really work. You'll also have an extremely useful palette of six colours at your disposal: cadmium red, alizarin crimson, ultramarine, cerulean, lemon yellow and cadmium yellow pale.

Before you start, arm yourself with all you need. Remember, you'll get through plenty of water and kitchen roll because meticulousness is all important. Always clean your brush before you put it into a pan of colour or wash, and keep a separate jar for mixing washes.

First of all, have a go at mixing the pure secondaries from the pairs of recommended primaries. Then try the muted secondaries. Mix ultramarine and cadmium yellow pale together, for instance. You'll end up with a colour that isn't a pure secondary but which is an interesting muted green all the same.

You've already seen neutral greys being made from mixtures of complementary pairs (see pages 51–54). The swatches of colour used there were all proprietary pigments. Re-create the exercise for yourself now, but instead of resorting to tube or pan colours for the secondaries, make use of the pure secondaries you've just mixed.

▼ A rich but subtle palette of warm and cool muted colours provides a foil for the brilliant unmixed red of the parasol.

Some of the pearly greys are mixed, while others have been created by laying one colour on top of another.

'THE RED PARASOL' BY KEN HOWARD RA, OIL ON CANVAS, 40 X 48IN, COURTESY OF MANYA IGEL FINE ARTS, LONDON

OPTICAL COLOUR MIXING

With the arrival of the Impressionists in the 19th century, there was a dramatic break with tradition. It was all to do with the way this group of artists used their colours.

Until the Impressionists, artists had gone about the business of mixing colours in the usual way – on the palette. Then there was a revolution.

It started with a Frenchman, Michel-Eugène Chevreul, who in 1839 published his scientific discoveries about colour. Among his observations was the theory of optical colour mixing – the idea that colours could be mixed in the human eye.

For the artist, the implications of this were tremendous, and the Impressionists made haste to put theory into practice. They set out to paint the effects of light in the knowledge that optical colour mixing could help them capture special luminous qualities. These were qualities that were unachievable by mixing paints on the palette, where the more you blend them, the more a blackish brown colour tends to emerge.

Instead the Impressionists used pure, simple colours, laying them down in tiny dabs side by side on the canvas. Viewed from a distance, these speckles of 'broken' colour merged together. So a mixture of red and yellow strokes, for instance, actually appears orange, and the paint surface as a whole is lively, vibrant and scintillating.

▲ As director of dyeing at a tapestry workshop, Chevreul identified a problem – colours weren't registering their full effect. It was nothing to do with the dyeing, however. He discovered that colours placed side by side have an impact on one another – a phenomenon known as simultaneous contrast (see pages 51–54).

► Optical colour mixing appears in an exaggerated form in the work of Pointillist painter Georges Seurat.

In his later paintings – such as this picture – he laid down tiny dots of brilliant colour, intending them to mix in the viewer's eye. Here they produce intermediate tints more luminous than those you get from pigments mixed on a palette. Meanwhile close-up, the picture surface is just a mosaic of dots. Try placing the life-size detail (above), for instance.

'THE HARBOUR AND QUAYS AT PORT-EN-BESSIN' BY GEORGES SEURAT, 1888, OIL ON CANVAS, 67 X 84.5CM

▶ Turn-of-the-century 'Fauve' painters, such as Vlaminck, were keen to explore optical colour mixing. His early paintings are characterised by small strokes of intense primary and secondary colours laid down with glimpses of bare canvas in between.

Here the brushstrokes follow and describe forms: small dashes and dots for fallen leaves; long, bold marks for the tree-trunk; and flowing strokes for the smaller branches.

'PAYSAGE AU BOIS MORT' BY MAURICE DE VLAMINCK, OIL ON CANVAS, 1906, 65 X 81CM, © ADAGP, PARIS AND DACS, LONDON 1994

Note

Other systems of optical colour mixing include:
- an underpainting or toned ground showing through;
- scumblings (thick and thin), where you apply paint over white, a toned ground or previous paint layers;
- hatching — a system of criss-crossed lines of coloured pencil or pastel;
- oil applied in dabs, strokes, or dashes.

In some media — such as coloured pencils or pastels — you can't really blend colour so you *have* to use one of the optical colour mixing techniques.

Pointillism

Chevreul's ideas dominated the use of colour by artists such as Vincent van Gogh and Camille Pissarro. But it was Georges Seurat who applied the theory of optical colour mixing in the most scientific and exacting way.

He carried it to extremes, building up whole pictures from tiny dots (points) of colour – a technique known as Pointillism or, less commonly, Divisionism. Close up, you can see all the individual dabs and dots, but stand back and they merge to present a rich and lively colour.

Seurat died young and this exacting system of working didn't last long. But it left an important heritage, creating greater freedom for artists. Such freedom led to uses of colour never before explored, particularly in the work of a group known as the Fauves.

The Fauves and afterwards

The Fauves painted at the turn of the century. They included Matisse, Vlaminck and Derain and they earned their name – which means *wild beasts* – because of their way of painting.

Their works were brilliant and highly coloured, with wild, exaggerated, heightened colours placed side by side. They painted cool shadows in cobalt blue, and delicate fleshy pinks in the brightest of scarlets. These were colours that expressed their feelings as well as describing what they saw.

But it's perhaps in the paintings of the Post Impressionists such as Vuillard and Bonnard that broken colour can best be seen. Working from the mid 1880s to the early 1900s, they employed colour in an exciting way, using individual brushstrokes to break up colour.

▶ This study by Seurat was painted three years before the one on the previous page. Here he uses broken colour, but with a greater variety of brushstrokes. Horizontal dashes of paint describe the surface of the water, while small dashes of colour laid in many directions are used for the grass (notice the touches of complementary red here, too).

'THE SEINE AT COURBEVOIE' BY GEORGES SEURAT, OIL ON CANVAS, 1885, 32¹⁄₁₆ X 25⁹⁄₁₆IN

Breaking a colour

You might come across another meaning of the term broken colour. It's one that's been around for centuries and it's also to do with mixing, but mixing on the palette rather than on the canvas or in the eye.

To 'break' a colour means to add a small amount of another colour to it. So you break red when you add a dash of yellow to it and end up with a warmer, brighter, broken red. You don't break red when you mix it with more than a touch of another colour – 50:50 with yellow, say, to make orange.

▲ In this painting the artist uses broken colour, but far more freely and less rigorously than Seurat, for example. The colour is applied in a variety of ways: wet paint is worked into wet paint; in other places it is scumbled loosely over underlying colour; and in others touches of crisp impasto add emphasis.

'ST MARTIN'S' BY GARY JEFFREY, ACRYLIC ON PAPER, 22 X 26½IN, COURTESY OF LLEWELLYN ALEXANDER FINE PAINTINGS, LONDON

In 1910 there was an exhibition in London called 'Manet and the Post Impressionists'. It brought bold new ideas to the British public and led to the foundation of the London Group, which included such artists as Harold Gilman (see left), Walter Sickert and Wyndham Lewis.

◄ To create this image the artist used vigorous brushstrokes and dryish paint dragged over underlying paint layers. The patches of paint are large and widely spaced, so that the more closely you approach the painting the more it dissolves. Seen from a distance, however, it is resolved. The picture has a fresh, shimmering and luminous quality.

'GIRL BY A MANTELPIECE' BY HAROLD GILMAN, OIL ON CANVAS, 12 X 16IN

GREYS AND COLOURED NEUTRALS

Neutrals are some of the most useful and versatile colours on the artist's palette – and what's more, they are easy to handle. There's a glorious range for you to choose from.

So far we have looked at the fully saturated hues on the colour wheel – the primaries, secondaries and tertiaries. But for the artist – and the interior decorator – the complex colours we call neutrals or greys offer a more fascinating palette. Indeed, some of the best colourists, such as Sickert and Bonnard, really display their quality in their use of neutrals.

In artistic terms, a neutral is a colour which has been muted, greyed, dulled or knocked back so that it is no longer pure (fully saturated) but still has an identifiable hue. The neutrals encompass an enormous range of beautiful colours, from slightly muted purples, olive greens and shades of terracotta, to the grey and brown neutrals we associate with stone and sand and the sky on an overcast, dull day.

Some pigments are naturally neutralised. The most obvious examples are the naturally occurring earth colours, such as yellow ochre, raw sienna, raw umber and terre verte, and also earth colours which have been heated to produce new colours – burnt umber and burnt sienna. Colours such as Venetian red,

Indian red and Mars red, which are based on iron oxides, are also neutrals.

A range of neutrals

There are many ways of neutralising a colour. The best way is to mix your colour with its complementary. Take a look at our colour wheel,

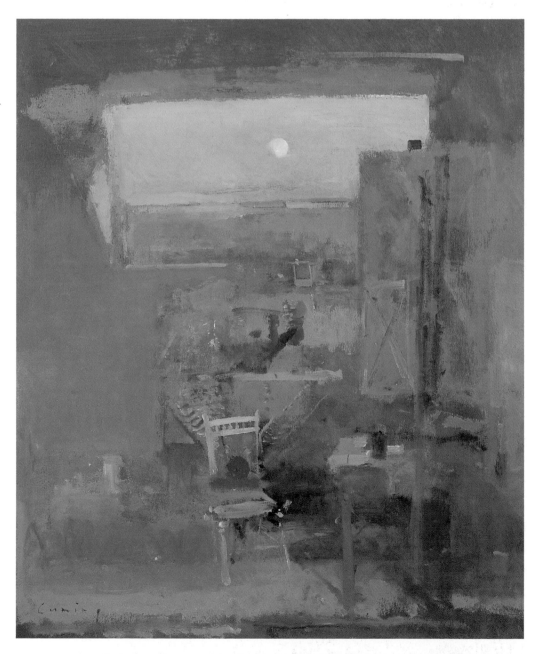

▶ If you study this picture section by section, you'll find a putty colour, a pale, cool grey, a lilac-grey, a rusty brown and so on – all colours which are difficult to describe. But what a wonderfully subtle evocation of shifting evening light the artist has created. And notice how the touches of unmixed colour sing out against the neutral ground – turquoise, lemon, red and orange.

'THE STUDIO, EVENING' BY FRED CUMING, OIL ON CANVAS, 24 X 20IN (COURTESY OF THE BRIAN SINFIELD GALLERY, BURFORD, GLOS.)

▶ The colours on the outer ring of this colour wheel are 'pure' colours – the primaries (we've used a warm and a cool version of each), secondaries and tertiaries. These are the most saturated colours, which can be modified but not intensified. (A pure orange can be made redder or yellower, for example, but it can't be made more intensely orange.) The middle ring contains the coloured neutrals, while the colours in the centre are greys and browns. These have all been made by adding more and more of the complementary colour.

▼ Sickert was a master of colour and often used a subtly orchestrated range of lovely neutrals as a base to give emphasis to strategically placed touches of gorgeous colour. Look how bright the golden yellow of the ornamentation is in this painting.

'THE OLD BEDFORD MUSIC HALL' BY WALTER RICHARD SICKERT, 1894-95, OIL ON CANVAS, 549 X 381MM

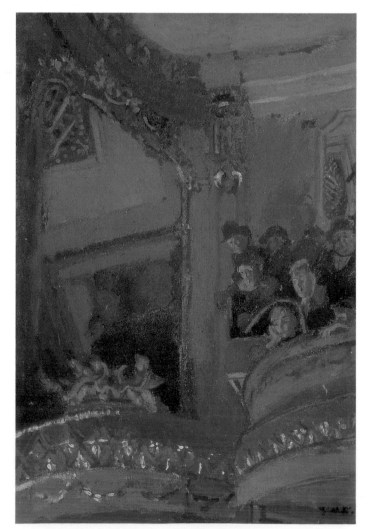

above, and you can see how this works. The colours around the outside are 'pure' colours – the primaries (red, yellow and blue), the secondaries (orange, green and violet) and the tertiaries (the remaining colours). Each colour is mixed with its complementary in the middle ring, and then more of its complementary in the centre of the wheel. Notice how this makes each colour greyer or browner.

If you mix a neutral in this way it will have a little of each primary in it – although not in equal proportions. Look at the colour wheel again and you can see how this works. Yellow is opposite violet (which contains blue and red), and if you mix these together to make a neutral, you've used all the primaries. Try it out for yourself, using any of the colours on the wheel. Remember, secondaries and tertiaries each contain two primaries.

You can also neutralise a colour (or reduce its saturation) by adding a little white (to make a tint or pastel) or a little black (to make a tone).

Using neutrals

Colour is a very personal thing. Set two artists in front of a subject and they will select a different range of pigments and interpret the subject with a different palette of mixes. Some people naturally opt for a high-keyed, vibrant palette, others choose a more subtle, muted range of colours. Your mood, your intention and

◀ Tertiary blue-greens and greeny blues, slightly muted, provide a vivid but cool foil for the warm, earthy flesh tones of the models. These aren't pure, saturated hues, but neither are they dull or dingy.

They illustrate very well the lively and vibrant colours provided by the range we call the coloured neutrals. Notice how bright the splash of red in the foreground looks, yet it is a fairly muted terracotta rendered vibrant by its context. Also notice the way it vibrates against the bright splash of aquamarine on the back of the girl on the right.

'THE TWO MODELS' BY TOM COATES, OIL ON CANVAS, 36 X 36IN

▼ Walter Sickert was a marvellous colourist. Here he demonstrates that paintings which exploit neutrals can be wonderfully colourful – he is concerned with the contrast between natural and artificial light, the individual and the crowd, the public and the private.

Sludgy greens, lilacs and rich, earthy reds provide a subdued foil for candy pinks and touches of bright lime green. In this context small patches of colour acquire a significance out of proportion to their size.

'BRIGHTON PIERROTS' BY WALTER RICHARD SICKERT, 1915, OIL ON CANVAS, 25 X 30IN

► The overall impression of this painting is of a sunny landscape. The colours look brighter than they are because of the play of complementaries – the blue-violet roofs against yellow bushes, and the orange tinges in the hills against greenish fields and bushes.

'BURLY COBB'S HOUSE, SOUTH TRURO' BY EDWARD HOPPER, OIL ON CANVAS, 23¾ X 36IN (WHITNEY MUSEUM OF AMERICAN ART, JOSEPHINE N. HOPPER BEQUEST)

▼ This painting has an almost abstract quality, though the subject of the painting is realistically described.

Again the painting is colourful – warm, rich browns and earths set off by cool, slate greys and greyed whites. Here the neutral palette holds a lot of disparate objects together so that you see the subject as a whole, rather than as a series of isolated elements.

'STUDY IN BROWNS AND GREYS' BY PAUL NEWLAND, WATERCOLOUR ON PAPER

the subject itself will also exert an influence. So while a vase of flowers in sunlight suggests a vibrant palette, a moody interior would probably be rendered in more sombre, muted tones. So basically you can choose whatever suits your mood, style and subject – you might even decide to exaggerate colours.

An all-neutral palette

By muting or neutralising colours you reduce their saturation. Because they are less intense, these colours have a natural harmony and are, in many ways, easier to handle than colours at full intensity. It takes great skill to balance a palette of fully saturated colours, each of which will jostle for attention.

If you use muted colours you will naturally achieve a sense of harmony. A painting in primarily pastel colours will have an intrinsic coherence – the colours will sit well together and nothing will shout at you. Although neutrals are, in many ways, easier to use, you also run the risk of producing an image which is lacking in emphasis.

You can create emphasis within a muted (neutral) palette by exploiting contrasts. The main ones are complementary contrasts, contrasts of temperature and contrasts of tone. These are important in any painting, but in a painting which uses coloured neutrals and greys, they are even more significant. So an earth red in a field of complementary sludgy green will have almost as much impact as the contrast of bright red and green in a more saturated painting. Lilac and blue shadows will give solidity to warm brick walls and figures. (The cool neutrals are greys, while warm neutrals are browns.) In paintings which are very low-keyed, the nuances of tone are restricted – very subtle shifts in light and dark are required, and in many cases will be emphasised by playing off warm and cool colours.

Artists like Gwen John and Giorgio Morandi produced exquisite paintings using a limited range of subtle, muted colours. They delight us with their infinitely subtle variations of colour and by the way warm and cool colours are used to describe form and suggest space. Their work has a wonderfully delicate and restrained quality. This same quality can be seen in the work of Fred Cuming on page 67.

Neutrals as a foil

You can also use muted colours to draw attention to stronger, more intensely saturated colours. In a rich and vibrant palette of bright, pure colours, the eye is constantly distracted, as each colour

▲ By carefully selecting her viewpoint and simplifying the subject, this artist emphasises the decorative, abstract quality of the vase of tulips on a table. The cool neutral palette creates a peaceful image; look closely and you will find many subtle nuances of colour and tone.

'WHITE TULIPS' BY ANNE-MARIE BUTLIN, OIL ON CANVAS, 15 X 11IN

◄ Whistler used very fluid paint mixed with plenty of medium which he called a 'sauce'. It was so fluid that he often worked on the floor to prevent it running off. His atmospheric and mysterious images were pulled from the paint surface with sweeping brushstrokes.

This palette of dark blue-greys evokes the confusion of twilight. The colour of the lights draws the eye to the tall ships, while a few reflections call attention to a group of shadowy figures standing on the quayside.

'NOCTURNE; BLUE AND GOLD; VALPARAISO' BY JAMES ABBOT MCNEILL WHISTLER, OIL ON CANVAS, 37⅛ X 27⅞IN

DID YOU KNOW?

Costly theme

Whistler painted several variations on his nocturnes theme (see left). However, they didn't all go down well. On seeing his 'Nocturne in black and gold, the falling rocket', Ruskin accused Whistler of 'flinging a pot of paint in the public's face'. Whistler sued him and won, but he only won a farthing (the smallest amount he could possibly have been awarded) and the costs left him bankrupt.

demands attention. But a dash of a bright pastel pink will really sing out against a field of muted pinks and greys, and its impact will be out of all proportion to its intensity and size.

If your painting lacks emphasis, you might find that by knocking back some of the background areas you give the focal points more importance. You could do this by mixing a bit of the complementary colour on to the background, for example, or by overpainting with an earth equivalent.

The artist Walter Sickert was a master at introducing surprising touches of colour into his paintings – and yet when you study them carefully, these apparently bright colours are in fact quite restrained. By placing them within a neutralised field, he really makes them tell.

◀ Washing dancing on a line in a pretty street makes an enchanting motif. The warm, sepia tones of the masonry provide a muted background for the blues and rusts of the washing, which seem quite bright in comparison. The artist uses a restricted palette to create an image which is restrained but engaging.

'PITIGLIANO' BY ALISON MUSKER, WATERCOLOUR ON PAPER, 15 X 11IN

▶ Tom Coates uses a range of warm and cool neutrals to describe the dissolving, shimmering forms of Venice on a wet winter's day. The warm brown of the support provides local colour in some areas – as in the fabric of the Doge's Palace – but in others it acts as a unifying element and a warm contrast which gives impact to the blues and greys.

'THE DOGE'S PALACE, WINTER' BY TOM COATES, OIL ON BOARD, 14 X 18IN

CHAPTER THREE

COMPOSING PICTURES

FORMAT – FIRST THINGS FIRST

One of the first decisions you make at the start of a picture is how to compose it – how you put together and arrange its different parts.

The basic element of any composition is the format (shape) of your support. This can greatly affect the mood, and even the final success of your painting, so before you start, make sure you take time to consider which shape is best for your subject. It can be any shape or size you wish, but at first you may prefer to stick to formats which are already well established.

A choice of two

There are two traditional formats – portrait and landscape. Both are based on the rectangle. When the longer side is upright the support is described as 'portrait'. Placed the other way (horizontally) it is called 'landscape'.

The names reflect the fact that the upright one is used most often for portrait painting, while the horizontal one is traditional for landscapes. In fact, you'll also find that most supports come ready made in these shapes.

There are sound practical reasons for these choices: using the horizontal format for depicting a landscape means you can fit in a wide, sweeping view. Using the vertical format for portraits means that you can follow the naturally upright human shape and – if you want to – focus on the subject matter since there is little peripheral space.

▶ In a classic portrait, the eyes are automatically sited quite high in the painting, and the upright format naturally leads your eyes up to meet the eyes of the sitter – conveying an instant feeling of intimacy.

'PROFESSOR FRANCIS CRICK OM, FRS, BSc' BY TOM COATES, WATERCOLOUR, 16 X 12IN

◀ The upright format of this picture focuses attention on the dramatic figure of the Arab and helps to enhance the close relationship between the man and the fine horse he is leading.

'ARAB AND RIDER, PUSHKAR FAIR, RAJASTHAN' BY CAROLYN PIETS, WATERCOLOUR, 12 X 17IN

▶ The horizontal format can convey a great feeling of space and calm in a painting of a landscape.

'EVENING' BY JOSEPH FARQUHARSON (1846-1945), OIL ON CANVAS, 18 X 30IN

portrait (vertical) format

◀ A quick way of seeing which format is best is to make a frame with your hands and then squint through it at your subject. The advantage of this is that you see your subject matter in isolation without the confusion of things around it. Here's the upright format shape for the Arab and horse painting above. Try it the other way as well...

Using format for effect

Format is important because certain shapes convey messages to the eye which the artist can exploit. For example, a tall, thin, upright rectangle tends to lead the eye up towards the top, which is where the main point of interest – the face – is. And a long, thin, horizontal format often gives a feeling of peace and quietness. The flowing horizontal lines across the picture are soothing and relaxing, and the wide horizons convey a sense of space and calm.

You can also use these shapes to create different effects. Some artists choose to paint a portrait on a 'landscape' support, while others prefer a 'portrait' format for landscapes. It depends on your subject, and how you wish to present it. For example, a running figure fits well in a landscape format, which allows the subject space to run into and gives a strong sense of movement to the picture. And a landscape in which the sky is to be the dominant factor may well look best in the upright portrait format.

If these shapes are used in the wrong way they can give false messages to the eye – that is, they can lead the eye away from the focus. It's no good using a portrait format that leads the eye to the top of the paper if all the action is going on at the bottom. The whole picture will fail to capture the mood you are trying to convey. With a little common sense, and a basic understanding of format, avoiding this kind of pitfall is easy.

When you have chosen a format, ask yourself why you have picked that one, and how you're going to make use of it. Think about the empty space in your picture. Is there too much or too little, or just the right amount for the mood you want to create? Follow your instincts, and try looking at your subject in different ways. The aim is to create a picture that is satisfying to look at and conveys a sense of excitement and pleasure.

▶ …and you should get an instant feeling of what looks right. In the painting above, the landscape format helps to evoke an atmosphere of serenity and peace.

Quickly sketch your subject using several formats if you are still not sure what works best.

landscape (horizontal) format

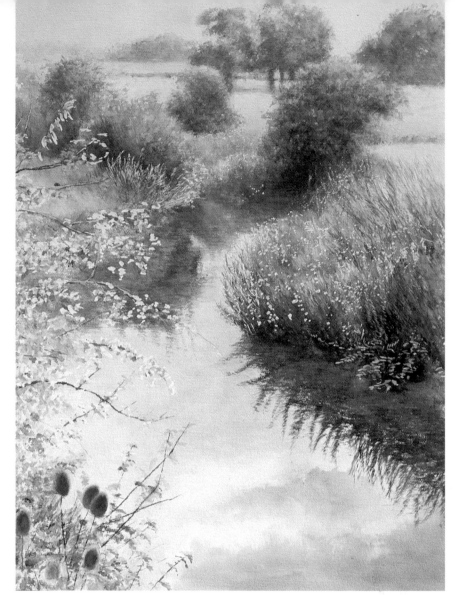

◄ There's no cast-iron rule that you must use a horizontal format for a landscape. If the subject dictates an upright shape, then make the most of it – as in this painting where the focus is fixed firmly on the meandering stream.

'WATER MEADOWS' BY GRAHAM PAINTER, WATERCOLOUR, 31 X 21IN

▼ There are also perfectly good reasons for painting a portrait of someone in a horizontal format. A reclining figure fits naturally into this shape, and makes a graceful, relaxed image.

DETAIL OF 'MRS WINSTON CHURCHILL WITH HER DAUGHTER, SARAH' BY SIR JOHN LAVERY, OIL ON CANVAS

PLACING YOUR MAIN FOCAL POINT

Follow a few useful guidelines and you'll soon develop an eye for where to position your main focal point. But before you start, consider all the options open to you.

Every picture needs at least one focal point – a point which draws the eye – otherwise the eye wanders from one spot to the next without knowing where to linger. So before you compose your picture it's always a good idea to ask yourself why you're doing it.

What has made you respond to the topic? Do you have a clear subject in mind? And what exactly is it you want to capture on paper or canvas?

When you know the answers you can start thinking about composition – and about what happens if you start manipulating focal points, placing them first in the centre and then trying them off-centre.

Going for the centre

Many people put the main focal point in the middle of the canvas most of the time. It's where the eye naturally looks first and so is the obvious spot for the important elements of a picture. It also creates a restful, well balanced image.

Because of this, a central focal point is particularly effective for something symmetrical – such as a classical building, perhaps. Traditionally artists have still often slightly offset a central focal point to avoid an uncomfortable 'cleavage' of the support which would otherwise be the case.

However, you may find that composing too many pictures with centrally placed focal points could start to look static and dull. Many paintings and drawings look stronger with the main interest to one side. This also ensures that you avoid repetition in your pictures.

▲ Placing the main focal point in the middle is a perfectly valid option, particularly where you want to stress symmetry. All the same, slightly offsetting it avoids an uncomfortable 'cleavage' of the picture.

'MADRID, SPAIN' BY TOM MCNEELY, 1989, WATERCOLOUR ON PAPER, 22 X 30IN

Why is composition so important?

Composition is often overlooked by people but the importance of good composition can't be overstated. By arranging the elements of a picture carefully you manipulate the viewers, enticing their eyes to travel around the painting's surface while also providing them with places to rest. The viewers look first at one part of the picture, then at another, roaming around or lingering as you intend. With a well composed image you can create a sense of excitement or produce a feeling of calm.

In this chapter on composing pictures, we look at the business of where to position the main focal point and how to lead the eye.

► With the main focal point on a vertical third your eye is guided around the picture – to the figure and across the swimming pool and then back to the figure again – rather than resting in the centre.

'VILLA POOL' BY ANDY WOOD, 1983, WATERCOLOUR ON PAPER, 10 X 14IN

► Whichever format – vertical or horizontal – you choose, putting the rule of thirds into practice makes for a stimulating picture that's pleasing to the eye. Interestingly, here – as in the picture above – the head is still the focal point of the picture though it's shown from behind.

'THE BACK OF CHARLIE' BY HENRY SCOTT TUKE, PRIVATE COLLECTION

The rule of thirds

The classic way of creating a satisfying composition is to divide an image into vertical thirds in your mind, and then position the main focal point roughly on one of the dividing lines.

This works whether you use a horizontal or a vertical format. The focal point doesn't need to be precisely on one of the lines. But by placing it off-centre like this you often create a more dynamic image than one with central emphasis. It's dynamic because it makes your eye move round the picture when you look at it.

Using the rule of thirds also lets you show a subject in context. A central subject usually needs to fill the picture to have any impact, while an off-centre one reveals the setting. Even when the subject is quite large its surroundings show.

Horizontal thirds

But it's not just vertical thirds that make good composition – you can also divide the picture into horizontal thirds. In a landscape, for instance, it can be distracting to have the horizon chopping the picture in equal halves (though it is possible to make this division work). By placing the horizon one third of the way from the top of a picture – or one third of the way from the bottom – you have an easy formula for a satisfying arrangement.

◀ Though your inclination might be to paint the horizon right across the centre of a picture, you can see how dramatic the effect when it's placed on a horizontal third, especially at the bottom. Here the large sky creates a feeling of airiness.

'WILD POPPIES' BY ROSALIE BULLOCK, WATERCOLOUR, 12 X 17IN

▼ Sometimes what looks like a fairly random design by the artist is actually a careful organisation of picture elements. The large amount of foreground in this picture puts the reclining woman on a horizontal third at the top, creating a feeling of remoteness from the viewer. Notice also that she is on a vertical third too, as is the lowest point of the sofa.

'MADAME HESSEL AND HER DOG' BY EDOUARD VUILLARD, 1910, OIL, 29 X 34IN

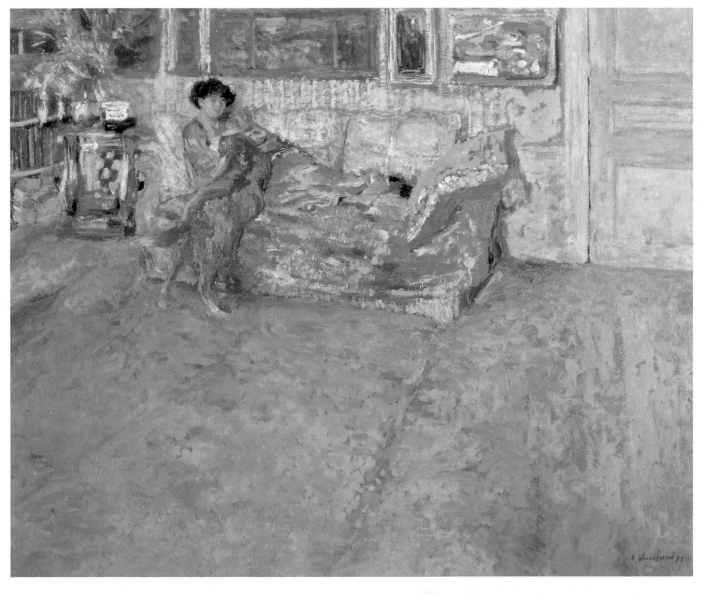

Moving subjects

Another reason for placing the main focal point off-centre is that when it's a moving subject it seldom looks right placed in the middle of the frame. It's not only a question of balance, but also that a moving subject needs space to move into – this may be space within the painting or, as below, it could just as well be space beyond the frame.

As well as involving the viewer, a subject with space in front of it suggests activity and direction. This is why pictures of moving figures or objects often have the main focal point off-centre, with space on the side of the frame or just beyond it for the object to move into.

► A centrally placed moving subject tends to feel static. To imply movement it should be placed to one side.

Here the artist has created a sense of movement by placing the boat far to the right so that it is cropped by the edge of the picture. In this way she suggests the space beyond the picture into which the vessel is moving.

'SCARBOROUGH SPA' BY BRENDA BRIN BOOKER BY COURTESY OF FIVE WOMEN ARTISTS, PLUS, 1993, ACRYLIC ON BOARD, 15 X 17½ IN

LEADING THE EYE

Guiding the viewer's eye to the focal point of your picture is easy – when you know how. Here are some of the most useful and common devices for achieving it.

One of the most important influences you, as the artist, have on viewers is to lead their eyes to the focal point of your picture. Most of the time you can pull this off with deceptive ease.

With a path
Make the most of a path, road, river or railway line to lead the eye to an important point. It's best if you 'break' the picture frame with it, meaning that the path should point out at the viewer and disappear into the depths of the painting, *beyond* the picture plane and to your focal point.

The eye has no trouble being guided in this way because paths and the like are all associated with travel anyway – the eye naturally follows a path to see what and where it is leading to.

Fences, walls, hedges and even buildings all have strong, straight lines or serpentine shapes that you can exploit. What's more, you probably won't have to 'create' one of these to do the job for you. It's more a question of seeing the possibilities and making adjustments so the composition works.

If you are painting or drawing directly from the landscape, for example, you can shift your position until you can see a wall or stream in a useful way. Perhaps by moving a bit to the right or left, or crouching down to change your viewpoint, you can make the wall appear to lead to a building on which you want to focus.

▼Nothing in this painting is coincidental. The path leads the eye from the space this side of the picture plane into the picture space beyond. From there a serpentine path takes you right up to the horizon, where you see the focal point, the horse of the title.

'VALE OF THE WHITE HORSE' BY RONALD MADDOX, WATERCOLOUR, 380 X 545MM

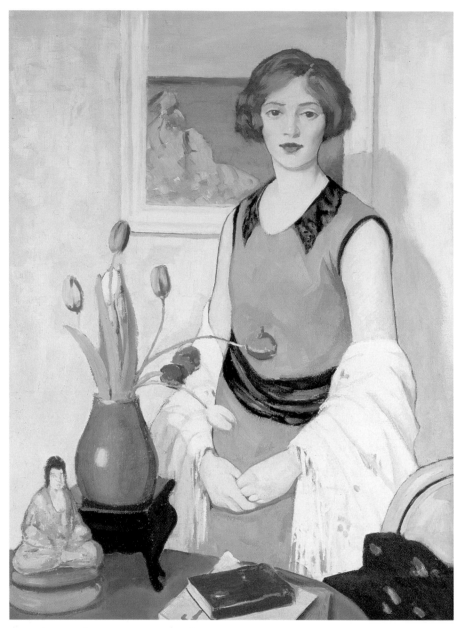

Experiment with these compositional possibilities by making rapid thumbnail sketches. You may find you need to remove a tree altogether or shift it slightly sideways so that the connection between the wall and building becomes all the clearer.

Another naturally occurring feature with a strong line to it is the horizon. This may be a dead straight horizontal – as in a seascape – but it could just as easily be undulating curves in a hilly area or steeply pitched angular shapes in a mountainous region.

In all these cases, you can use the outline to draw the eye from the edge of the picture to a focal point.

Framing the focal point

One way to draw attention to a special area of a picture is to frame it in some way. In a landscape you could use a pair of trees, a single tree with overhanging branches or an avenue of trees forming a tunnel. A bridge is yet another possibility – make use of its span or spans as individual frames.

Interiors, too, offer a host of framing opportunities. Doorways and windows in particular create a picture within a picture. But there are also more classical architectural devices such as porticos, arches and niches.

Colour and tone

You can use a carefully placed area of colour to remarkably good effect. Try setting off a bright colour with muted tones, for example, or use a 'hot' colour in an otherwise cold picture and vice versa. Even the smallest dash of colour can have a dramatic impact out of all proportion to its size.

▲ Your attention is drawn to this woman's head by the framed picture behind it. In effect she's framed twice – once by the frame of this painting and again by the landscape on the wall.

'PORTRAIT WITH STILL LIFE' BY GEORGE TELFER BEAR, OIL ON BOARD, 1003 X 742MM

► A dot of hot red sings out of a field of predominantly muted colour – an example of a little doing a great deal.

'VENETIAN LAGOON' BY HERCULES BRABAZON BRABAZON, WATERCOLOUR AND BODY COLOUR ON PAPER

SPACE IN PAINTINGS

The world exists in three dimensions. But how do you go about conveying this sense of space on a flat support such as paper, canvas or board?

Over time many conventions have evolved for describing space and for indicating the relative location of objects in that space. This visual language varies from culture to culture.

The art of Ancient Egypt, for instance, sought to provide the maximum amount of information. So faces were portrayed in profile, with eyes seen frontally. The torso was also painted frontally, but the legs, feet and arms were shown in profile.

The visual language we use today derives from the Italian Renaissance, which started in the 14th century. It depends on representing the appearance of things as seen from a single, fixed

POSITION ON THE PICTURE

The farther away an object is, the higher in the picture you place it. This was one of the first devices used by artists to convey an impression of distance. You'll see it a lot in medieval paintings.

viewpoint in space. It's a system that's called single-point perspective. In recent years many artists and artistic movements have deliberately broken away from the Renaissance commitment to this single-point perspective. Cézanne, for instance, separated space into basic planes and shapes without maintaining a fixed viewpoint. The Cubists went even further and showed several views of an object at the same time.

Here, though, we look at some of the devices you can use to indicate space, and location in space, in your pictures. Just which you go for depends on the subject and your intentions. You might, for instance, be delighted by the shapes and colours within a still life group. You could draw attention to these shapes and colours by simplifying the tonal arrangements and flattening the forms. This would emphasise the abstract qualities of the arrangement and do much to play down the spatial side of things.

RELATIVE SIZE

Things look smaller when they are far away and larger as you get closer to them. So when you draw three trees that are the same size in real life but are disappearing into the distance, you do them different sizes. The viewer automatically judges the smallest one to be farther away than the largest one.

► In this delightful painting the spatial descriptions are secondary to the abstract and decorative elements. But there are clues. The white horse cut into the chalk hillside is larger than the real horse in the field, but we understand that it is farther away simply because it is higher up in the picture area and nearer the horizon.

'WHITE HORSE WITH WHITE HORSE' BY RUTH STAGE, OIL ON GESSO BOARD, 20 X 25IN

COMPARISON WITH THE PICTURE FRAME

The relationship between an object and the picture frame can also give you information about spatial arrangements.

If you crop into an image – especially if the subject now 'breaks' the frame – the viewer sees the subject as close to the picture surface. (Think of a tree very close to a window.)

On the other hand, if you place the subject in the middle of the picture area, the viewer assumes that it is farther away from the picture surface. The small size of the tree in this situation also helps to reinforce the feeling of distance.

tree close up

tree farther away

► By cropping right into the sunflower heads in this picture the artist leaves the viewer in no doubt that they are close to the picture surface. The apparent difference in size between the foreground flowers and those in the background creates a dramatic sense of recession.

'SUNFLOWERS' BY GODFREY TONKS, CHARCOAL, COLOURED INKS AND PASTEL, 22 X 30IN

DID YOU KNOW?

Your point of view
Most children instinctively draw objects from the viewpoint that gives the most information. So they draw a house from the front, but a lorry from the side – because it's from there that you can see the cab, trailer and wheels.

OVERLAPPING OR INTERPOSITION

When objects are almost behind one another, you overlap them. The picture to the near right is generally seen – according to convention in Western art – as three complete trees, one behind the other. But you could also interpret it as three adjacent shapes: one complete tree, and behind it two others with bites taken out. It's a measure of how completely – and unconsciously – we accept the convention that most of us simply don't see these three adjacent shapes.

three overlapping trees?

or one whole tree and two with bites out of them?

TEXTURE GRADIENT

The closer you are to a textured surface the coarser – more detailed – it seems. So when you're painting a tree in the foreground you show as many of the individual leaves as you can. When you're painting a tree away in the distance, you do a greenish, untextured blur instead. You can use this device together with atmospheric perspective (see below) to create a convincing sense of space in landscapes.

◀ The dabs of bright colour in the foreground of this picture are larger and more defined and have more texture than those in the background. Texture here becomes a useful device for emphasising the foreground in favour of the background, and so suggests recession in an immediate, clear way.

'UNTITLED NO. 124' BY TREVOR NEAL, OIL ON CANVAS, 22 X 18IN

ATMOSPHERIC PERSPECTIVE

Objects in the distance not only appear smaller, they also seem less bright and less clear. So when you're painting trees in the foreground they're vivid green. Those in the distance, however, have a bluish quality.

▲ Atmospheric perspective helps create a sense of recession in landscape paintings where there are no obvious linear elements to give you clues. By making the hills on the horizon paler and bluer than those in the middle distance, the artist here has created the illusion that they are farther away. The more detailed texture of the trees in the foreground brings that area forward.

'LAKE GARDA' BY GRETA FENTON, WATERCOLOUR ON PAPER, 22 X 12IN

◀ Many pictures by the surrealist artist Magritte are disquieting because they challenge our assumptions on the way we see and understand the visual world. Here two subjects are shown realistically – a room and an apple. But by putting the two together, Magritte creates an ambiguity – are we seeing a tiny room with a normal size apple in it, or is it a normal size room with a huge apple?

'THE LISTENING ROOM' BY RENÉ MAGRITTE, 1958, © ADAGP, PARIS AND DACS, LONDON 1994, OIL ON CANVAS, 38 X 45.8CM

TONE

Light reveals form, so the way you disperse light and dark tones about an object gives clues to its shape and solidity. In fact, you can create images which appear to have volume and take up space by using tone only – as the second of the two trees shown on the right demonstrates.

▶ In this sensitive head and shoulders study in graphite, the play of light and dark across the forms is rendered mainly in tone – with little help from line. Careful modelling with many subtle light and dark tones has enabled the artist to create the illusion of a convincingly solid, three-dimensional image.

'SALLY' BY JACQUELINE HINES, GRAPHITE ON PAPER, 28½ X 23¾IN

LINEAR PERSPECTIVE

This is one of the best-known clues to depth. Put simply, it means that parallel lines appear to converge as the lines recede horizontally away from you. It calls for the distortion of objects. Take a cube. The laws of single-point perspective turn the sides into trapezoids. And a circle (eg. a plate) becomes an ellipse. Usually we see this distortion of objects as perfectly 'realistic'.

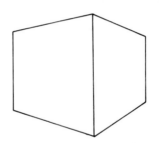

cube – horizontally receding sides appear trapezoidal

circular plate – appears elliptical when viewed from an oblique angle

◀ This well known painting is famous for its inspired use of single-point perspective. It's not just that the trees nearest the horizon appear smaller than those nearest the viewer. You'll find that lines drawn through the tree tops on either side of the road appear to descend towards a point on the horizon, while lines through the tree bases appear to ascend to the same point.

'THE AVENUE AT MIDDELHARNIS' BY MEINDART HOBBEMA, (REPRODUCED BY COURTESY OF THE TRUSTEES OF THE NATIONAL GALLERY, LONDON), OIL ON CANVAS, 40¾ X 55½IN

PERSPECTIVE MADE EASY

Far from being the daunting thing most people think it is, linear perspective is really very simple. What's more, you'll find you probably have a fairly good grasp of it already.

The basic principles of linear perspective are mechanical and very straightforward. So, once you've mastered them, you can put them to use freely and creatively.

You may argue that your perspective drawing is already excellent, working as you do from pure observation. But a sound knowledge of linear perspective still comes in handy because it helps you understand what you see. What's more it's an invaluable aid for troubleshooting and for correcting mistakes. So let's now look at what linear perspective is all about.

Linear perspective is no more nor less than a system for creating an illusion of three-dimensional space on the flat surface of a support. When it's done successfully, the relative position of objects in the picture, and their relative size, appear to the eye just as they appear to the eye in real life.

One of the most striking examples of linear perspective is the way parallel lines – such as the top and bottom of the side of the building in the picture below – seem to join together at a point on the horizon.

Before we can look deeper into perspective we need to define a few terms (see overleaf).

▼ The workings of basic linear perspective are easy to grasp. Imagine you're looking through a window at a building, and drawing on the glass. The building is parallel to the window, with its sides at right angles. Notice the way the top of the side slopes *down*, while the bottom of the side slopes *up*.

eye level (same as horizon line)

ground plane

Ground plane, horizon line and eye level

The flat extension of the ground you're positioned on is the **ground plane**.

The height of your eyes from the ground is your **eye level** – it always coincides with the **horizon line**. So when you're sitting down you can see less of the ground plane, and the horizon line seems nearer than ....

..... when you're standing up. Standing up, you can see more of the ground plane and the horizon line seems farther away.

centre of vision

vanishing point

Centre of vision

A child sees less of the ground plane than a standing adult can, but about the same as a seated adult.

The point on the horizon line which is directly in front of the viewer's eye is called the **centre of vision**.

Vanishing point

The point on the horizon line at which parallel lines – like those of the furrows – seem to converge is the **vanishing point**. The vanishing point for all lines which recede at right angles from the picture plane coincides with the centre of vision.

ONE-POINT PERSPECTIVE

Looking again at the picture on the opening page of this chapter, you can see that the converging lines of one side of the building meet at the vanishing point. This point is the same as the artist's centre of vision and it's also at his eye level and on the horizon line.

This sort of perspective is known as one-point perspective because the converging lines of one side of the building can be extended to meet at one point (the lines of the front of the building always remain parallel, however, because of your viewpoint).

One-point perspective is sometimes called central/parallel perspective and it's the simplest form of linear perspective. Later in this chapter we look at two more complex forms of linear perspective.

▶ This witty picture plays games with the illusions used in conventional painting, especially with the idea of the picture plane.

'THE DOMAIN OF ARNHEIM' BY RENE MAGRITTE, 1949, OIL ON CANVAS, 99.4 X 81.3CM

Defining a few terms

The picture plane is an imaginary vertical plane which coincides with the surface plane of your picture. Another way to visualise it is as a sheet of glass between you and the subject. On the next page you can read more about the picture plane.

The ground plane is the horizontal plane that you, the viewer, are positioned on (or imagine you're positioned on).

The eye level is the height of your eyes from the ground as you view the scene. A tall person's eye level is obviously higher than a short person's, and an adult's is higher than a child's.

Eye level defines how far you can see — if you are taller or higher up you can see farther than if you are shorter, sitting down or crouching.

The eye level assumes you are looking straight ahead. It does not change when you tip your head back or look down. It simply tells the viewer how high up you were when you did the drawing.

The horizon line is the line at which the sky meets — or appears to meet — the ground. It coincides with your eye level, so if your eye level changes it affects the horizon line. If you are tall or high up, for instance, you can see farther so the horizon appears to be farther away. If you are short or crouching, you can't see quite so far so the horizon appears to be nearer.

The vanishing point is the point on the horizon line at which parallel lines seem to converge.

The centre of vision is a point on the horizon which is directly in front of the viewer's eye.

▼One-point perspective performs two functions in this painting – it creates a sense of space and acts as a compositional device. The building is the focal point of the picture and it's placed in the upper third of the painting, leaving the lower two-thirds relatively empty. The pollarded tree at the front connects foreground to background, while the converging rows of vines ensure that the eye is led to the building.

SEE FOR YOURSELF –
THE WINDOW PICTURE PLANE

Demonstrate for yourself the principles of linear perspective by looking through a window and tracing what you see. You need a sheet of transparent material such as glass, perspex or – as we used here – acetate (it's available from art shops). It doesn't matter which; this is just an exercise. You also need something to draw with – a chinagraph pencil, a permanent marker or some acrylic paint and a brush.

Fix the transparent material to the window with tape – this is now your picture plane. Close one eye and start to trace what you see. You'll have to stand very still or you'll find the drawing begins to wander. It's a good idea to select a particular line as your base point – the corner of a building, say. Establish this base point and keep checking that the drawn line is over the actual line.

Continue with the tracing. When you have finished you will find that parallel lines do converge, and that your drawing obeys the rules of perspective and is a convincing depiction of the scene.

More one-point perspective

When it comes to drawing and painting, you're as likely to be working indoors as outdoors in the open air. So the question of getting the perspective right is just as important.

One-point is the simplest kind of perspective, and you can put this into action for yourself indoors by standing in a square or rectangular room.

Position yourself with your back exactly in the centre of one wall. Now look at the far end. Notice how the side walls appear closer together the farther away they are from you. If the far end weren't there at all and the side walls continued on and on, they'd appear to meet. The place they'd seem to meet at – the *one point* of *one-point* perspective – is known as the vanishing point (see **step 1** below).

Now, still with your back to the wall, move towards one side of the room. You're still seeing one-point perspective (because the far wall is parallel to the picture plane), but your view is rather different. That's because your centre of vision has moved with you (see **step 2**).

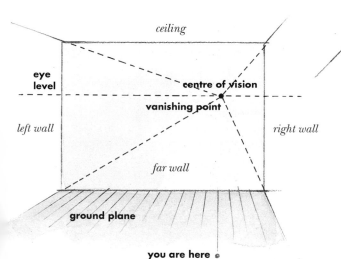

ceiling

eye level

centre of vision

vanishing point

left wall

right wall

far wall

ground plane

you are here

◀ **1** With your back in the middle of one wall, look at the far wall parallel to it. Notice how the side walls appear to converge, and how the lines below your eye level slope up, while those above it slope down. If these lines were to continue beyond the far wall, they'd appear to meet, and that point is called the vanishing point. Notice how the vanishing point is at your eye level and also at your centre of vision, which is the point directly opposite where you're standing.

▼ **2** With your back still against the wall, move to one side. Your whole view has now changed. As you moved, your centre of vision moved with you. The vanishing point has moved as well. It's still at eye level, but the lines of the side walls now converge at different angles – more steeply on one side than on the other.

eye level

vanishing point

horizon line

▲ With a window in the far wall, you can see that the vanishing point of the converging side walls is on the horizon line – proof, if proof were needed, that the horizon line always coincides with your eye level.

ceiling

eye level

centre of vision

vanishing point

left wall

right wall

far wall

ground plane

you are here

Now over to you – draw a room in one-point perspective

Here's the right wall of a room in one-point perspective. To complete it, you need to extend the converging lines of the wall and find the vanishing point (it's the same as your centre of vision). Then draw in:

☐ the left wall
☐ the far wall
☐ a window in the far wall
☐ the horizon line/your
  eye level

If that's all plain sailing, draw a door in the left wall, a window in the right wall, and the floorboards of the ground plane. And if that presents no problem, draw another sketch where your centre of vision is to one side of the room, as it is in step 2 on the previous page. See how simple one-point perspective really is!

One-point perspective plus

Useful as one-point perspective is, it doesn't cover all eventualities. That's because the far wall of your room isn't always parallel to the picture plane. But before we go into that, let's look at the table with the box on it in the foreground of the room below.

If you were drawing the table, the rules of one-point perspective would apply because its front edge is parallel to the picture plane. When it comes to the box, though, it's an entirely different story.

Looking at the box, you can see two sides at the same time, and neither of them is parallel to the picture plane. The box is in fact drawn in *two-*point perspective, and you can read more about that on the next page.

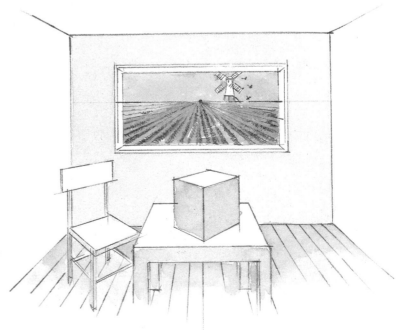

▶ With its converging sides, and front edge parallel to the picture plane, the table is clearly in one-point perspective. But what about the box on top of it? It has *two* sides with converging lines and therefore two vanishing points. We call this *two*-point perspective. See the next page for more about it.

Two-point perspective

In the sketch below, you can see two sides of the same building. You could of course see two sides of the building in the one-point perspective sketch (see pages 89–92), but the difference here is that *both* sides have converging lines because neither is parallel to the picture plane. And with two sets of two converging lines there have to be two vanishing points – one on either side of the building.

Notice that both vanishing points are on the same horizon line, which means they're also at the viewer's eye level. (Notice, too, that all vertical lines stay parallel.) This time, though, neither vanishing point coincides with the viewer's centre of vision.

You may ask how our room looks in two-point perspective. Well, to get two vanishing points you have to imagine moving into one corner of the square or rectangular room and looking from there directly into the opposite corner. The converging lines of the right wall would meet at some point far to your left, while those of the left wall would join at some point on your right. Both these points would be at your eye level and on the horizon line. And neither of them would be at your centre of vision.

▼ When you're depicting a building that isn't parallel to the picture plane, you have *two*-point perspective. That's because the visible sides both have converging lines – these meet at two separate vanishing points. Both vanishing points are on the horizon line and at your eye level. Neither coincides with your centre of vision.

▲ In this gouache painting of a view of farm buildings in Cumbria there are two vanishing points – both outside the picture area.

All-important are the precise angles at which the lines of the roof and those of the walls ascend or descend to the vanishing points. These could certainly be measured with a pair of angle-measuring scissors, which you can read about on pages 97–100.

Three-point perspective

If you stand at the bottom of a tall building such as a skyscraper or cathedral tower and look up, you'll find that the vertical lines are converging. So in addition to the two vanishing points of two-point perspective there's a third vanishing point – making this three-point perspective.

You also see things in three-point perspective when you have a bird's eye view, looking down on a tallish building from an even taller one.

Three-point perspective isn't something you come across all that often – but you just might, particularly if you were producing a technical perspective drawing of a building.

There are occasions when you might choose to ignore three-point perspective, such as when you're drawing a terrace of tall houses from a viewpoint across the street. This is quite acceptable.

► Imagine looking at a tall building in two-point perspective and then glancing up. In addition to the vanishing point to your right and the one to your left, you now have a third one, way up in the sky where the converging verticals of the building meet. This is three-point perspective. As you can guess, its applications are fairly limited.

Getting the angle right

Getting perspective right is often just a matter of observing and drawing angles correctly. In the case of a building viewed absolutely front-on, this is quite straightforward because most of the angles are right angles (of 90°). But when you're looking at the same building in two-point perspective, life becomes somewhat more complicated – because all the angles are now greater or lesser than 90°. This is where a pair of angle-measuring scissors comes in handy. Fortunately they're very simple to make, and even easier to use.

Tip

Check your perspective
You might well have seen artists holding up a pencil to the scene they're drawing. This has as much to do with getting

◀ **1** To make a handy pair of angle-measuring scissors, all you need is a piece of stiffish card and a paper fastener. Cut the card into two strips about 5cm wide and 25cm long. Fix these two strips tightly together with the paper fastener. You're now ready for action.

5cm

25cm

angles right as it does with measuring, which you can read about for yourself in *Making Measured Drawings* on pages 23–26. (See also the Nine Checks on pages 40–42)

◀ **2** To use your pair of angle-measuring scissors, start by imagining there's a sheet of glass vertically in front of you. This is like the window picture plane you read about in Composition 8.

Now hold out the scissors at arm's length. Most importantly, make sure they're flat against the imaginary sheet of glass.

Use your other hand to move the two arms of the scissors until they match the angle you're interested in – here it's the line of the roof compared with a vertical line. Remember, the scissors should be flat against the imaginary glass.

▶ **3** Holding the scissors tightly so you don't lose the angle you've just measured, transfer them to the right spot on your canvas. Align the vertical scissor-arm with the edge of the canvas, then draw in the angle. There you have the correct angle for the rooftop!

Aerial perspective

A simple, effective way of creating the illusion of space in your landscape painting is to mimic aerial perspective.

Aerial perspective – sometimes called *atmospheric* perspective – describes the way the atmosphere affects light travelling through it. Far from being a vacuum enveloping the world, the atmosphere is actually made up of gases, moisture and tiny particles, and it's these that have an impact on light.

There are several effects of aerial perspective, all of which vary with location, time of day and time of year.

● Among the most notable of these effects is the

the intense blue of the sky pales towards the horizon

in the distance there is less contrast of tone in the vines

the vines in the foreground have strong contrasts of light and dark tones

way colours appear cooler and bluer with increasing distance – check for yourself.
● They also seem less bright, so a red pillar box appears browner and less red as you move away from it.
● What's more, there's less contrast between the lightest and darkest areas of an object.

● And its outlines and details appear increasingly blurred and ill defined.

Below is a landscape painted in watercolour by our artist. In it he makes good use of the effects of aerial perspective to create an extremely convincing sense of space. We show you exactly how he pulled it off.

the most distant hills are pale and blue

nearer, the hills are darker and less blue

the converging lines of the vines and posts imply recession

a touch of 'hot' red brings this area forward

the detailed texture of this area brings it towards the picture plane

Turner and aerial perspective

Aerial perspective gives you the opportunity to introduce light and space into landscape paintings which might otherwise have few clues to spatial arrangements. It's a device much exploited by Turner, one of Britain's greatest and most influential painters.

Joseph Mallord William Turner (1775-1851) was a genius with light. His later landscapes in particular have a fleeting, insubstantial quality in which forms are dissolved by light so there are few solid objects, and details are hard to make out. Sunlight is dispersed through a misty, hazy atmosphere and the subject is enveloped in – and devoured by – dazzling light.

It was Turner's treatment of light that attracted the interest of the Impressionists and Post Impressionists. Both Monet and Pissarro visited London in 1870-71 and Turner's influence can be traced in their work. Like him, they were concerned with the scrupulously exact observation of nature, and the most fleeting phenomena of light.

The French artist Henri Matisse (1869-1954) said of Turner: he 'lived in a cellar. Once a week he threw open the shutters, and then, what incandescences! what dazzle! what jewellery!'

▼This painting is full of ambiguities – just as you begin to find the forms of the sailing ships, they appear to dissolve on the shimmering surface. There is, however, a definite sense of space and recession, with your eye travelling over the water and away to the pale horizon.

'PEACE: BURIAL AT SEA' BY JMW TURNER, 1842, OIL ON CANVAS, 87 X 86.7CM, TATE GALLERY LONDON

CREATIVE CROPPING

Usually all the compositional decisions are made at the beginning of the picture-making process, but sometimes it's not until late on that you realise how things could be improved.

However carefully you plan a composition, there can be times when you want to make changes at a later stage. Your picture might look too symmetrical, perhaps with a horizon line passing through the exact centre; or it might be unbalanced, with too much empty space on one side. Both problems may be too fundamental to change with paint or pencil, but both can be solved with judicious cropping – literally chopping off part of the picture to improve it.

Successful cropping may involve nothing more than trimming a narrow band off one edge of a picture. Or it can be altogether more radical – you may decide to remove a substantial area from two or more sides. (On a more creative note, it's not unknown for artists to cut a picture in two, getting two pictures out of one. You might even decide to cut up a large picture and make it into several smaller pictures.)

Cropping can be creative and fun – a positive part of picture making – and it's also useful as a damage limitation exercise. Some artists crop their pictures quite frequently, finding it gives the images new energy and vitality. However, cropping should never become a lazy habit or a substitute for planning a composition properly in

the first place. After all, you won't always be able to rectify a bad composition by cropping it.

When you crop a painting or drawing you are effectively creating a new composition – the principles are exactly the same as those for good composition. You can crop at any stage in a painting or drawing, but it's important to think carefully about what you want to do, and why.

Once you've decided to crop, stand back from the work and take some time to plan the new

▼ Although this portrait works perfectly well as it is, the artist thought that he might crop the picture just below the girl's elbows or even crop right in on her head and shoulders (below left) to create a more eye-catching and focused image.

'LYDIA' BY DENNIS GILBERT, OIL ON CANVAS, 30 X 25IN

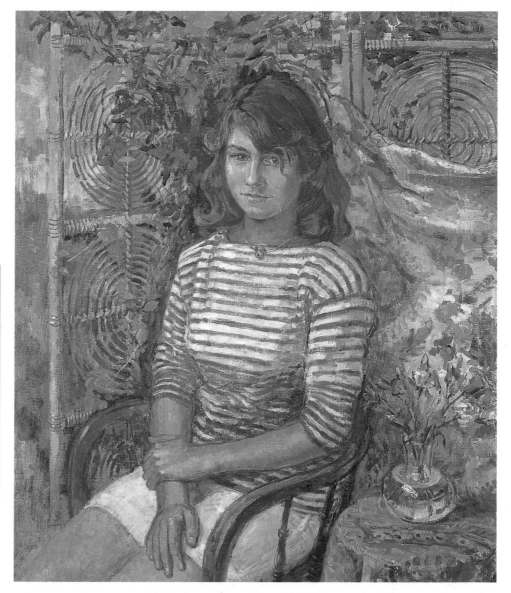

composition. If the work is small enough, use L-shaped brackets, moving them about until you frame the composition you want. On a larger work, it's easier to use strips of card or paper to mask out the unwanted edges.

Don't make your crops too drastic at first. If in any doubt, cut off too little rather than too much. You can always trim off a bit more, but you can't put back what you've already taken away.

Watercolours don't allow you to make major changes because you can't cover over or remove colour. When things go drastically wrong with a watercolour, cropping is the only available means of making significant changes. Fortunately, works on paper and thin card are easy to crop.

Once you have decided where you want to cut, use a T-square to get a perfect right angle with the edge of the paper. Draw the proposed cutting line

▲ This painting of the Festival Gardens on the South Bank of the Thames is packed with many cropping possibilities. If required, it could be made into many successful but smaller paintings instead of one large one.

'BIG BEN' BY DENNIS GILBERT, OIL ON CANVAS, 40 X 30IN

► Don't fall into the trap of thinking only in terms of standard portrait or landscape rectangles. Long and thin or short and wide formats can be really eye-catching. This view of the river seen through trees, for example, makes a delightful cameo.

◀ This crop concentrates on the most recognisable landmark in the painting – the Houses of Parliament on the other side of the river. Notice that the river cuts the picture horizontally along one of the thirds, and the clock tower is also placed off-centre, creating a pleasingly natural balance.

▼ This area plays just a small part in the painting, so it's probably not the first thing that would come to mind as a composition in its own right. However, by moving the L-shaped brackets around, the artist discovered its potential. Notice how our attention is drawn by the children in the front and how we are then led via the zigzagging wall through the trees to the river.

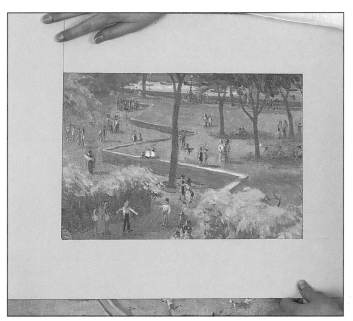

▼ The slide was the focal point for this attractive scene in the playground area of the gardens. If the artist wanted to, he could isolate this portion and make two or three other pictures out of the rest of the painting. In fact he could get all four of the compositions on this page out of the one painting.

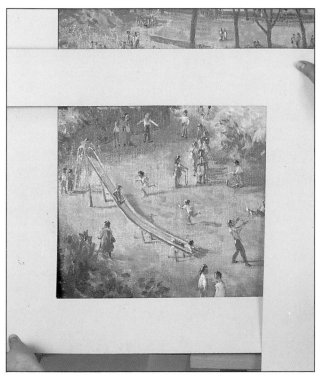

▼ A secluded spot in the garden provides privacy for this pair of lovers. The picture captures a fleeting moment in the couple's lives, and reminds us that the larger painting comprises a series of little incidents in the lives of the characters shown. Each incident could make a painting in its own right.

lightly with pencil, then take a second look to make sure you're cropping in the right places. Cut paper and thin card with a guillotine or craft knife held against a metal rule. Avoid scissors – they don't produce a really straight line.

Acrylics and oils With opaque media, such as oil and acrylic, compositional changes are usually made with the paint itself by rubbing back or overpainting. However, there may be occasions when you want to change the size or proportions of the support, or to chop off part of the composition without altering the work you've already done.

Paintings on plywood or hardboard can be cropped, but the paint must be completely dry. You will need a fine saw – an electric jig saw on a '0' setting is ideal, or a tenon saw if you are doing it by hand. The sawn edge will be slightly jagged, especially on the underside, so make sure your painting faces upwards as you saw. Smooth the sawn edge with fine sandpaper – framing the picture will hide the sawn edge.

▶ Like the painting on the previous pages, this picture of Piccadilly Arcade in London includes many people involved in their daily life, some of whom could be the focus of a painting. The different architectural areas of the picture could also be divided off. For example, the top of the painting, from the arcade sign upwards, would make an interesting picture.

'PICCADILLY ARCADE' BY DENNIS GILBERT, OIL ON CANVAS, 40 X 30IN

▼ This crop focuses on the lower right corner of the painting, including two police officers, one of whom is pointing to a mysterious gentleman in a fur hat. His portfolio gives him away – he is the artist who painted the picture. If you study the painting on the previous pages, you'll see that he appears in that scene too!

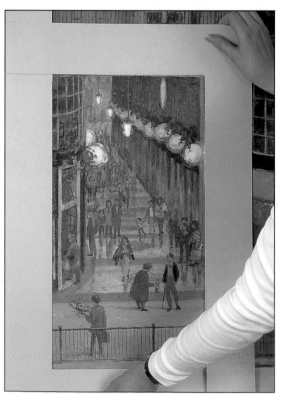

◀ This is an obvious part of the painting to isolate. There's plenty going on in the foreground, with the lady collecting for charity and the man with the bouquet of flowers who is clearly waiting for someone. The diagonal of the arcade also provides a good compositional device to lead the viewer farther into the scene.

CHAPTER FOUR

WORKING FROM COLLECTED MATERIALS

AIDS TO COMPOSITION

A good composition will help you hold the attention of the viewer. Here we look at some simple devices to help you select, edit and decide what to emphasise.

Many artists' tools are expensive, so it's delightful to find ones which are useful yet cheap. Two such tools are a viewfinder, which can be made from card, and a pair of L-shaped brackets, also made from card.

A viewfinder is basically a piece of card with a rectangular hole in the middle – like a picture mount – which helps you frame and isolate your subject. A landscape subject, for example, is daunting because you

are presented with so many possibilities – you can select from a 360° panorama and any point from the ground at your feet to the sky above. A viewfinder makes the process much easier. By scanning the vista through this card frame, you can isolate small sections and consider their picture-making potential.

A viewfinder is useful for considering almost any subject – an interior, a landscape or even a figure study. In fact, once you've used a viewfinder, you'll feel lost without one.

▲ A viewfinder is a useful tool which enables the artist to assess his options quickly. Yet it's inexpensive and easy to make for yourself from card.

Our artist's version measures 20 x 17cm with a central opening of 12 x 9cm (the frame was 4cm wide all round). He divided his viewfinder into a grid with rubber bands which makes it easier to assess positions. The rubber bands are a third of the way in along each edge of the aperture, and are held in place by grooves cut in the card.

► Our artist made three quick thumbnail sketches before deciding that this was the composition he wanted for his painting. A large sketch, with a few colour scribbles, backed up with a photograph, is all he needs as reference for a painting.

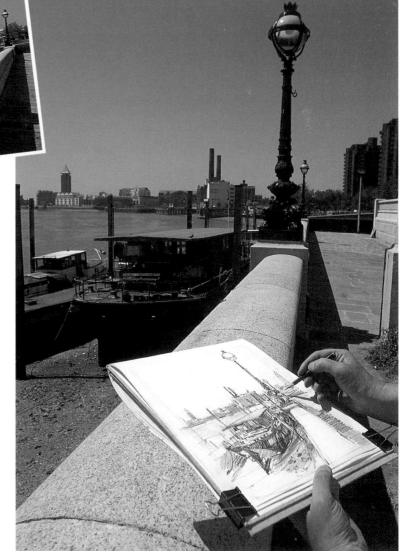

A viewfinder enables the artist to consider the way the image will fit within the rectangle of the support. Should the subject occupy the centre of the support or fall on the third? Should it break the paper at the top or bottom or is it more effective if it is contained within the picture area? By bringing the viewfinder towards you, you'll be able to see more of the vista – and less as you hold it farther away from you. A few thumbnail sketches will record what you see so that you can compare the options or even revisit them at a later date.

You can also use your viewfinder to experiment with different formats – will the composition be most effective as a portrait or landscape, or even as a square?

L-shaped brackets are simply L-shaped pieces of card which you can form into an adjustable rectangle or square, using bulldog clips or your fingers to hold them together (see below). The great advantage of this sort of viewfinder is that you can manipulate the Ls to create larger or smaller windows, or to change the format from a long rectangle to a square. The Ls can also be dropped over compositional sketches in the field to check the composition. Or you can use them to isolate a section of a drawing to see how it will work as a painting.

Your hands provide the easiest 'viewfinder' and will cost you nothing at all. You can frame an image between your thumbs and forefingers (below left) but this method is not as easy or as effective as using Ls or a viewfinder.

▲► Our artist assessed the scene through his L-shaped brackets which he formed into a viewfinder. He held them together with the bulldog clips he uses to hold down the pages of his sketchbook on windy days. His Ls were 6cm wide, with legs 20cm long.

▲► Your fingers and thumbs make a makeshift viewfinder (above) which you can use if you haven't got a viewfinder or pair of Ls handy.

A viewfinder is easy to use and if you divide the aperture with elastic bands or threads it will help you position the important features of your sketch (right). Our artist put elastic bands a third of the way in from each edge. This is also helpful if you wish to position your subject in accordance with the rule of thirds.

◄ A quick thumbnail sketch showed our artist where the basic elements of the view would fall in a landscape format.

► Now our artist tried a portrait format. He decided that he liked the strong vertical element of the river wall and lamp from his first thumbnail sketch, so he kept this in, but he didn't add any more to the height of the composition – he merely cropped into the landscape version.

▲ For his third thumbnail sketch, our artist decided to show more of the area to the right of the lamp, bringing the lamp further into the picture.

◄ Our artist liked his last thumbnail sketch best so he prepared a larger, more detailed version, adding a little colour for reference. He believes it is very important to name and date his sketches for future reference.

Chelsea Reach
15th June '94

Thumbnail sketches

Even when you're fairly happy with the view through your viewfinder, it's worth doing a few thumbnail sketches of alternatives so you can consider different options. Work quickly, looking for basic geometric shapes, repeated shapes and angles, and the way areas of light and dark are distributed across the picture.

Light is an important element in any painting or drawing, so use your thumbnails to consider the direction of light. Screw up your eyes and look for the areas of light and dark. Scribble these in broadly so they read as abstract patterns. If the light is behind you, the colour will be heightened but the modelling of forms will be minimised. Side lighting, on the other hand, highlights the three-dimensional quality of the subject.

▶ A camera is a wonderfully useful tool, which you shouldn't overlook even when you are sketching in situ. Although it's always better to paint from life, your photographs will provide excellent additional information about details and colours.

Our artist had an old Polaroid camera which meant that he could check his photos immediately and compare them with the scene.

▲ Our artist was attracted by the strong lines and wonderful colour of London's Albert Bridge, a little way up the river Thames from where he made his previous sketches. He used his Ls to assess the format.

▲ This suspension bridge is much more difficult to draw than it may look because of the complicated arrangement of cables and the angles of the towers, bridge and steps. So our artist used the elastic bands on his viewfinder to help him.

▶ Now he tried a landscape format. This gives the bridge more context than the tight square format he tried first (above).

WORKING FROM PHOTOGRAPHS

If the scene you want to paint is constantly changing or highly complex, if the weather is inclement or if you have simply run out of time, then a photograph is definitely in order.

There's nothing new about using a photograph as a reference. More than a century and a half ago, Turner (1775-1851) saw some of the very earliest photographs. He was so captivated by a print of Niagara Falls, which showed the effect of refracted light on frothy water, that he was inspired to try the same effect with paint. The resulting studies of light and colour are generally considered to be the direct forerunners of Impressionism and one of the major influences on painting today.

Since then photography has had a direct influence on many other artists, including the French painters Corot (1796-1875) and Courbet (1819-1877). Both worked from photographs – Corot learned from photographs how to create the impression of light using tiny flecks of white paint; Courbet preferred a photograph to real life because he felt it provided him with a more objective image.

Today artists have all the benefits of advanced photography – colour film, fast film, zoom and wide angle lenses, and so on. The drawback is that the photos can take over, and the artist can rely too heavily on them. They should never become a substitute for looking at the subject itself.

▼Courbet is known to have used several photographs as references for this complicated painting. They helped him achieve the realism that he is famous for.

'THE PAINTER'S STUDIO', 1854-5, BY GUSTAVE COURBET, OIL; ON CANVAS, 359 X 598CM

► If you take a series of connecting pictures, like these, you can stick them together to form a wonderful panorama with plenty of detail. You can even carry on taking shots until you have a full 360° view. These composite photographs make excellent reference material.

Making the most of photographs

The rectangular format of a photograph is not necessarily the best shape for your composition. So to give yourself more scope for manoeuvre, don't cramp your subject; allow more background area than you think you'll need, so that you can play around with the composition later by cropping into it.

The other thing you might try is to compile a series of pictures, giving you good details of a large area. To do this, just stand in one spot and take several pictures, moving your camera round so that each picture just overlaps the one before – you can get a full 360° view this way. You can also move the camera up and down to take in more sky and land. When the prints are assembled you will have a panoramic jigsaw, which you can paint as a single large picture or pick and choose from, exactly as if you were working from life.

If you have a projector at home, you may like to consider using slides instead of prints. Slide colours are usually more natural because the transparent image retains the qualities of light and shade. The flattening effects found in printed photographs are thus minimised.

◄ For this photo montage, all the photographs were taken from one spot – except the picture of Canterbury Cathedral. Nevertheless it fits its place convincingly, and the resulting picture by John Harvey (below) captures the changing scene which you would see as you near the cathedral.

Canterbury, Kent — John Harvey

Why work from a photograph?

There are many occasions when working from a photograph is simply easier than working from the actual subject. For example, *light* and *weather* are remarkably changeable, and you might start a landscape painting in brilliant sunlight only to find that the light has changed dramatically and you are painting in the pouring rain. Not only are you getting very wet, but suddenly the scene in front of you is completely different from the one you started painting. And even if you are working indoors, the light can shift, your model may change position or your flowers may wilt.

A photograph taken before you start work gives you a *permanent record*

of the subject and enables you to complete the work in your own time. You might even consider investing in a Polaroid camera so you can get your pictures straight away. Then, if you are painting outdoors, you can take a picture of the sky, say, and use the photograph for reference to paint

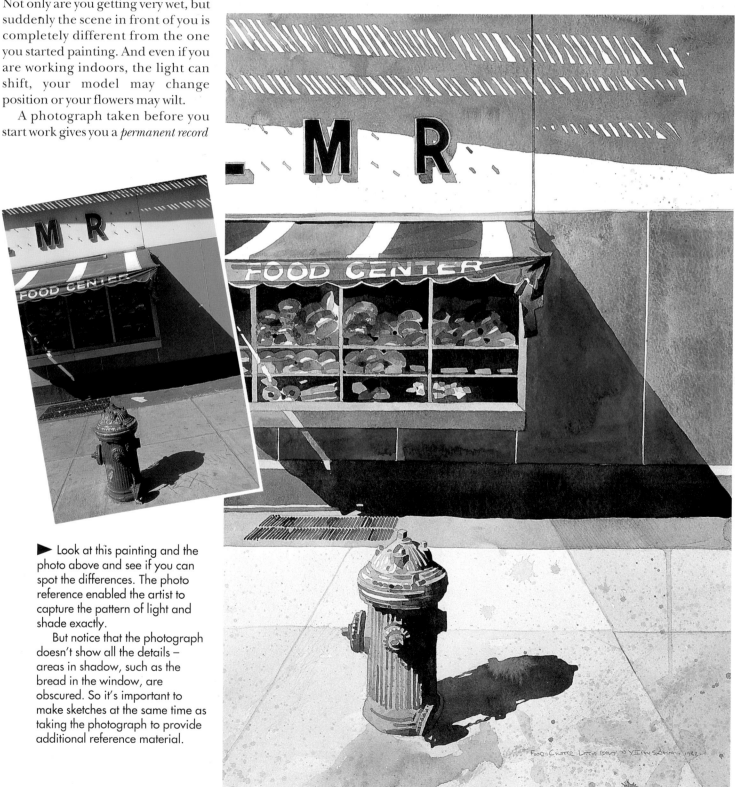

► Look at this painting and the photo above and see if you can spot the differences. The photo reference enabled the artist to capture the pattern of light and shade exactly.

But notice that the photograph doesn't show all the details – areas in shadow, such as the bread in the window, are obscured. So it's important to make sketches at the same time as taking the photograph to provide additional reference material.

the sky exactly as you first saw it, even if the clouds have completely blown away by the time you come to putting in the details.

Perhaps a camera is most useful when there is lots of *movement* in a scene. Think of a busy market scene, with lots of people rushing about, of ships swaying to and fro at sea or cars zooming around a race track. If you want to capture any of these subjects, you'll find it much easier to freeze them in a photo. And even for something like a portrait, you can use a camera to freeze that elusive smile on a young woman or the sleepy expression of a child.

You may also want to use photographic references if your subject is very *difficult*. Have you ever looked at a painting of waves or a babbling stream, or marvelled at the rippling surface of a David Hockney swimming pool? And did you wonder how on earth the artist managed to recreate the effect of moving water so convincingly? You will find these effects much easier to paint if you have a photograph showing clearly the patterns of light, shade and colour on the surface of the water. The moment is fixed in time, enabling you to study the

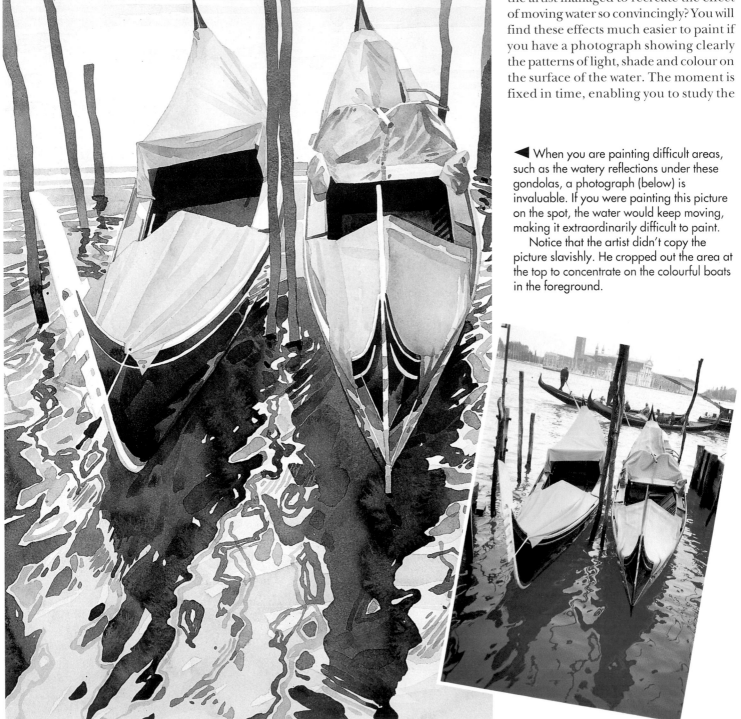

◄ When you are painting difficult areas, such as the watery reflections under these gondolas, a photograph (below) is invaluable. If you were painting this picture on the spot, the water would keep moving, making it extraordinarily difficult to paint.

Notice that the artist didn't copy the picture slavishly. He cropped out the area at the top to concentrate on the colourful boats in the foreground.

subject at leisure and make thoughtful decisions about the best way to capture the effect of movement in your painting or drawing.

On *holiday* your camera can again prove invaluable. Not enough time to finish a painting or even to start one? A quick sketch backed up by a few photographs should give you enough information to make a painting at home.

It's a good idea to carry your camera with you whenever possible to back up your sketches. Use it to photograph any incidents or scenes which particularly interest you and to record details of everyday subjects – anything you feel might be included in a future painting. This way you will build up a personal collection – a source of subject matter to draw on at a later date.

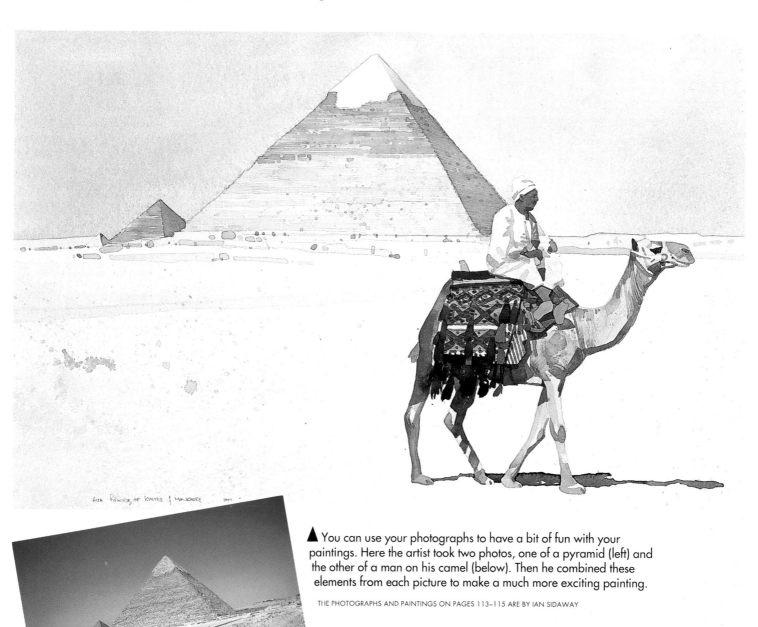

▲ You can use your photographs to have a bit of fun with your paintings. Here the artist took two photos, one of a pyramid (left) and the other of a man on his camel (below). Then he combined these elements from each picture to make a much more exciting painting.

THE PHOTOGRAPHS AND PAINTINGS ON PAGES 113–115 ARE BY IAN SIDAWAY

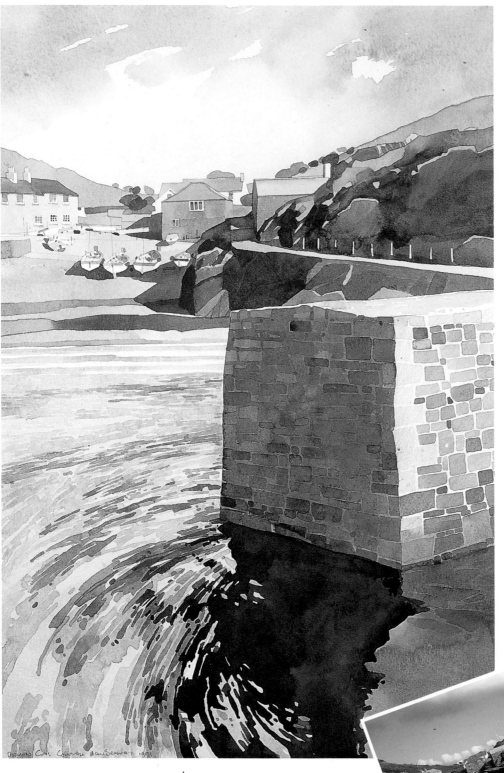

What a camera can't do

All this sounds as if the camera is one of the artist's most important pieces of equipment. But in fact it should never become so important that it takes over. After all, if you are just going to copy a picture exactly, you'd be better off with the original – the photograph itself.

The camera is not like the human eye. Unless you have a sophisticated one, it doesn't focus on a chosen area, leaving the surrounding areas hazy and blurred. The image can look flat, and landscape photographs in particular often lack a sense of space.

Also photographs can actually miss subtleties, especially where there is a high contrast between light and shade. Whereas the human eye can make out the details in a shady room and still focus on the bright view outside, a camera might capture the same scene with the view in focus but the room interior in total darkness, or the room in focus and the view represented as a white blur.

When painting from life, you are making decisions all the time, both consciously and unconsciously. You respond to the subject, emphasising points of interest and leaving out things you dislike. Lines, tones, shapes, textures and colours may all be exaggerated, simplified or rearranged. The camera does none of these things. It produces an unedited image – but it is an image you can control, to select from or interpret as you please.

▲ This painting is a refined version of the photograph on the right. At first glance they look very similar, but notice how the artist has elaborated and emphasised the sweeping curve of the foreground ripples and perked up the colours of the background features, yet has made good use of the basic skeleton provided by the photograph. Can you see other differences?

A Day at the Zoo

Join Stan Smith at Regent's Park Zoo in London for a fruitful, educational and enjoyable day's drawing.

The beauty of a zoo is that you have a rich, varied and virtually inexhaustible source to draw from. There are over 500 species of animal here and some – such as the Sumatran tiger – have become so scarce that the only place you are ever likely to meet them is in a zoo.

Armed with sketchpads, pencils, putty rubber, Conté pencil and a few tubes of paint, we're going to wander around, sketching whatever takes our fancy. The idea is to make quick sketches rather than detailed drawings, aiming to capture the spirit and character of the type of animal in question. (Later, if you want to make pictures, you'll find sketches like these indispensable.) Now subjects that pace or swing, bound, swim, slither, waddle or pounce – in short, moving subjects – present a special challenge, but with a bit of forethought you can imbue your drawings with movement and life.

Often, a line of just the right rhythm and stress laid along the animal's underbelly or

◀▼With no bars, a low wall on which to rest my pad and an obliging juvenile jackass penguin, this enclosure made a convenient first port of call (left). I drew a preening pair (below) but didn't see any swimming birds.

▼ A fluid line down the belly, a more considered silhouette over the head and beak and an abrupt line down the back of the stubby, flipper-like wing give the dynamics of this chap (below left). Scribbled tone adds bulk and form.

▲ These two sketches took about a minute each (above) and they're just the kind of scant but lively images that would add spirit to a more carefully composed picture.

back is worth a hundred tentative marks, and with practice you can often sum up the whole gait with one line. This makes the job of fleshing out the animal in tone and adding a few lines to describe movements of legs and tail, say, much easier. I'll show you quick ways of recording colours too.

Animals often repeat patterns of behaviour – some frequently. So if you are drawing the haunches of a big cat, for example, you probably won't have to wait long before you see them adopt a similar position. Finally, remember that the animal has survived because it has evolved and however peculiar it looks, its characteristics serve a need – allowing it to feed, evade predators and breed. So if you are drawing a bird of prey, say, make the hooked beak look as though it is capable of tearing flesh, and if you are drawing a jackass penguin, make it look like a strong-swimming, pilchard eater rather than the head waiter at your local restaurant!

"Remember the animal has survived because it has evolved."

Head and shoulders above the rest

Snapshot This pair of giraffes were galumphing around their enclosure when I arrived but soon settled down together under their acacia tree. As such they make a rather attractive couple.

Before you start, sit and watch your beast for a minute or two to gain an insight into its mood and behaviour. If it is preening or feeding (like one giraffe here), its movements will be confined.

1 Draw the giraffe on the left pretty much as you would take it in if you looked at it for the first time (see snapshot). Try it – follow the line from the head down the back of the neck to the rump and then down the back leg. Then look to the front leg and back up to the head. (Notice that the head doesn't hold your attention until you've taken in the rest of the animal – probably because it's so small). By scribbling on some rich, brownish red pencil you can quickly add bulk and hint at the overall colour.

2 A giraffe's markings camouflage it from predators such as lions, and each animal has a unique pattern. You can't hope to describe it fully, so just draw a few of the patches as I'm doing here. Work briskly rather than frantically – towards the hot end of your own pace.

◀ **3** If the animals move (as mine did), don't worry. You aren't aiming to freeze a moment in time, and there's no fixed set up to work from. In any case, false starts on the same page can help to capture the rhythm of a movement or facets of an animal's character.

Bear in mind what I said about the function of an animal's parts. A giraffe's legs might be long but they aren't spindly. (Look at the joints of the front legs in the snapshot.) Likewise, the neck is extremely flexible and powerful – capable of wielding the head to deliver a club-like blow, in fact!

One way to record the colour of these fishes is to scribble with coloured pencils. Another way is to write notes. Try inventing your own descriptions for colours. You might base them on food – pickled cabbage red, toffee brown, butter yellow or sherbet lemon, for example.

◀ **4** If you have time, try to get in a little of the animal's surroundings. In this case the tree and arched doorway give a sense of scale (more so had I included the edge of the slates on the roof – see the snapshot). Scale is important with small animals such as birds and insects too, not simply with sixteen-footers like these.

Used intelligently, vegetation can be particularly useful. For example, if you are drawing an orang-utan standing on a branch, not only is it logical to draw the support but you can use the branch to show off the highly dextrous grip of the ape's foot.

Tyger tyger…

◄ **Snapshot** The tiger must be one of the most beautiful animals on earth. Sadly, in many areas it has been hounded virtually to the point of extinction. (Cures for acne, laziness, impotence and fevers caused by ghosts are among some of the uses to which various parts of these animals have been put.) The closeness of this female and the regularity of her movements made her a perfect subject.

▶ **1** I've used a clean cotton rag dipped in turps and some 'burning bright' cadmium orange oil paint to wipe in the rough shape of the head, shoulders, legs, rump and tail. Now I'm working back into it with black Conté pencil. The rag/paint method is great for moving subjects because you can capture the movement so quickly – poking your fingers into the rag and using it like a glove puppet to control the paint, or scrunching it up to apply it more haphazardly.

Don't smother the animal in paint – try to hint at the form by grading the tones. Use Conté or charcoal for adding detail and tightening your drawing (inset).

▼ The rag/paint technique is quick and fun. Give it a try but if you are working with oil paint, use good-quality, heavy cartridge paper. (You could try acrylic paint if you prefer but remember that it dries quickly – which means you can't push it about as easily as oil paint.)

▲ **2** By leaving the lower half of the flank white and using the stripes as contours, I'm able to give a sense of the animal's form as it tucks under the belly and, rather luckily, I can even hint at the colour of its belly. The tiger continued to pace as I worked but often returned to the same spot, allowing me to gather more and more information each time.

▲ **3** Look for the essential details. Apart from this animal's striking colour and stripes (which camouflage it from its prey), notice how thick the legs are above its paws (capable of bringing down a deer with one swipe), the powerful shoulders which undulate as it walks and its haunches – again powerful but raked for speed.

You might find a large sketchpad cumbersome. A pocket-sized sketchbook does the job perfectly well and has the advantage of not attracting unwanted attention. You can use it instead of, or in addition to, a camera.

Beauty in the beast

It isn't always the highest profile performers – the apes, big cats and elephants, say – that make the best subjects. Birds, reptiles, fish and even insects can be equally fascinating to draw – and sometimes easier. Snakes and lizards tend to keep very still and because they are housed in smallish spaces and behind glass rather than bars, you can scrutinise them in minute detail. Fish, too, will often provide the most beautifully shaped and coloured subjects.

◀ These lappet-faced vultures are hardly the prettiest creatures I've come across today, but they're still irresistible to draw. Their bald heads serve a function – allowing the bird to feed on carcasses without becoming caked in gore.

▶ The slow, robotic movements of this iguana meant I could sketch it quite carefully from different viewpoints. The folds of skin around its body give a clue to the oval cross-section of its form.

◀ This little Chinese alligator from Shanghai remained well-hidden and, like many of the reptiles, perfectly still. The only difficulty you are likely to encounter when drawing the reptiles is people walking between you and your subject.

FROM START... TO FINISH

The inspiration to paint a picture can come at any moment, so make the most of the time you have to gather material that will help you produce a finished work.

An inspirational scene – perhaps a beautiful summer landscape or a busy street market – might make your fingers itch to get started on a painting or drawing. But, as any artist can tell you, a good rendition of a setting needs some solid reference material to work from.

For artists the material gathered in their sketchbooks is an invaluable source of inspiration and information. This raw material can be used as the basis for a painting, or as reference for details within a painting. It may be worked up immediately or at a later date – maybe even several years later. And in most cases the final image will be developed from several sources, the artist making adjustments, editing and adding in order to create a successful composition.

▼ Sketch No. 1 This is our artist's 'jumping off point': a first, quick, unedited sketch of the street scene as he saw it, with buildings, people and trees in place.

Note that he has included details of shadows and tones. Studies like these are a great help when it comes to making the tones in the final picture look convincing.

► Snapshots not only record what's going on in the scene, they also make excellent colour references.

Rule number one is to have your sketchbook with you at all times. You never know when something will catch your eye. It may be a broad scene – a stretch of rolling countryside, say, or a railway station where you are waiting for a train. Or it could be a detail, a single figure sitting on a park bench, or a dog asleep in a doorway, caught in a shaft of sunlight. Whatever it is – jot it down. Don't worry if you are pushed for time; even the simplest notes will help you to call a scene to mind later.

If possible, carry a camera with you as well as a sketchbook. A few pictures of the scene from different angles give you alternative views, and snapshots record all details, providing you with factual references. Similarly, pick up any relevant postcards or posters you can find.

With all or some of this material you can develop a finished painting or drawing back at home. The important thing is to make a picture that works – that is well structured, entertaining and captures the quality of the scene that first drew your attention. The picture is your invention so don't be afraid to put things in, leave things out or move items around. In the example shown here, for instance, the artist has taken a

► Sketch No. 2 is a group study, made on quite a different occasion (it's one of many in the artist's sketchbooks) – but he thought the figure on the right ideal for his market scene, and promptly 'borrowed' it.

▼ Sketch No. 3 The artist made this study in his studio. He's combining several elements from various sketchbooks and also exploring composition, mapping out a strong, squarish format and placing the big tree boldly in the centre.

figure from an entirely different location and successfully incorporated it in his composition.

For the sequence of images on these pages, our artist has made the most of a series of trips to France in which he filled several books with sketches. The main thing to note is that he has made free use of material from different sketchbooks, working up some in his studio and trying out a variety of different compositions. He then incorporated all the images he wanted into his final picture. The result beautifully captures the essence of a busy French street market.

Putting it all together

The detailed sketch (No.1) on the first page is an unedited record of what the artist saw. He noted the main elements of the scene: the location of the market stalls, the trees, the buildings in the background and some of the figures. He also indicated some areas of light and dark – for example, the dark tones on the tree trunks and foliage and the shadows cast by the two figures in the foreground.

Our next sketch (No.2) is one of many of various people, places and objects that the artist made on holiday. This group study was made on quite a different occasion from the first sketch, but he 'borrowed' one of the figures (the man on the right) for his final drawing.

Study No.3 was made later, in the artist's studio. At this stage he was keen to explore the compositional possibilities of the market scene, combining elements from several sketches, and experimenting with a squarish format. In particular, he tried out a bold composition – placing the big tree near the centre of the image to divide the picture plane in two.

The more detailed study (No.4) was also worked up in the studio from drawings made on different occasions in the artist's sketchbook. He was interested in the relaxed figure of the man on the bench, as well as in the shape and texture of the melons. Both were successfully included in the final picture.

Drawing No.5 (overleaf) is based on sketch No.3. The artist has decided to go for the composition with a strong central axis. He has developed the row of vegetables, leading the eye from the foreground to the tree in the middleground. He has also refined

some details, including the windows and the shutters on the buildings in the background and the foliage of the tree. He decided to make things less symmetrical by placing the foreground figure on the right hand side, moving it farther to the right so it didn't crowd the woman sitting on the car bumper.

In drawing No.6 you can see how the artist has finally brought together information from a variety of sources. His colours came not only from memory but also from reference notes and snapshots taken on the scene.

▶ Sketch No. 4 Two more studies from the artist's sketchbooks. He worked them up from quick jottings before including them in the composition shown opposite.

▶ Sketch No. 5 Here the
artist has resolved his
composition, retaining the
strong central axis he tried in
Sketch No. 3 by developing
the display of vegetables that
now helps to lead the eye
from the foreground to the
tree in the middleground.

He has also inserted detail
in the buildings at the back
and in the tree foliage.

▼No. 6 Coloured pencils provide a bright, fresh
medium which reflects the informal, bustling nature of
our artist's favourite French street market.

BABIES AND YOUNG CHILDREN

Whether absorbed in play, mesmerised by a new discovery, grinning mischievously or sleeping peacefully, the innocence and freshness of young children are a delight to capture in your sketches.

Childhood is a fascinating subject to explore, even if you're not a parent yourself. The results can be touchingly sentimental, sometimes humorous and always appealing. And if you do have children, you'll get an invaluable personal record of their development which they'll be pleased to own one day.

Besides their highly individual characters, young children provide a source of wonder. Consider the semi-transparent quality of their skin with its delicate tones and textures; their rounded features and soft colouring; their rapidly growing bodies and developing skills; their range of expressions; and last but not least, their incredible vitality.

▶ The fluid pencil lines in this lovely sketch pick out the form of the baby's body inside the folds of the fabric. Soft pastel colouring on the face contrasts well with the bright, colourful clothes and complements the line work. The sketch catches perfectly the way young children abandon themselves to sleep.

PENCIL AND PASTEL SKETCH BY MALVINA CHEEK

▶ Very young babies can't move around much, which makes them easier to sketch than a three-year-old on the move. Rapid pen lines give this baby's head form, as do the shadows on the face, while outlines show the frog-like legs characteristic of young babies.

BALLPOINT PEN SKETCHES BY STAN SMITH

▼ Sketching is all about seizing the moment. The artist here hasn't concentrated on details – there's no need. His confidently drawn ballpoint outlines give plenty of information and capture this moment of peace and relaxation for mother and baby.

Look hard at the developing features of children before you start to draw. Their proportions are different from those of an adult. The cranium grows faster than the rest of the face, resulting in a large forehead. Nose, mouth and chin are small and less developed, and the jaw is soft and undefined. Ears are also large in relation to other features, and cheeks are usually full and round. As a child gets older, the nose lengthens, and the eye-line rises as the jaw develops. It's important to get these proportions right if you want your sketches of children to look convincing.

The hair of young children can range from non-existent to plentiful, wispy patches, curls or straw-like straightness. A few well-placed lines may be all you need.

Be prepared to work quickly. Attempting to keep an inquisitive and energetic child still is a lost cause! There's little point in trying to get him or her to pose – you'll get an unnatural position instead of capturing the real mood and expression, which can be done with even a few quick lines.

▲ Capturing character is simple when you look for individual habits, like this sleepyhead sucking her thumb. Notice how a few gentle strokes of graphite stick are enough to show the depth of the eye socket. Look, too, at the way the shape of the head is shown clearly, under the hair.

▲ This eight-day-old baby girl has been sketched in loving detail by her mother, whose close observation has helped her portray the tiny new-born features – puffy eyes, minuscule nose and mouth, curled up fingers and rounded chin. Even the detail on the blanket fringe has been drawn with care to give us an impression of warmth and cosiness.

◄ When you have the opportunity to sketch a child unawares, you can catch some interesting angles and viewpoints. Notice how, from this extreme angle, the shape of the toddler's head is elongated. The artist uses simple, yet effective graphite marks to depict the beautiful, long eyelashes and the soft, ruffled hair.

If you want to make longer, more detailed sketches, catch your subjects when they are asleep! Even if they stir, it's quite likely they'll return to the same position – if not immediately, perhaps at another nap time – so you can resume your sketch. As you can see from the sketches here, children take on relaxed, abandoned positions in sleep. Try to convey expression and the smoothness of the skin as well.

As always, choose a medium to suit your subject. Stick to quick items which you can pick up and use with little or no preparation before the moment is lost. A graphite stick enables you to vary the thickness of your lines as well as block in areas of tone swiftly. A well-chosen range of graphite pencils gives you the choice of frail, light lines to dark, bold marks. If you want to use colour, you'll find the delicate quality of coloured pencils particularly well suited to drawing young children. You can make fine lines as well as build up areas of colour quickly by scribbling and cross hatching. Charcoal, pastels, Conté crayons, chalks, technical pens and felt and fibre tips are also excellent alternatives.

GRAPHITE STICK SKETCHES ON THESE TWO PAGES ARE BY SUSAN PONTEFRACT

▲ Peace (at last) after a day's frenetic activity! Graphite stick, with its fine lines and soft shading, describes the lines and tones in each strand of hair and each fold of fabric.

◄ The beauty of sketching is that you can do whatever you want – there's no 'finished' painting or drawing to worry about. Here, the artist has focused in tight on the little girl's face, concentrating on getting her expression of trusting restfulness right.

▲ This is a simple sketch, with quickly scribbled lines and areas of loose tone drawn with the flat edge of the tip of a graphite stick. Yet it is effective, showing the rounded podginess of the cheeks and the snub nose of the toddler.
   All the sketches on this page and the one opposite were done by the same artist who has five children – plenty of material for sketching!

► Several mixed studies make for full and interesting pages. Do as this artist does – begin another study as the child moves in sleep. Keep your sketchbook handy so you can grab the opportunity to continue sketches when the child returns to the same, or a similar position.

▶ Choose a coloured medium and you bring an extra dimension to your sketches. The artist here chose to work in pastels which, with their softness and velvety texture, suit his subjects.

Notice how this baby's face is not simply pink, but a subtle mixture of blues, purples, greys, yellows, white and pinkish reds.

PASTEL AND COLOURED PENCIL SKETCHES ON
THIS PAGE BY HUMPHREY BANGHAM

◀ Though done at speed, with a view to catching the essence of an expression or effect, sketches should still include form and tone as well as line.

Colour and tone are built up to great effect with loosely hatched lines. The highlights where the baby's plump cheek has caught the light help give it form, while the dark background throws the head forward to give it a convincing three-dimensional quality.

▼ Gentle strokes of overlaid colours illustrate the transparent quality of this young child's eyelids. The fine, dark lines of the closed eyes and mouth combine with subtle colour to create a warm, tender and extremely expressive drawing.

CHAPTER FIVE

DRAWING WITH VARIOUS MEDIA

THE APPEAL OF LEAD PENCILS

Lead pencils are the most familiar drawing tools of all. Perhaps that's why we don't always appreciate them for the wonderful implements they are.

Most of us learn to handle pencils as children, and then promptly forget their usefulness and flexibility. This is a great shame when you consider the vast range available – from pencils so hard they produce the palest of grey lines, to soft pencils, perfect for dark velvety shading.

But it isn't only the hardness or softness of the pencil you use that affects the kind of drawing you produce. There's also the sharpness of the tip to think about, and whether it's rounded or chiselled. Add to that the amount of pressure you exert on the pencil – and the surface of the paper itself – and you're nearly there. All except for the little matter of the *way* you apply the pencil of course!

Pencil lines can be soft and sinuous, vigorous and bold, or controlled and crisp. And your drawings might be subtle and detailed, with carefully graded tones, or energetic works in which the expressive flowing lines are important.

Softest to hardest

Artists' pencils come in 20 grades, ranging from the softest (8B) to the hardest (10H), with F and HB being in the middle.

As a rule of thumb, hard pencils (H - 10H) are best for very fine lines because they can be sharpened to the finest of

► With its range of descriptive marks, this sketch is pencil drawing at its most expressive.

'TRASIERRA, NEAR SEVILLE', BY ALBANY WISEMAN, PENCIL SKETCH, 12 X 18IN

round pencil

hexagonal
pencil

clutch pencil

9H

7H

4H

HB

F

B

2B

3B

4B

8B

round
graphite
sticks

putty
rubber

hard pencil
erasers

unsharpened
sketching
pencil

sharpened
sketching
pencil

hexagonal
graphite
sticks

points. They also keep this point for a long time, which means they're good for lines of a constant thickness.

Soft pencils (B – 8B) are in many ways more flexible than hard pencils because they have a tip that quickly blunts. When sharp, they make a fluid line of thicks and thins. When blunt, their marks become broad and dark.

Types of pencil

Most pencils are available in a standard 18cm length, though the shape of the shaft may vary. Which you use largely depends on your own personal preference.

Hexagonal pencils are the most common drawing tools. They give you a firm grip, even when you're shading with the flattened side of the tip (a round pencil used like this would roll in your hand).

Round pencils have great flexibility because the slightest turn gives you access to another side of the tip.

Sketching pencils (sometimes called studio pencils) are like traditional carpenters' pencils – rectangular in shape. With these, you can produce a line of varying width just by turning the pencil slightly.

Clutch pencils are like propelling pencils – the lead can be extended by releasing a clutch lock or by clicking the end. They come in the complete 8B–10H range, but need a special sharpener.

Graphite sticks are available in two forms – hexagonal sticks of pure graphite and rounded 'pencils' with a protective outer coating that stops you getting your hands messy. With a range that runs from HB to 9B, they lend themselves beautifully to such techniques as smudging and blending. This is particularly true of the uncoated kind of stick whose sides and flat end are excellent for shading.

You'll also find that pencils come with different sized leads. Most are 2mm in diameter, but some have cores as thick as 5.5mm – invaluable for making bold thick lines.

Erasers

These familiar items are useful for rubbing out mistakes, and come in just as handy for creating highlights in areas of tone. There are two different sorts.

Putty rubbers are used to erase soft pencil marks. They are kneadable so they can be worked to a fine point to rub out precise details.

Hard pencil erasers work best with hard pencil marks.

One pencil does it all!

Drawing textures is a challenge for any artist, and here's a still life that positively abounds with them. There's the basket itself, with its mass of weaves and plaits. Then there are the intricately grained logs and bark. To capture all of these, you need just one pencil and six kinds of mark.

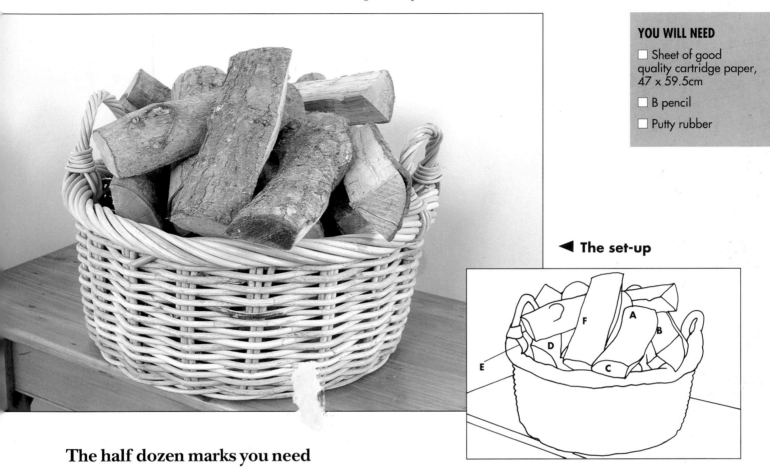

◄ The set-up

The half dozen marks you need

Practise these six marks and you'll have all you need for the *Fireside basket*. Don't devote too much time to each one, though, or you'll lose spontaneity. Rather, do them quickly, using your B pencil and a sheet of cartridge paper.

◄ A Hold the pencil as you would to write. Now draw short lines close together. Adjust the pressure to give three weights, and vary the direction. You'll use this *hatching* to describe bark.

◄ B Hold the pencil fairly lightly and draw a series of long tremulous lines. These represent the wood grain.

◄ C Work the side of the pencil tip to a flat edge, then lightly shade with it – let the texture of the paper show through. This represents the grain of the wood at the end of some of the logs.

◄ D Blunt the tip of the pencil, then make crisp black lines with it, exerting lots of pressure. This useful line adds definition.

◄ E Hold the pencil as in **A**, press hard and scribble. Do this in several directions and in several layers to build up good dark tones for the shadows.

◄ F As you hold the pencil on the paper, roll it in your hand. Then, by varying the pressure, you'll end up with a squiggly line of thicks and thins, perfect for the bark on some of the logs.

Warming up

Now you've practised the basic pencil marks, continue as the artist did – with some warm-up sketches (there's no particular order to them).

As you're doing them, you'll have the chance to study the make up of the still life, which will prove invaluable when you come to draw the picture for real. You can also work out the best angle to draw from.

For the best results, keep your pencil fairly blunt most of the time. You'll still have to sharpen it first, though. Once you've done this, rub it back and forth on a scrap of paper or glasspaper to blunt the end slightly.

◀ You can either set up your own still life log basket or work from the photograph on the previous page. If you're arranging your own, start by positioning yourself comfortably a few feet from it. Then make sure that the set-up is well lit and that you can see it properly. Also check that you have plenty of light to draw in.

Work into a pad of cartridge paper or on to a single sheet attached to a drawing board with pins or tape.

▲ One of the most prominent and fiddly features of the set-up is the wickerwork weave of the basket, so it makes good sense to sketch it beforehand. Start by loosely indicating the verticals, then draw in the horizontal canes.

▲ With its loops, curls and plaits, the handle of the basket is another excellent drawing to do in its own right.

◀ This preliminary viewpoint of the set-up proved rather an awkward one, so when it came to doing the picture proper the artist decided to draw from a different angle.

SHARPENING YOUR PENCIL

When it comes to sharpening your pencil, penknives, craftknives and scalpels have the edge over common-or-garden pencil sharpeners, whatever their design. Using a blade, you can cut away more of the wood to expose more lead, which means you don't have to attend to the tip so often. You also have more control over the shape of the tip, making it fine, chiselled, blunt or rounded, exactly as you wish. Rubbing the sharpened tip on a sheet of glasspaper makes it even finer – or blunt.

Fireside basket of logs

Once you've practised the pencil marks and have completed some warm-up sketches, you're ready to have a go at the drawing proper.

Equip yourself with a big piece of paper – it's good to work on quite a large scale. This doesn't mean you have to put in lots of detail. Instead, get into the habit of standing back from your drawing to assess it from a distance. Above all, resist the temptation to overwork your drawing.

Make your marks quite lightly to begin with. As with watercolour, you're working from light to dark. There's plenty of time to make things heavier as you go along, and the actual putting in of darker marks over lighter ones helps you build up interesting texture. With the B pencil and a textured paper, drawing the shading is easy. So don't press too hard or you'll make an indent that no amount of rubbing out will shift!

1 Fix the paper to the drawing board with pins or tape. Sharpen your pencil, then rub it back and forth on a scrap of paper to blunt the end slightly (you'll get the best results in this picture by keeping your pencil blunt like this most of the time).

◀**2** Working freely from your elbow, roughly and lightly draw in the outline of the whole image, making sure your composition fits neatly on the page. Don't worry about fine detail at this stage.

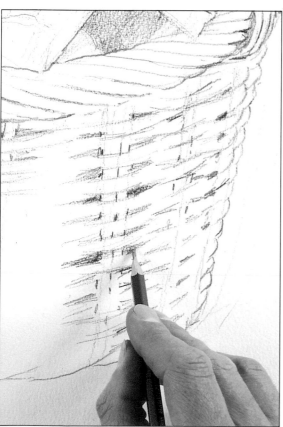

◀**3** Draw in the twisted rim of the basket. Now start on the wickerwork itself, on the right side of the basket. Because this is actually quite a complicated design, you need to simplify it. Look closely at the basket for its broad forms. Loosely indicate some verticals first, then start to establish the horizontal canes. Don't get too caught up in working on one small section – try to keep the whole thing going at once.

Don't worry either about putting in every detail – in this version not all the shadows are there, for instance, but the eye is deceived into thinking they are.

YOU WILL NEED

☐ A 47 x 59.5cm sheet of good quality cartridge paper

☐ One B pencil

☐ Putty rubber

☐ Spray fixative

▶**4** With one side drawn in, turn your attention to the tones on the logs. Define the darker edges by laying in some crisp black marks with the pencil lead fairly pointed. Shade in the shadows, but don't make them too dark yet – the texture of the paper adds to this here and there. Draw a series of lines for the grain of the wood. Roughly describe the bark with patches of scribble running in a variety of different directions.

▲ **5** Draw in the other side of the basket. As before, put in the verticals first, then draw in the horizontal wickers in panels, using lighter and heavier lines to indicate the different tones and shadows.

◄ **6** Now sort out the tones of the whole picture. Darken some of the shadows, for instance. It may help you to see where these are if you stand back from the drawing and look at it with half-closed eyes.

▼ **7** Hold the pencil loosely and lay in some more scribbles for the bark. Work over it in little clusters to capture the slightly varying surfaces. Create some vertical shadows on the basket by smudging the pencil lines downwards with your finger.

Once you've put in the final touches, fix the drawing with spray fixative, following the manufacturer's instructions.

DISCOVERING COLOURED PENCILS

If you haven't used coloured pencils since you were at school, give them another go. They have graduated from the classroom to the studio, and are now a refined and versatile drawing medium.

You'll be surprised by the beautiful results you can get with just a handful of coloured pencils and a few basic techniques. They're good for line drawings and illustrations and you can even achieve some painterly effects with them. You can use them in either a loose, expressive way or produce some very subtle, considered works.

Coloured pencils are easy to use, cheap and you don't need a lot of equipment to get started. There's no messy mixing to do, and they don't smudge easily. And the mark you make is the mark you get – unlike paints which often dry lighter or darker. On top of this, coloured pencils are small and easily portable, so you can take them with you when you go sketching, and store them without trouble.

▲ Much of the charm of coloured pencils comes from their sheer versatility. In this lively drawing bold, loose scribbles, pressure techniques and careful colour mixing combine to portray the bright, sunny atmosphere of a French village.

'LA GARDE FRINET' BY IAN SIDAWAY, CARAN D' ACHE COLOURED PENCILS ON PAPER, 58 X 85CM

◄ Most art shops carry a wide range of coloured pencils – some hard, some soft and in an impressive array of colours. Try out as many as you can to find the type you prefer.

You're also spoiled for choice when it comes to paper. With so many tempting colours and textures, there's a perfect paper for every subject.

Two-colour mixing

The colour mixes here are worked in Lyra Rembrandt Polycolor coloured pencils.

▲ This vibrant orange is mixed from vermilion and lemon cadmium.

▲ Mixing lemon cadmium and Paris blue makes a vivid light green. Lighten it with more yellow, or darken it with more blue.

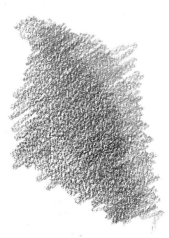

▲ Light carmine and vermilion combine to produce a moody violet.

▲ You can make a neutral grey by laying vermilion over true blue.

▲▲ A cooler, darker green results from mixing Prussian blue and lemon cadmium.

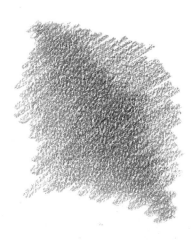

▲ Viridian and vermilion combine to make a darkish brown.

Hard or soft?

Some coloured pencils are softer than others, depending on how much wax they contain. The 'lead' or core is clay, coloured with pigment and bound with wax. The higher the wax content, the harder the pencil. With a soft pencil the core is softer, so the colour comes off smoothly and evenly. A hard pencil lays down colour quite lightly – ideal for delicate work. Try out different ranges to see which you prefer. Many artists use both types – harder pencils for fine line work and softer ones for laying areas of solid, bold colour and for pastel-like effects.

You can buy coloured pencils in large sets of 72, but you only really need a set of 12 to mix a wide range of colours. If you prefer to buy them loose, a good limited range of colours for mixing are ones that approximate to cadmium red, cadmium yellow, cobalt blue, ultramarine, alizarin crimson, Prussian blue, black and white.

When buying, look for well constructed pencils, with firmly set, well centred leads. Make sure colour builds up quickly and uniformly without any grittiness or squeak. You will also need a craft knife or pencil sharpener and a putty rubber for erasing and rubbing back.

Pressure points

As with lead pencils, you create different grades of tone by varying the amount of pressure you put

PENCIL PRESSURE

light pressure

medium pressure

hard pressure

The amount of pressure you put on the pencil affects the tones in your drawing. Hard pressure gives a dark tone; medium pressure, a medium tone; light pressure, a light tone. Use the sharp point of the pencil for fine lines. For soft lines and broad blocking in, work with the side of the core.

on the pencil. Pencil pressure also controls the final effect. Coloured pencils are most often used on cartridge paper which has a slight tooth. With light pressure the colour catches only on the 'peaks' of the irregular surface, producing a granular finish.

Under heavy pressure the colour is pushed down into the 'troughs' of the paper surface. It spreads more evenly and the texture of the paper is slightly flattened so you're left with a smooth, fluid finish.

Colour mixing

Coloured pencil marks are semi-transparent so one colour laid over another makes a third. For instance, strokes of blue laid over yellow make a green. This green is more subtle, lively and interesting than the flat colour you get with a green pencil.

You can vary this green by controlling the amount of blue or yellow you put down. And you can modify it further by adding some strokes of brown or any other colour you choose.

Combining colour mixing with different types of strokes can produce various effects, from regular and neat to loose and scribbly. Controlled cross-hatching – overlaid criss-crossed lines – produces a crisp image, while layers of

free-hand scribble in two or more colours are effective for backgrounds and large expanses. For small areas, use dense flecks or dots. Experiment to discover the effects you can achieve.

Use the right paper

Your choice of paper governs the final result of your drawing, so give some thought to the kind you use. Cartridge paper with a slight tooth is the most popular of all. Coarser papers can take more layers of colour than smoother ones. Very smooth surfaces – such as hot-pressed water-colour papers – are not suitable for coloured

▼ Coloured pencils aren't exclusively for illustrations and pale, delicate subjects. In this dramatic portrait, vigorous, expressive pencil marks and imaginative use of colour make a drawing bursting with energy.

'PORTRAIT OF ANNIE' BY SARAH DONALDSON, AQUARELLE COLOURED PENCILS ON WHITE PAPER, 15 X 20CM

Tip

Using fixative
If you prefer to work with heavy pressure techniques, spray your work with a couple of light coats of fixative, or you'll find within a week or two that it looks dull and foggy. This is because the wax has seeped to the surface. If this happens, rub the surface lightly with a soft cloth to remove the wax.

THREE-COLOUR MIXING

This brownish green was made by laying true blue and lemon cadmium over vermilion. Notice that the one on the left is lighter in tone than the other. Although the same pencil pressure was applied, the colour on the left is on NOT watercolour paper with a good tooth. The one on the right is on smoother cartridge paper with a very slight tooth. The different tones are the direct result of the different paper textures.

pencil work except for fine line drawings.

Highly textured, granular papers such as handmade and NOT watercolour paper produce equally granular drawings. These are excellent for loose, linear work but are not good for detailed work or laying areas of flat colour.

Many toned and tinted papers, such as Canson and Fabriano, have a slight texture (tooth) and are excellent for coloured pencil drawing. Both come in a wide range of colours.

▼ In this beautiful, carefully considered still life, the artist has captured the distinct character of many different textures – shiny metal saucepan and kettle, organic vegetables, transparent bottle and solid wooden board.

The fine detail in the build-up of form and tone shows what can be achieved with these pencils.

'STILL LIFE WITH VEGETABLES' BY JOE FERENCZY, CONTÉ COLOURED PENCILS ON PAPER, 38 X 51CM

▲ Sensitive use of coloured pencil strokes helps build up a solid shape from many different layers of blended colour. The directions followed by the pencil strokes appear to 'feel out' the shape of this yellow pepper.

◀ At their best, coloured pencils can combine many of the qualities found in both drawing and painting. The onion and leek here are both drawn in precise detail, while the complex build-up of colour on the crumpled skin of the onion adds a fine touch of realism.

USING WATER-SOLUBLE PENCILS

Water-soluble pencils are extremely flexible and a delight to use. They give you the control and precision of a pencil combined with the blending, soft edges and washes you get with watercolours.

Water-soluble pencils have all the qualities of regular coloured pencils – you can use them for linear work, hatching, laying blocks of colour or mixing colours optically by overlaying them. But their water-soluble quality gives them another dimension – by blending the marks with water you can produce soft gradations of colour and tone, as well as areas of delicate colour washes.

These pencils are ideal for coloured subjects with intricate detail. For instance, they're good for drawing birds, animals and plants – flower studies can gain much from the line and wash combination.

The following three basic techniques for these pencils are simple to follow. Try laying down some colour, then washing over it with a wet brush. This gives a range of blended effects and washes. Soft pencils create intense, even washes, while harder pencils give paler washes, and the drawn marks tend to remain visible.

You can also draw on to damp paper, or into wet, pre-blended colour. The lines are softer than those drawn dry-on-dry, and the pigment dissolves less than brush-washed colour.

You can even dip a pencil into water and draw on dry paper with the moistened tip. This is only practical for small details since the tip absorbs very little water. But if you're prepared to keep dipping, you can build up areas of texture – fur or feathers, for example.

◀▲ As a general rule, water-soluble pencils are softer than conventional pencils. The degree of softness also varies from brand to brand. It's worth buying a few singles first to see which range suits your style. If you concentrate on linear and textural qualities, with limited areas of blending, go for a harder variety. If you like to work boldly and loosely, using larger washes, you're better off with softer pencils.

When you have chosen your pencils, spend time exploring their character. Try different papers – the results can be remarkably diverse.

Thistles and nigella

▶ **The set-up** A combination of delicate details, soft tones and a splash of bright colours make this arrangement of nigella (love-in-a-mist) and thistles perfect for a drawing in water-soluble coloured pencils.

If you're interested in textures, there are plenty for you to experiment with here – the crisp tissue paper, the crinkly nigella petals, the spiky thistles and the solid wooden table top.

Pencil marks

 blue-grey

 Prussian blue

 smalt blue

 light violet

 bottle green

 May green

 zinc yellow

 primrose yellow

 raw sienna

◀ **1** Start by roughly placing the objects very lightly on the paper with the bottle green pencil. Then, using Prussian blue, draw the outlines of the flowers and tissue paper. Try to show the crinkly edges of the nigella petals and the shapes of the centres. Indicate a few of the stems and circle in the main thistle heads.

Now draw the table top in raw sienna, suggesting the quality of the wood grain with irregular strokes.

▶ **2** Dampen the flat brush with clean water and start to blend the marks. Use horizontal strokes for the table top. Then do the same with the edges of the tissue paper.

Notice how the water deepens the blue lines, giving them a rich, velvety quality.

Three ways with water

◀ **3** Pick out some of the darker stalks, drawing them in with bottle green. Then blend the outlines of the nigella petals and centres with the brush and clean water. The colour spreads out gently and unevenly, giving the flowers softly graded tones. Soften some of the outlines of the thistle heads with water too, before you begin to develop them further.

▲ Draw, hatch or scribble with a pencil on some watercolour paper. Blend the colour by washing over it with a wet brush and clean water.

▶ **4** Now you've laid in the basic composition, start to introduce more colours. Don't be afraid to work over the areas you've already washed down. Draw into the nigella flowers with light violet, showing the way their petals overlap. Add more stalks with the side of the blue-grey pencil, then strengthen the outlines of the thistle heads – some with light violet, others with blue-grey. Scribble these two colours onto the thistles in varying amounts, then blend in the scribbles with some clean water.

Don't use your colours according to a formula. Vary them – and their amounts – on all the flowers so they don't all look the same. This creates a much more interesting picture.

▲ Wet the paper with some clean water and a brush, then draw into an area with a dry pencil. The marks bleed, yet still retain their main shape.

▲ Dip the tip of your pencil into some water and draw on dry paper. The wet pigment crumbles off to leave a highly textured mark.

◀ **5** Bring some brighter colours into the picture. Use May green to add lighter stalks, washing them down with clean water. Notice how this green turns towards yellow when diluted.

Now work up the flowers, starting at the bottom right of the picture. Scribble varying amounts of May green and primrose yellow on to the thistle heads for lighter tones and soften the scribbles with water. Then stroke in spikes on the thistles with blue-grey.

Add touches of primrose yellow for light tones on the nigella centres. Reinforce the petal outlines using blue-grey and bottle green. Change the pressure you apply on the pencil for varying tones.

6 Put in more stems with May green, making strong, jagged lines with the side of the pencil. Remember – you can be selective about which stems to include.

Stand back and assess your progress. You now need to work around the picture in the same way as you have been doing to build up all the elements. Rest your hand on a piece of tissue paper to avoid smudging your drawing.

7 Develop the thistles by blending varying amounts of the same colours as before. For the spikes, use blue-grey, smalt blue and light violet. Use both greens to strengthen the stems, washing down the lines as you go. Add zinc yellow to some nigella centres.

Use your technical pens for fine details. Add dark spikes to the thistles, and outline some nigella petals. Draw fine scribbles on the petals for their crumpled texture. Add black dots to the nigella centres for texture.

8 Build up the table top by laying more raw sienna at a different angle over the existing marks. Allow the paper's texture to show through. This contrasts well with the delicate detailing on the flowers and hints at the texture of the wood. Add more stalks with bottle green and May green.

The finished picture shows both qualities of water-soluble coloured pencils. The subject demands attention to fine details, such as the tiny spikes on the thistle heads. Yet the areas of softly blended colours add a sense of delicacy to complement the subject. They also give the flowers a more rounded quality, suggesting the gentle folds of the petals.

DRAWING WITH CHARCOAL

By far the oldest drawing medium still available on the market today, charcoal sticks and pencils are simple to use and lend themselves to expressive, spontaneous work.

The perfect medium for beginners, charcoal is nearly always the starting point of any art course – students are encouraged to pick up a piece and start sketching big, bold images right away. This is because working with charcoal can teach a great deal about drawing textures and creating different tonal areas – essential before starting with colour. And it encourages artists to think about the subject as a whole and not about fiddly detail.

Charcoal is made from burnt vine, beech or willow twigs and is available in natural or compressed sticks, in pencil form or as a powder. Vine charcoal produces a brownish black colour, while willow and beech – more commonly used in Britain – make a bluish black mark.

There are varying degrees of hardness – soft, powdery charcoal blends easily and is useful for tonal areas, while the harder sticks are ideal for linear work and details.

The sticks come in various thicknesses, so you can create a range of marks – from broad, sweeping strokes to fine details. In its pencil form – sticks of compressed charcoal encased in wood – charcoal is much cleaner to use, but you soon lose the feel of the traditional sticks because you can use only the point, not the sides.

Paper and accessories

Charcoal works well with any type of matt paper with a textured surface. But don't use it on smooth or glossy papers because it simply won't adhere to the surface. Canson or Ingres are the best papers for drawing with charcoal, but for everyday practice sugar paper is a suitable alternative.

willow charcoal sticks in various thicknesses

charcoal in pencil form

fine sandpaper

coloured and white drawing paper

torchon

GLASSPAPER BLOCK
WINSOR & NEWTON
Made in England, London HA3 5RH
for pointing pencils, charcoal, chalks etc.
7000 572

putty rubber

LARGE KNEADED PUTTY RUBBER
WINSOR & NEWTON
7000 618

craft knife

fixative

Aerosol
Fixative

USING CHARCOAL

Smudging Charcoal smudges easily, allowing you to produce smooth, velvety effects. Use the side of the stick to make a series of lines. Then with the tip of your finger – or with a torchon – gently rub across the charcoal from one side to the other, creating light and dark tones by varying the pressure as you go.

Cross-hatching Another way to build up tone with charcoal is by using a series of loose strokes known as cross-hatching. To practise this technique, make a series of parallel lines, then cross them with a series of others at a different angle. Vary the size and closeness of the lines to each other to produce different tones.

Soft blending Instead of smudging the charcoal with your finger or a torchon, use the wide tip of the stick to create lines and marks which blend into each other. Sharpen the tip slightly first on a piece of glasspaper, then hold the stick near the top end. Vary the pressure as you scribble so you get a range of lights and darks.

To begin, you need only the bare minimum of equipment – a few sticks of charcoal in different thicknesses, paper and fixative (essential because charcoal smudges so easily). Buy proper fixative from an art shop or use ordinary hairspray.

You'll need fine sandpaper or a sharp craft knife to sharpen the point of a charcoal stick, and a putty rubber to create highlights and correct errors. Fingers are ideal for the job of blending, but you can use a torchon – a piece of paper rolled tightly to a point – to avoid dirtying your hands. Cheap alternatives include paper tissues, scraps of rag or cotton wool buds.

Wash your hands after using them to rub charcoal into the paper – the dust can work into the skin of your fingers and then you'll make a mess of the paper surface.

Experience will teach you the amount of pressure needed for the different grades of thick or thin sticks. Too much pressure on a thin stick causes it to break frequently, splattering charcoal crumbs over the paper.

◀ Charcoal is ideal for life studies because it is so easy to erase and correct mistakes. You can also create a whole range of tones with it.

This study was made with medium and thin sticks of willow (the artist finds thick sticks too bulky). Sweeping lines define the contours of the form while smudges and blended tones give the figure bulk and create an entertaining picture surface.

'WOMAN CLEANING' BY SARAH CAWKWELL, 1987, 30 X 32IN

PENS, INKS AND PAPERS

Even experienced artists are daunted by the bewildering choice of pens, inks and papers on the market today. Here's a selection of materials to whet your appetite and get you on the right track.

Thanks to recent manufacturing developments, there are hundreds of pens and inks available, and you can work with them in literally countless ways – from simple monochromatic drawings in traditional black Indian ink to detailed paintings in brilliant colours. But whatever your interests, it's important to choose the proper materials for the result you have in mind.

Traditional drawing pens

Pens made from natural materials – quills, reeds and bamboos – were for many centuries the only types available. But they are still popular today because they're pleasurable to use. If you look after them, they can last a long time. They all make their own, characteristic marks, and they're cheap, easy to handle and widely available.

▼ Indian ink allows you to create boldly expressive and finely detailed drawings. The artist used very fine lines for the details of the statues and decorative objects.

'VIEW THROUGH AN ARCHWAY' BY JOHN WARD

◄ There's a wide range of nibs and papers on the market to choose from when working with Indian ink. Experiment with a selection of mapping, round and square nibs to find out what works best for you. To begin with, use sized papers to prevent the ink from bleeding. When you've gained more experience, move on to NOT papers.

Quill pens – made of the large flight feathers of such birds as swans, turkeys or crows – are light, flexible and responsive. Swan quills, usually imported from the United States, are the best and most expensive. But turkey or goose quills are a cheaper alternative.

Because quills are soft, you have to trim their nibs (or points) frequently to keep them sharp enough to make a fine line. Use an ordinary craft knife for this, or buy a traditional quill knife in a specialist art shop.

To prepare a nib, first slice off the natural tip of the stem at an oblique angle. Then scoop out the soft central material. Make a slit in the centre of the nib and cut it on both sides to shape it like the nib of a conventional fountain pen.

Reed pens – superb for producing short, chunky strokes – have flexible nibs, making them especially satisfying to draw with. But the fragile nibs chip very easily, and once this happens the pens are useless.

Bamboo pens are the toughest of all the natural material pens. Because the nibs aren't flexible at all, these pens work best for thick, short lines. They need little care to keep them in good order and, provided you wash them after use, they should last a long time. Some nibs are as quite wide, making them useful for drawing thick, bold lines.

▲ Pens with fine nibs are superb for drawing thin lines and making many precise details – notice, for example, the balconies and windows here. After the forms were mapped in, thin washes were added for the tonal contrasts.

'A PAGE FROM THE SKETCHBOOK' BY ANNE WRIGHT

◀ This fine portrait of an Alsatian was drawn with a mechanical pen. The artist used a technique called stippling – applying hundreds of tiny dots and flecks of ink. Stippling is time-consuming, but it allows you scope to consider the tones carefully.

'MICKEY' BY SUE SMITH, INK ON BOARD, 21 X 30CM

▲▼A turkey quill (above) and reed pen (below) are very responsive to the touch and a pleasure to use. They allow you to draw smooth, fluid lines.

Mechanical pens (with an assortment of nibs) are used for engineering and architectural drawings. They aren't really suited to fine art drawing, though you can hatch and stipple with them easily enough.

Dip pens and their nibs

There's a wide range of nibs for dip pens on the market to choose from. Detachable steel nibs for dip pens are extremely flexible and come in myriad shapes and sizes.

Brush pens have nibs made from two wide, spatula-like plates of metal. They are excellent for making wide, bold lines and heavy shading.

Mapping pens have fine, pin-point nibs for drawing precise detail and extremely fine lines for maps and technical artworks.

Script pens have pointed, round or square nibs and are mainly used for calligraphy, but you can use them for drawing, too. Round nibs are the most suitable for really thick work, while square ones give a fluid, ribbon-like line. Both types come in various sizes. Script nibs are split into sections so that you can change the width of a line as you draw it. Some nibs have two slits and some three for even broader work.

It takes practice to make a fluent line with a script pen. Start with a pointed, two-slit nib and work at developing tone and shading in simple sketches before you tackle the round and square heads. The variations in line width allow you to create a beautifully free style of cross-hatching.

Cartridge pens

Instead of dipping the pen into an ink well every few minutes, you can buy pens with ready-flow cartridges for convenience and easy use.

▲ In this portrait the artist used many lines to describe the form of the model. Very dilute washes of black watercolour paint provided the dark tones.
'NAOMI' BY JOHN RAYNES, PEN AND WASH ON PAPER, 54 X 42CM

▼ Expressive textures and tones are achieved by hatching and cross-hatching in selected areas.
'FARMHOUSE SCENE' BY GORDON BENNETT

▼ Bamboo pens (below) come in a range of sizes. They are superb for making thick, bold lines but aren't really suited to drawing very precise details. A fountain pen (above) is portable and easy to use – the perfect choice for sketching out-of-doors.

▲ Combining ink with other media – pastel in this case – really helps to bring out the details of the composition.

'CUSTOMS HOUSE, KINGS LYNN' BY JOHN TOOKEY, PASTEL, WATERCOLOUR & INK ON PAPER, 11 X 15IN

▼ The artist worked solely with burnt sienna ink to create this beautiful monochromatic image.

'STILL LIFE WITH PRIMULAS' BY DENNIS GILBERT, 16 X 12IN

▲ The artist here has simplified his painting to its basic tonal elements, then worked over the architectural features with pen and ink to add detail. Notice the variety of lines in the church – they give spontaneity and freshness to the whole composition.

'NORTON ST. PHILIP CHURCH' BY STAN SMITH, GOUACHE AND INK ON PAPER, 15 X 11IN

▼ Use the same brushes for working with inks as you would for watercolours. Round sables in various sizes work well – they're responsive and can hold a lot of ink. Why not use a brush for making whole drawings with inks? It's the most expressive instrument you have.

◄ Skilful use of watercolour gives texture to the buildings and street, while the Indian ink adds detail to the bricks in the cobbled road and the planks in the large wooden doors.

'TIMES PAST, SOUTHWARK' BY GILLIAN BURROWS, WATERCOLOUR AND PEN AND INK ON PAPER, 16 X 11 IN

▼ Inks are available in many different colours – both opaque and transparent varieties. You can apply them in much the same way as watercolours, using standard watercolour brushes or even Chinese brushes (below) for long, expressive, fluid strokes.

Technical pens have tubular stainless steel nibs in many sizes. They produce a line which has an even width – giving a rather mechanical feel. You can use them for stippling and shading, but they aren't suited to free-hand artworks.

Re-fill fountain pens You can also use fountain pens for drawing; some are marketed as sketching pens. They have a pump-action for drawing ink into a reservoir within the pen, and come with a fairly wide range of nibs.

Indian and coloured inks

Indian ink (which actually originated in China) is pitch-black, waterproof and dries fast. The bottles are available in a range of sizes, but a little ink goes a long way. There's no need to splash out on huge quantities at once.

Chinese ink sticks come ready-ground in powder or stick form (which you have to grind yourself with a mortar and pestle). The sticks give you the freedom to make watery or thick ink.

If you want to work in colour, buy a few small bottles while you develop your own artistic style and preferences. There are basically two types of inks – namely, waterproof and non-waterproof (sometimes called brilliant watercolours).

Inks offer brilliant, unparalleled colours – they are made from dyes, not pigments. You can buy both opaque and transparent colours, and they all dry very quickly. But their big disadvantage is that most fade in time. Since they aren't all lightfast, manufacturers don't

▼ Brilliant concentrated liquid watercolours are water-soluble inks which aren't generally lightfast (not to be confused with watercolour paints). They come in a range of unparalleled colours with handy dropper cap bottles.

recommend them for long-term, fine art drawings, but they are excellent for work which is to be reproduced. Don't use them for work which will be permanently displayed. 'Permanent' on a label means the ink is waterproof or water-resistant, not necessarily lightfast.

Start with a small range of about six colours – we suggest lemon yellow, vermilion, ultramarine, brown, black and white. You can use these to make a wide range of other colours simply by mixing them. If you want to thin the ink, use distilled water, which has fewer impurities than tap water, but bear in mind that thinning may affect the vibrancy of the colour.

Some transparent inks, such as non-waterproof Indian ink, are less light sensitive than permanent ones. As a general rule, drawing inks do not work well in fountain pens, although you can buy specially formulated calligraphic inks which flow exceedingly well.

You don't have to use ink on its own. With its fluidity and staining properties, coloured

▲ As a result of a recent technological breakthrough, liquid acrylics are generally more lightfast than coloured inks and are ideal for fine artists.

'HIGHGATE JUG, HAMPSTEAD TULIPS' BY JENNIE TUFFS, LIQUID ACRYLICS ON PAPER, 29 X 41IN

inks add tone and atmosphere to pastel and watercolour paintings. You can also use inks in an airbrush to create pictures that have velvety smooth textures.

Papers for pen and ink work

Sized papers used to be the traditional choice for ink drawing because they prevented the ink from bleeding (or being absorbed into the paper). Today, you can buy several types of ready-stretched, coated papers and boards.

Stiff cartridge paper and NOT paper are also available. These work well, provided you allow for some bleeding at the edges of your lines. Whatever paper you choose, prepare it in much the same way as you would for a watercolour.

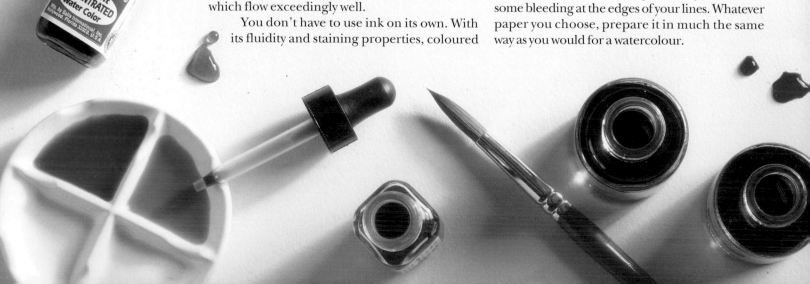

PORTRAIT IN DOT AND LINE

The delicacy, fine control and subtle range of marks on offer with pen and ink make it ideal for portraits, helping you achieve great expression and character in your drawing.

One of the joys of drawing with a pen is the wonderful flow of ink through the nib – it means you can keep a continuous line going and call on dots, hatched, broken or continuous lines, thick and thin strokes, blobs, stipples and shading to give a huge variety of effects. And these help you render the subtle nuances of a person's features, expression, hair and skin with great sensitivity – and economy.

Remember, though, that pen and ink is very difficult to correct. The wonderful sense of fluency you achieve with pen and ink comes from the freshness and immediacy of its application, not from a laboured build-up of ink. Each line must ring true from the start. Underpinning your drawing with pencil can be dangerous because once

you have made a pencil drawing you often merely reiterate – rather than re-invent – the lines, which results in a flat, 'dead' picture rather than something fresh and lively.

If you want to keep a lovely fluency in your pen work, you must find a method to help you make measurements and establish the proper relationship between all the features on the face. A good way, chosen by our artist here, is to dot in the main features very lightly at the start, with no pencil work at all. The dots don't detract from the drawing, nor do they need covering up. Every mark put down brings its own quality to the work.

Here, the dots (in very dilute ink) make a vital link from one position to another across the mask of the face.

▶ With any portrait, concentrate first on getting the relationships of the features right. The width between the eyes is critical – if you don't get that right, nothing else in the drawing will work (there should be roughly one eye's width between the eyes).

Once you've dealt with this, let yourself go and have some fun – take your line for a walk and explore the marks available!

'MARCUS' BY ALBANY WISEMAN, PEN AND INK ON PAPER, 16 X 12IN

Making a mark

Practise different marks with your pen before you start on the drawing. Our artist diluted the ink with distilled water to help the ink flow smoothly and give a softer, greyer line for unobtrusive but helpful guidelines. The light grey lines can be strengthened later on if needed.

fine dotting to establish planes and positions

thin strokes for outlines and shading

tighter shading for darker shadows

scribbled lines for mass and detail

continuous line for contour and 'exploration'

cross-hatching and strong, dark lines for emphasis

strong cross-hatching for the darkest tones

light swirls and dots for variety and interest

YOU WILL NEED

☐ A 56 x 38cm sheet of good quality cartridge paper

☐ A fountain pen with a flexible nib (our artist preferred a tried and trusty old plunger type fountain pen – not a cartridge refill type, but this is optional; choose a pen and nib that YOU are comfortable with)

☐ Drawing board and gummed tape or drawing pins

☐ Bottle of Indian ink

☐ Bottle of distilled water

☐ Kitchen towel/paper tissues for wiping pen and hands

Naomi in a hat

▶ **The set-up** The hat framed our model's face attractively and gave some intriguing shadows. When working from life, take into account that the model sometimes has to move – try to make her as comfortable as possible.

▼**1** Lightly dot in the eyes, eyebrows and the far cheekbone and the hat brim in dilute Indian ink. Emphasise the far eye and brow to establish the basic form. Using the dots, search for the exact relative positions of eyes, mouth, nose and cheek.

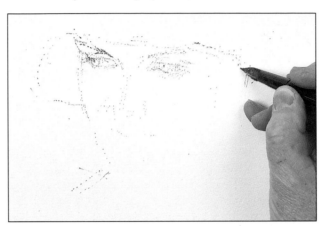

▼**2** Establish the shape of the hat and the line of neck and shoulder in light strokes, using the dots as guides. Dot in nose, nostrils and lips in darker ink. Revisit the far eye and eyebrow, strengthening them so you can read the eye sockets and the eyes travelling back into them.

▼**3** Continue drawing the hat, shading a little on the far temple. Strengthen the eyes and eyebrows again, and begin the central flower motif on the hat brim. The remaining guideline dots bring a happy freshness to the picture – rather than impede, they help your eye read the lines. There's no need to scrape them out.

▶**4** Now, with very dilute ink, start scribbling in the flower on the hat and the hat itself, which is very floppy against the hardness of the cheekbones and the soft chin and nose. Use very dilute ink – a very grey, light line. Drop in a line or two at the bottom of the nose and along the far cheekbone.

▶ **5** Reinforce cheekbone and the far eye, eyebrow and eyelashes. Note that because the eye is spherical, the eyelid must travel around the sphere.

Work up the flower motif on the hat. The dilute ink is recessive while the pure ink lines now shaping the hat are assertive, creating a three-dimensional feel.

◀ **6** Strengthen the line between the lips, then sketch in the blouse. Put in the chin with a stronger line. (Note our artist was happy to correct the line of the neck.) Travel around from eyes to hat, back to the eyes and down to the mouth and chin.

▲ **7** Return to the hat again and firmly establish its shape and contours. The darker ink lines contrast well with the pale grey dilute ink marks. With all the features in place, our artist now produced a livelier, freer line – breathing a real spirit of life into the drawing.

▶ **8** Establish the shoulders and neck relative to the face in free, loose lines. Put in some assertive points – ensure the line between the lips is correct, draw in the nostrils and strengthen the near cheek.

Work up the flower in the hat in stronger, darker lines (no more dilute ink), using loose swirls and scribbles for mass and shape. Suggest the puckered band on the hat with a few angled lines.

9 Finish off final details round the neck and the side of the face. Using a fully charged pen and a bit more pressure, emphasise the lines indicating the right side of the neck and shoulder (the side nearest to you). These strong, dark, lively lines around neck, shoulder and hat point up the very careful, delicate treatment of the face itself. (If you treated the whole head like the face, it might not have so much vitality.)

10 With such economy of line, every stroke counts in this portrait, as do the lightness or darkness of the lines. Notice that there's no heavy shading to indicate tones or shadows.

Our artist has fully achieved a sense of three dimensions, at the same time suggesting the attractive character of the model. Positioning every feature in its correct place has produced an extremely good likeness, and he has retained a freshness, fluency and vitality in his use of pen and ink that gives great charm to the whole drawing.

Tip

Pen and ink tricks

Turn the pen wrong way up, with the nib down, so you get a strong flow of ink and therefore a strong line. Dip the pen into some distilled water from time to time to improve the flow.

When diluting Indian ink, it's important to use distilled water – ink contains shellac which, if mixed with ordinary tap water, causes the pigment to 'throw out', granulate and eventually become unusable.

CHAPTER SIX

WATERCOLOUR
PAINTING
TOOLS AND TECHNIQUES

THE MAGIC OF WATERCOLOUR

Watercolour is justly regarded as one of the most beautiful of all the painting media. For centuries painters have loved its freshness and translucency and today it is as popular as ever.

At its best, watercolour looks effortless. That's why so many people are tempted to try their hand at it, and why almost as many are disappointed with the results.

There are some basic principles and techniques to watercolour painting. Once you've mastered these, you'll find you can create successful watercolour pictures.

Laying flat washes, controlling colours flooding into each other and creating textures with an almost dry brush are all part of the process of discovering just how versatile watercolour is. You'll find that deliberately blurring several colours together can create some beautiful effects, while painting on damp paper produces a soft-edged look that is most appealing.

This doesn't stop you taking full advantage of the unpredictable. Chance marks and happy accidents bring sparkle and spontaneity to your painting. When such things occur, leave well alone – let the picture itself 'talk back'.

The characteristic translucency of watercolour comes from the whiteness of the paper showing through the transparent colour. This is the only white available in watercolour, which is why artists choose to work mostly on white paper.

▼ All the magic of watercolour is here – transparent washes, soft gentle colours blending subtly together and sparkling white highlights.

'CHÂTEAU IN BRITTANY' BY ALBANY WISEMAN, 140LB PAPER, 18 X 24IN

Pans or tubes?

Watercolour is available in two main forms – semi-moist cakes of paint in pans, and soft paint in tubes. There are pros and cons to each.

Pans (and half pans) are most often available in assorted boxes of 12, 18 and 24, but they can also be bought singly, so you can have just as many or as few as you like. Useful if you need a whole range of colours to hand, they're ideal when you're keen to carry the bare minimum of equipment around with you.

Tubes are sold individually or in boxes. They have the edge over pans when it comes to covering large areas because you can buy big tubes and squeeze out as much paint as you need, but working on a small scale can be a tedious business as you constantly stop to squeeze different colours from the array of paint tubes.

Artists or students?

Whether you plump for pans or tubes, you'll need to choose between artists' quality watercolour and students'. Be prepared, though – it may be your pocket that does the deciding!

Students' colours are aimed at the beginner and in consequence are the cheaper of the two. All the colours are the same price.

Artists' colours, made from vastly superior pigments, cost four to six times more than students', depending on the colour you choose.

When it comes to the crunch, go for artists' colours if you can – with watercolour, more than any other medium, buy the best you can afford. Cheaper colours can't always produce the same effects as the more expensive ones.

One final word before you commit yourself to a choice of paints – buying a selected range of colours in a box does have distinct advantages. For a start, it is easier to transport than a whole bundle of loose tubes or pans, brushes and palettes. But more than this, a box stops the paints drying out. And many have convenient built-in mixing palettes in the lid.

Getting started

Bear in mind when starting out with watercolour that you require a *thin* wash, not a thick, opaque layer. If you use the paint straight from the tube or pan, you're liable to get through it far too fast – working with watercolour paint correctly is very much cheaper.

By dissolving the paint in water you create washes of different intensities – more water gives a paler wash, less water gives a deeper colour. You can also use layer upon layer of these transparent washes to build up the colours and shapes you want on the paper.

Tip

Keeping a record
As soon as you've taken the wrappers off your new pans of watercolour, paint a blob of each one on a sheet of paper and label it. Then when you pick up an unidentifiable pan, all you need to do is moisten the tip of your finger, dab it in the paint and test the colour on a piece of paper. Then take a quick look at your home-made chart to tell you what colour it is.

BRUSH STARTER KIT

Keep things simple. You don't need many brushes to start with – one No. 12 round brush is all that's required for the landscape painting on page 166. It can cope well with washes and most other basic techniques. For finer work you'll find a No. 6 round and a No. 2 round useful. Buy all three in a sable/synthetic fibre mix – pure sables are very expensive.

►Preparing a pan colour wash

Using your brush, transfer a little water from the jar to one of the wells of the palette or to a saucer.

Wet the paint with the brush and mix the colour well. Now load the brush with paint and transfer to the water in the palette.

Mix well, then add more paint or water as needed until you have a wash of the right colour – but remember that watercolour dries paler. Test the colour on a scrap of paper.

◀ Start off by mixing some paints – remember you need two jars of water, one for cleaning brushes, the other for mixing paints. Change the water regularly so your colours don't turn muddy.

▶ Preparing a tube colour wash

Squeeze a little watercolour paint into one of the wells of the palette or into a saucer. Dip your brush in the jar and load with water. Transfer to the palette and mix well with the paint.

Add more water with your brush until you have a wash of the colour you want – remember, though, that watercolour dries paler. Test the colour on a scrap of paper.

Laying a flat wash

YOU WILL NEED

☐ A No. 20 round sable/
synthetic fibre mix brush

☐ Sheet of paper
(pad or stretched)

☐ Natural sponge

☐ A tube of Winsor blue

☐ Clean water

☐ Saucer

The secret of laying an even wash is to work confidently, without pausing. It is cheaper to use 130gsm NOT paper and stretch it than to use heavier paper which doesn't need stretching. But if you don't wish to stretch paper, work straight on to a pad of 210gsm NOT which is thick enough not to cockle when damp. Remove any dirt from the paper with a putty rubber.

Work flat or angle the board slightly to help the paint flow down the paper. Don't angle it too much, though, or your wash will end up darker at the bottom. Choose a large brush which holds plenty of paint and covers the paper in a minimum number of wide strokes. You can't get an even wash over a large area with a small brush.

Keep your water, mixing palette and saucers together, so that you can move from one to another without carrying your brush over the paper. Water or paint spilt on to the paper can be removed but still affects the result.

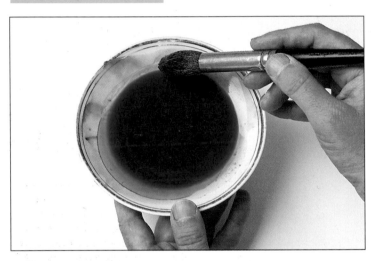

▲**1** Squeeze a dab of paint on to the palette and transfer a little to a saucer with your No.20 brush. Dip the brush into clean water and add some to the paint. Keep adding water until the puddle covers the bottom of the saucer. The more dilute your paint, the lighter your wash. If you want a darker wash simply add a little more paint from the palette. Mix plenty so that you don't run out half way through.

▲**2** Soak the natural sponge in clean water and squeeze out the excess. Starting at the top edge, draw the sponge back and forth, working down the paper. Don't press too hard or water will run from the sponge, flooding the paper. Use just enough pressure to wet the paper evenly. Don't worry about going right up to the edge. If the paper is very absorbent you may need to go over it again.

▲**3** Apply the colour wash before the paper dries. Using the No.20 brush, stir the paint and mix it well. Load the brush with paint and, starting at the top left hand corner, draw it across the top of the paper. When you reach the end, draw the brush back below the previous band. Overlap only slightly so you catch the paint above just enough to coax it down the paper. Don't stop until you reach the end.

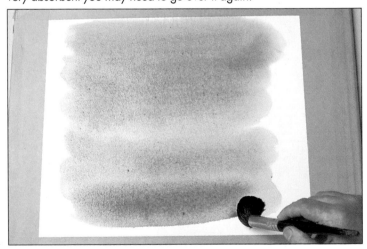

▲**4** When the wash is finished, put the board on to a level surface and leave the paper to dry. This might take about an hour – it depends on how thick the paper is. Don't worry about small gaps between the bands of colour; the dampness of the paper helps to close them. Any attempt to rework the surface while it's still damp results in flaring. As the paper dries the wash gets lighter and more even in tone.

Practising watercolour

For this exercise it's best to work on stretched paper. If it is not stretched, even fairly heavy paper – such as 220gsm NOT – may cockle if it becomes excessively wet.

The aim of the exercise is simply to see what happens when you put wet paint on wet paper. So make the paper fairly damp – bordering on wet – to start with. You can repeat the exercise with different degrees of dryness/wetness later. Try a number of strokes to see what happens as the paint spreads.

There may be times when you wish the paint would stay just as it was when wet – but of course, it never does! Learning how effects change as the paper dries, and anticipating the result, are things that only come with practice.

SOLVE IT

Lifting out paint

You may find it convenient to tilt your board slightly. The drawback is that when working into a wet surface, the paint may run and come to rest against a dry edge in a small puddle. If allowed to dry the puddle forms a patch of darker colour and may spoil the effect. The answer is to lift out the excess paint with a piece of kitchen towel. Don't overdo it though, or you'll leave a light patch.

▲**1** Dilute some sap green paint in a clean saucer with the No. 20 brush – plenty so that you can charge the brush fully. Wet an area of paper with a clean sponge or a large clean brush. (You may need to go over the paper a couple of times if it is particularly absorbent. Make sure the surface is clear of any specks of dust or hairs that might spoil the result.) Now drop some paint on to the paper.

▲**2** Notice how the paint spreads straight away. Individual blobs start to join up, leaving lighter areas between. Here you can see that because the board was tilted slightly, the paint ran and collected in a line at the bottom of the wetted area. Now leave the paint to dry.

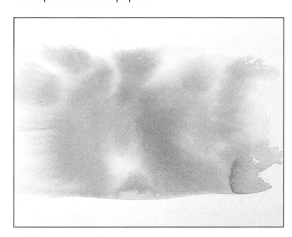

▲**3** Compare this step with the previous one and then the first one. See how much softer the shapes are now that the paint is dry. Heavy, opaque drops of colour in the first step have dispersed and dried to form transparent areas of colour only marginally darker than the surroundings. Here and there some of the pigment has separated slightly to give a yellowish tinge. At the bottom of the paper the paint has dried to a crisp line.

▲**4** Mix up some alizarin crimson in a clean saucer, then use some more water to wet your paper again. (Notice how the green remains unaffected by the water.) Load the brush with paint and drop in some crimson blobs. See how the paint radiates from the tip of the brush to form brilliant circles of colour – like ink on wet blotting paper.

Mixing colours: summer trees

To paint a simple landscape, find a pleasing view or do what our artist did and paint from the photograph he had taken.

If you've never worked with watercolour before, start by mixing up a few washes and allowing yourself time to get the feel of the brush and the paint.

Before you begin, make sure you have all the equipment to hand. Set up plenty of palettes for mixing washes, and don't forget you need two jars of water – one for mixing and another for cleaning your brush.

Our artist chose a heavy piece of watercolour paper for this painting and taped it to a board. As an alternative to a single sheet, you could use a glued pad to hold the paper taut.

He also picked a sheet of paper larger than he needed to give space for testing colours. If you prefer, use a smaller piece and paint right up to the edges. You can test your colours on scraps of paper.

Keep things as simple as you can. Break down the landscape into broad areas of colour, then work with just a limited range of paints. The large brush won't lend itself to putting in fine detail anyway.

At all costs avoid overworking – the paint and paper surface are actually quite delicate. If the paper starts to get really wet, don't panic – you can always blot it off with kitchen paper.

Finally, do have faith. It's sometimes hard to believe that everything will be all right when the paint dries, but you'll be pleasantly surprised at the final result.

1 Mix two washes for the sky – a lighter one of cobalt blue and a darker one of diluted Payne's gray. Test the colours.

◄2 Load the brush with cobalt blue. Quickly lay a band of colour at the top of the paper. Don't worry about covering all the paper – any white showing through will stand for clouds.

Now load the brush with Payne's gray and, starting below the cobalt band, lay the colour across the paper. Angle it in all directions to get a modulated colour – full of lights and darks. Allow colours to flood into one another so you lose brush marks. Paint grey to the horizon.

To create an impression of distance here, lose some colour by laying a clean wash of water over the bottom of the sky. Add warmth to the sky with a yellow ochre/Payne's gray mix. Leave to dry.

►3 Mix up three washes for the foreground. One of sap green with a little cadmium yellow; another of sap green; and a third of sap green with some brown madder alizarin.

Working quickly, lay a band of the first mix. Then lay a band of the second mix below. As with the sky, allow the colours to flood into one another. Finally, lay a band of colour with the third mix.

▲ **The set-up** Our artist used this photo as his starting point, but didn't copy it slavishly (he left the car out, for example).

◀ **4** For the near foreground, add a little Payne's gray to the wash of sap green and use it to lay a fourth band of colour.

Then paint more bands underneath, adding more and more Payne's gray as you approach the bottom of the paper – this darker colour will create the impression of closeness. Don't worry too much about the effect – this is all underpainting which you'll paint over later. Leave to dry.

▲ **5** As you paint, remember that your colours will dry much paler – as in the foreground here.

▲ **6** For the centreground trees, make a wash of sap green with a touch of brown madder alizarin. Paint them in, remembering that you're simplifying the shapes.

▶ **7** For the base of the trees, make an intense mix of sap green and Payne's gray. While the first tree colour is still wet, flood in plenty of the new wash. At the bottoms of the trees, pull the paint down with the brush to describe the tree trunks. Leave to dry. (As it dries, notice how crisp edges form where the paint gathered on the paper in small puddles.)

◀8 Still using the intense mix of sap green and Payne's gray, lay in the trees on the horizon on the left. Leave to dry (20 minutes to half an hour).

▼9 Paint in shadows under the trees with the sap green and Payne's gray mix.

Then, using one of your darker green washes, lay some patches of colour on the trees. Avoid moving the paint around – you want puddles which will dry with hard edges to describe clumps of foliage. Paint the smaller trees in the background using the same technique.

Now step well back and assess what your picture needs. Here the underpainted foreground looks rather thin and flat, so the artist added texture to it by laying more sap green and Payne's gray mix over it. Again, he didn't work it too much because he wanted some crisp edges to form. Leave the finished painting to dry.

WORKING WET-IN-WET

The technique of painting wet-in-wet produces beautiful, soft, blurred colours. You can combine various wet-in-wet washes to build up form with several layers of tonal shading.

Painting wet-in-wet is simple to learn (as we saw on page 165), but the art lies in controlling it. You are dealing with liquid colour on top of liquid – the mixing of two wet layers which results in softness and blurring. It's essential to start with stable, heavy watercolour paper, which prevents too much movement and soaks up the water. You must stretch the paper beforehand, or as here, use a very thick 444gsm sheet which won't buckle with the wet washes. Wet-in-wet blending can be controlled in various ways – for instance by regulating the amount of water or colour wash you apply. The more watery the layers, the softer and more rapid the blending. You can apply a clear water wash or tint it lightly, and use contrast colours or the same colour but in increasing intensity.

If you restrict the water content of the top layer you can watch the top colour slowly 'star' out into the base watery wash. And blotting the wash as soon as it starts to blend gives a 'frozen' effect with a crisper, sponged look.

▼ Large, nondescript areas, such as the background here, can be transformed into lively, vigorous parts of a painting by applying washes of colour to wet paper and letting the paint flow wet-in-wet.

If you need to prevent a wash spreading where it's not wanted, one good method is to leave a thin, dry white line as our artist has done around some of the apples.

'STILL LIFE WITH APPLES' BY PENELOPE ANSTICE, WATERCOLOUR ON PAPER, 21 X 14IN

Fruit and flower still life

It always helps to practise a technique several times before applying it for real. Experiment with these washes until you gain a feel for what will develop. Keep a scrap of paper at hand to try them as you paint. (Even our experienced artist used a spare piece of paper to loosen up her brushwork.) You need to start painting with a confident, large, loose stroke and the practice run can help you get rid of tension in your arm.

Watercolours dry lighter, so load plenty of colour into the washes if you want strong effects. Dry watercolour can easily be revived – if you don't like the effect, or want it to appear more intense, re-wet it and repeat.

YOU WILL NEED

☐ A sheet of 444gsm Rough watercolour paper

☐ Four synthetic round brushes: Nos. 12, 10, 6 and 2; and a 19mm flat wash brush

☐ Two jars of water; paper tissues

☐ Drawing board and tape or pins

☐ A water-soluble green coloured pencil

☐ Twelve artists' quality watercolours: cadmium lemon, cadmium yellow, permanent rose, alizarin crimson, vermilion, cerulean, ultramarine , sap green, emerald, Winsor violet, indigo and black

▶ **The set-up** The combination of an attractive ceramic vase, fruit and some flowers makes a classic still-life subject – here given a modern look with clear, unfussy lines and the contrasting brilliant blue background.

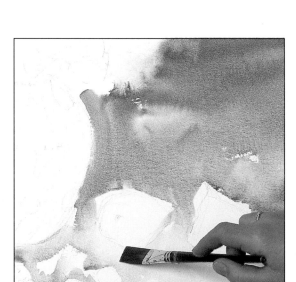

◀**1** Sketch in the composition with the water-soluble coloured pencil. Start with faint direction lines, then add the main shapes with a firmer line.

Roughly cover the top three-quarters of the paper with lots of clean water. Mix a pale wash of ultramarine/cerulean and fill in the background with the wash brush. (Don't let it go over the vase, fruits or palm fronds.) Use loose strokes, pulling the colour round the shapes with your brush.

▶ **2** Dilute some sap green to make a thin wash. Using the side of the wash brush, stroke the colour out along the palm fronds. Let the shape of the brush itself define the foliage. Try not to let the blue and green washes touch here. Leave a line of white, but if it touches slightly, just pull the resulting blur in the direction of the frond.

◀ **3** The fruit and vase now need a base wash. Using the large round brush, mix a thin cadmium lemon/sap green wash and roughly fill in the pears. Don't allow this colour to bleed into the blue. Do the same for the cherries, using a dilute red and painting partial cherry forms in curved brushstrokes.

Paint in the deeper blue of the vase, leaving the pattern unpainted, then fill in the fruit with cadmium yellow (a stronger yellow than that used for the pears). Note that this vase is almost a mirror of the larger composition but with more intense colours.

▶ **4** Mix several light washes with the No. 10 brush for the other fruit and leaves on the vase. Make a bluer green using emerald for some of the leaves, and try the pale lemon colour already mixed for the pears on others; then create a mix of rose and crimson for the pale pink flowers and use the same mix for the cherries on the vase. Just go for the broad shapes – more details will go in later.

▼ **5** Change to the No. 6 brush. You now need stronger colours, but still wet enough to blur softly. Outline the flower stems in sap green and the buds in a softer, yellower green. The flowers have twisting buds, so try to show this in the outlining.

BRUSH SIZES

Different sized brushes can help create variation in wet washes. You can sweep a light wash over the paper in soft bands with a large brush – ideal for skies and backgrounds. Smaller brushstrokes with intense colour give a different feel – try this for varied foliage effects.

Blobs of paint produce stars which vary with the amount of water and the depth of colour. Leave them to dry and you sometimes find unexpected little filigree patches developing later when a strong colour sits on a lighter wash.

►**6** You are now moving on to richer washes. The preliminary light washes are down, and the sharper details of the stems have been picked out, so now the stronger shapes need sharpening. Apply a darker version of the blue on the vase, and also pick out the patterns in stronger washes of yellow and green.

Mix a fairly intense blue-green wash and, with the No. 6 brush, stroke in the leaves of the pink flowers. Use the shape of the brush for the stroke, pressing down for the width and off for the thin end. One stroke per leaf gives you a lovely leaf shape.

Step back now and take an overview. Check the composition. The background wash still needs to be deepened to strengthen the painting.

►**7** Apply another wash of clean water right round the vase, then paint a darker but still loose blue wash on top. Use the wash brush for the bigger strokes, but take care that you don't distort the outline of the vase.

Crisp up the shapes of the spiky palm fronds, using the No. 10 or No. 12 round brush to pull the darker blue wash tightly in between each leaf. At this stage you can adjust the leaf shapes, but exercise great care and control as you do so. You don't want to paint a leaf out of existence!

◄**8** The fruit now needs attention. First apply a darker shade of the yellow-green wash on the pears, adding cadmium yellow for a deeper colour. Apply a warm red wash (alizarin crimson with vermilion) on the top side of the three pears on the right. The colours will bleed slightly, blurring the edges. Control the blurring to imitate the blush on the pear.

Paint the cherries in a darker crimson wash. These don't need the same wet blurred effect – a drier application of paint gives firm shapes. Add just a touch of violet to the crimson to deepen the colour on the underside of the curves.

◄**9** Using your smallest brush with indigo or black, lightly touch in the stalks and dimples of the cherries and pears. With the same colour make some quick flourishes around the outlines of the shapes on the vase to crisp them up.

Re-wet the right side of the background for the triangular shadow, using the wash brush and clean water. Once this water is painted on, stroke on a strong blue shadow. Make sure the edges of the stronger colour blend in with the background. Soften the edge with more water if necessary.

◄**10** You may find that this deeper colour unbalances the picture. Take a look at the flowers and check that they are strong enough. Our artist found that the background blue behind needed to be deeper in tone to bring the flowers forward again. She carefully painted in another blue wash behind the flowers, among the stems and petals.

▼**11** The flowers and buds also need work. Strengthen a few petals and stems with a thin, strong line in sap green, using the No. 6 brush. Deepen the rose-pink wash in some areas and apply touches of violet-pink to the inside of the flowers to give them some depth.

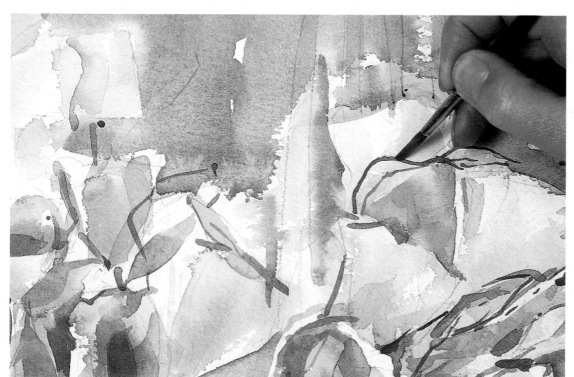

LIQUID ADDITIVES

Various proprietary liquids are available to help the washes flow. Traditionally **oxgall** was added to the water to improve flow. Now there are several modern additives (similar to detergents) that do the same thing, such as Winsor & Newton's watercolour medium. These break down the water tension which means you can get blurring effects with smaller amounts of water, helping to keep your watercolour paper in better condition.

▶**12** Crisp up the edges around some of the flowers by applying another layer of blue. Don't overpaint this exactly – let the different blue tones show in some areas to create a halo effect around the flowers which makes them shimmer slightly.

Strengthen the blue-green foliage by adding a more intense wash to some of the leaves.

▼**13** Take a good look to see where your painting may be unbalanced. Make sure the fruit sits forward in the painting, retouching with another deeper layer of colour if necessary. Notice that the pink flowers have been deepened in this way. The layers of washes start to outline each other, creating broken-colour effects which contrast with the soft blurring of the backcloth. Once you are satisfied with the picture, apply one last coat of clear water over the entire painting to soften any last-minute changes.

In the finished picture you can see how well the informal and deliberately loose style complements the wet-on-wet technique.

WET-ON-DRY TECHNIQUES

Achieve crisp, clean effects by building transparent layers of paint on a dry surface.

In the wet-in-wet technique (see pages 169–174), you apply paint to a wet or damp surface. The result is a shape with a soft edge. With wet-on-dry, you work on to dry paper or paint and the effect is entirely different. Here shapes are sharply defined – often with a very crisp edge. Whether you apply paint with a stroke of the brush or drop it on to the paper, you can work in a far more controlled and detailed way.

The quality of an edge is important in watercolour. With wet-on-dry you can use a clearly defined edge to capture form – a close-up of a leaf, for instance, or a range of mountains.

The wetness of the paint has an effect on the result too. For example, dilute green stroked on to the paper dries with an even tone. A wet blob of the same colour dropped on to the paper dries with a clearly defined edge because some of the pigment tends to migrate to the edge of the shape, reinforcing the outline.

If you are new to watercolour you might be tempted to work wet-on-dry all the time – for the sake of control – but you would be to lose much of the joy of the medium. It's the spontaneity and unpredictability of paint on a wet or damp surface which give watercolour its special quality. So it's often good to combine both techniques – working wet-in-wet in the early stages and then applying some detail wet-on-dry to pull the painting together later on.

▼ The warmth and light of this Mediterranean scene are captured perfectly by the wet-on-dry technique.

Crisp but smooth-edged shapes describe the dappled shadows of the leaves, while the vine leaves themselves are built up from ragged-edged patches of transparent and nearly opaque paint.

'VINE SHADOWS' BY ILANA RICHARDSON, PAPER, 1992, 28 X 38CM, COURTESY OF CCA GALLERIES, LONDON

Church by the sea

YOU WILL NEED

☐ A 28 x 38cm sheet of stretched 130–210gsm NOT paper

☐ A B or 2B pencil

☐ Three round brushes: Nos. 10, 6 and 3

☐ Several jars of clean water

☐ Mixing palettes

☐ Ruler (optional)

☐ Seven colours: cobalt blue, Davy's gray, Payne's gray, yellow ochre, cadmium orange, cadmium red, sap green

▶ **The set-up** Our artist is a compulsive drawer and has a great many sketchbooks of scenes that he has come across on holiday. For this painting his inspiration was a small sketch of a Moorish church at Collioure in south-west France. He used a flat Derwent sketching pencil to get a great variety of marks, and took notes of the colours.

1 Sketch out the composition using a fairly soft pencil. Don't make the drawing too tight. The idea is to treat the subject in flat areas of colour and then put a little texture over the top. Just map in the main shapes.

◀ **2** Dilute some cobalt blue. Wet the paper where the sky is to be. Starting at the top of the paper, use your No. 10 brush to lay a flat wash. (It helps to angle the board slightly towards you.)

Keep the brush on the move so you can complete the sky before the paper dries. Use a dry No. 6 brush to catch excess paint collecting at the bottom of the wet area. Leave to dry.

▲ Paint on the palette looks very much darker than it does when applied to paper. Once the paint is dry it is paler still and bears little resemblance to the colour seen in the palette. You'll get used to this as you gain experience.

▶ **3** Dilute some Davy's gray in the palette and, using the No. 6 brush, start to put in the main shapes: the buttresses on the church, the tower, church wall, quayside and the rocks in the foreground. Leave some of the white of the paper to represent bricks in the quayside wall. Leave to dry.

◄ **4** Paint in the water using cobalt blue and the same brush. Rest your hand on a piece of clean scrap paper to protect the watercolour paper from grease and excess paint.

You can make freehand strokes or use a ruler if you wish. Our artist used a bit of both. If you find it difficult to get into the corners, then turn the board around. Leave to dry.

► **5** Here you can see how the dry Davy's gray shows through the layers of transparent blue. If you look at the horizontal blue strip across the middle, you can see how the edges have dried slightly darker, creating the clean, crisp shape typical of the wet-on-dry technique.

◄ **6** Dilute some yellow ochre and then add a little Payne's gray to make it less intense. Still with the same brush, use this mix to put in the remaining triangles between the buttresses and the church wall.

Now strengthen some of the previous greys – the strips to the right of the church, the quayside wall and the shadow up the side of the tower. Don't be afraid to go outside the original areas and to leave some gaps so the existing grey shows through. Leave to dry.

DID YOU KNOW?

Davy's gray

So far Payne's gray has been used a lot in our demonstrations. Davy's gray is another useful one for your palette. Made from powdered slate, it is much lighter than Payne's gray and dries to a slightly warmer – greenish – hue.

▶ **7** Dilute some Payne's gray and, using the same brush, darken the rocks and the wall next to the church.

   Try to avoid entirely solid blocks of colour. Notice how the artist leaves gaps in the wall to represent bricks and in the rocks to create the impression of an undulating surface.

▶ **8** Using the No. 3 brush and the same grey, paint in the church windows and a few of the bricks on the end of the quay. Flecks of white in the rock on the right serve as foam and help to break up this dark, dominating shape.

▲ The artist made this sample sheet of the colours in his painting. He sometimes laid several washes of the same colour one over another.

   Here he has repeated a stronger tone on the right to give an idea of the range: cobalt blue (1), Davy's gray (2), Payne's gray (3), yellow ochre and Payne's gray (4), cadmium orange and cadmium red (5), sap green and Payne's gray (6). Compare these dry painted colours with the paint on the palette two pages back and you can see how much lighter they dry.

◀ **9** Assess the tones in your painting. Unless your first washes of cobalt blue were exceptionally strong you'll need to intensify them. If you still have some on your palette, make sure that it is well mixed and, using the full width of the No. 10 brush, put some bold strips of colour over the sky.

   Now do the same for the sea using thinner strips and the No. 6 brush. Notice how paler strips left in the sky lend depth to the painting.

◄ 10 Mix some cadmium red and cadmium orange in roughly equal proportions. This exciting tangerine colour placed among the cool greys and blues really brings the painting to life. Use your No. 3 brush to paint the roofs. Leave the paint to dry.

► 11 Reassess the tones. You might find – as our artist did – that some of the reds need another wash. Don't overdo it, though. Try leaving the dome – the most prominent form – palest of all.

You might need to intensify some of the greys too. The artist used his No. 3 brush and Davy's gray to strengthen the base of the church tower, wall, windows and the causeway in the foreground. Leave to dry.

▼ 12 Dilute some sap green and knock it back with just a hint of Payne's gray. Using the No. 3 brush, put in the parasol pine to the left of the buildings and the wedge shape to the right of the church. A broad band of green around the edge of the rocks in the foreground suggests weed.

Tip

Flat colour
Because the artist wanted to exploit flat, uniform areas of colour, he added oxgall solution to the paint. Just one drop added to diluted paint in the palette breaks the surface tension of the paint and actually improves the wetability of the paper itself, helping the pigments to disperse evenly over the paper.

◀**13** So far, most of the shapes are geometrical and flat. Now use some freer brushwork to give a looser feel. With the tip of your No. 3 brush and some Payne's gray, work some texture into the rocks in the foreground. Leave to dry.

▼**14** The few slight adjustments needed to finish the picture are more a matter of personal choice than necessity. Perhaps the most significant are laying another wash over the water to make it the most intense of the blues and strengthening the shadow on the left side of the tower. Detailing on the church turrets and the tower's reflection – using Davy's gray – and a second wash over the green wedge, help to engage your attention.

USING A LIMITED PALETTE

Although it's wonderful to have a mass of colours in your paintbox, and a quiverful of brushes, it's often worth limiting yourself – you'll find a selective palette can give your painting more cohesion.

You've already seen what you can do with a very limited palette consisting of just three primary colours (see Chapter 2) but often you'll want to use more. It takes skill to mix up a range of good colours from the primaries, and if you are new to the idea you can spend more time mixing than painting.

You don't, however, need to rush out and buy dozens of extra colours. Using a *selective* range has great advantages. For a start, your painting is much more likely to harmonise, particularly if you let the colours flit over the painting. You're also less likely to have jarring elements because you aren't tempted to dip into colours which have no business to be there. Of course, experienced artists often limit the colours they use automatically, even if they have a huge range on the palette in front of them, but for beginners it can help to be selective from the start.

The range of colours you select should suit your subject, mood and style of painting. Choose only the colours you think you really need – you can always mix them to make new ones.

For her painting of the Australian bush (overleaf) our artist chose strong colours to capture the light, hot atmosphere and vegetation of the area. Her palette comprised cadmium yellow, two reds and two blues plus a good strong green and one earth colour. To these she added two inks to increase the vibrancy of the painting.

In rendering this scene, our artist maintained a freshness which is often lost when working from a photograph in the absence of natural light. She avoided this problem by making a note of the colours on site, so it didn't matter if they were changed by the photographic process. In addition, she worked fairly quickly, without breaks, combining many techniques with a spontaneous approach.

▼ A carefully selected palette of blues, greens and greys plus a basic yellow is all you need to paint a landscape like this one. As usual in transparent watercolour, the white of the paper provides the highlights.

'AMBERLEY CHALK PITS, SUSSEX' BY ROGER SAMPSON, WATERCOLOUR ON PAPER

Australian landscape

▲ The set-up Our artist used a photograph and some quick colour references as her starting point. She made the colour references while on site, in case the colours in the photograph didn't come out true to life.

► 1 Lightly pencil in the main elements of the landscape. When you're happy with the composition, use the masking fluid and your old brush to block out areas you wish to leave white, such as the stems of the bushes and the tree trunks. Clean the brush immediately in warm, soapy water.

Mix ice blue ink with French ultramarine and cerulean blue, adding plenty of water. Fill in the sky with your wash brush, starting at the top and adding more water as you go down – this line of lightest blue on the horizon helps to create a sense of distance.

About three-quarters of the way down, dab your brush into a touch of permanent rose to create a sunset mood. Blot off any excess water with some kitchen paper and blend over the hills so you don't create a hard, unnatural edge.

◄ 2 Add a touch more blue ink to your wash and use it to paint in the rivers, aiming for a flat finish to suggest still evening water. Take the colour to the very edges so that when the foliage is laid on top, the river can be seen through it. Again, blot with kitchen paper if the painting becomes too wet.

For reflections in the water, use the clean 12mm flat to lift off a little blue.

YOU WILL NEED

- ☐ A 77 x 57cm sheet of 140gsm stretched NOT watercolour paper
- ☐ A drawing board
- ☐ Gummed paper
- ☐ Two jars of water
- ☐ White china plate or palettes
- ☐ A craft knife
- ☐ Pencil eraser
- ☐ Hair dryer
- ☐ Masking fluid
- ☐ Kitchen roll
- ☐ HB pencil
- ☐ Four brushes: 12mm flat, No. 6 round wash, No. 4 round and an old brush for the masking fluid
- ☐ Seven watercolours: cadmium yellow, cadmium red, permanent rose, Hooker's green dark, cerulean blue, French ultramarine, burnt sienna
- ☐ Two Ecoline inks: olive green and ice blue

► 3 Use the wash brush to apply a loose wash of burnt sienna to the mountains. Working wet-in-wet, dot in a little cadmium red, mixing straight on to the paper. This darkens the mountains and sends them into the distance. Quickly dab on some ultramarine and Hooker's green to suggest the gum trees on the mountains. See how they have already taken shape.

◀ **4** When you move on to a new area and don't want the colours to bleed into each other, make sure that the first colour is absolutely dry. A hair dryer is handy to speed things up.

When the rivers are dry, apply a wash of burnt sienna to the land, including the islands in the river. While this is wet, add extra touches of burnt sienna to the main land area so that you create a marbled effect.

▲ An ordinary white plate makes a perfectly acceptable palette, although you'll need something deeper if you want to mix large washes.

▶ **5** When the mountains are dry, add more details with the same four colours used earlier – burnt sienna, ultramarine, Hooker's green and cadmium red. You can have a lot of fun with this, turning and dabbing the brush freely to create interesting colour combinations. Leave to dry, then soften and blend the colours with clean water. If the mountains create a hard line where they meet the sky, soften the edges when dry with clean water too, using your 12mm flat.

▼ **6** Deck the hills in greenery with your 12mm flat, using mixes of Hooker's green, cadmium red and olive green ink. Rinse your brush, then add clean water to blend the edges into the plain.

Now you can have some fun flicking paint to give an impression of scrubby foliage. Charge your 12mm flat with paint and flick it at the paper with your fingers from about 15cm away. Use less water where you want more detail. This natural-looking effect helps add form and dimension to the hills.

7 To create darker greens, add more ultramarine to the mix; add more cadmium red for warmer greens. Where the foliage is dense along the side of the river, use a strong, dark green wash and your flat brush, wet-on-dry.

Once the specked hills are dry, add more details with the same washes.

Tip

When accidents happen

In step 4 you can see that our artist accidentally washed blue over an island in the foreground. To rectify this she lifted off a little colour with the 12mm flat, then cleaned the brush and scrubbed over it again to lighten the tone. You can use this method to rectify any mistakes you make – but you must act quickly, before the paint has a chance to dry.

◀ **8** Here's another chance to experiment with your palette. Be bold in your approach and work quickly to maintain freshness. For the eucalyptus bushes in the foreground, dampen the paper, then drop cadmium yellow on to the sunlit areas and ultramarine on to the shadows, wet-in-wet. You can work freely because the masking fluid protects the bush twigs from the paint.

9 Our artist now stippled over the bushes with the clean, wet edge of her 12mm flat to blend and soften the colours. Other colours can be added using the same technique to block in shady areas.

◄ **10** Stand back and look at your painting. See how the different techniques have created depth and texture. Notice, especially, how the clear water blending has created atmosphere and the way the blues combine to send the mountains back into the distance.

▼ **11** Now start work on the foreground. Dampen the paper with clean water, then use a fairly dry brush to dab in strong blue and green washes. Aim to create a variety of tones and textures, adding green ink for vibrancy, and ranging from wet to dryish paint.

▲ ► **12** Add shadows to the river by dampening the area with water, then adding pure ultramarine with your 12mm flat. Add cadmium yellow to areas which need lightening, then dampen your brush in clean water and use it to blend the edges of the colours.

Use your greens – mixed from Hooker's green, ultramarine, cadmium red, cadmium yellow and burnt sienna – to paint the leaves of the gum tree (above). Dab on some colour with your 12mm brush, then spatter on more colour with a fairly watery mix to suggest individual leaves (right). Work into the splatters, wet-on-wet, adding cadmium red for darker areas and cadmium yellow for lighter ones.

▲ **13** Carry on working into the tree foliage wet-on-wet, adding olive green ink for darker shades and softening the edges of the foliage with a clean, wet brush. Use the sides and flat edge of the brush for greater variety. Finally, paint in the fine lines of the branches with olive green ink, making use of the flat edge of the brush.

Notice how you can create a wide range of greens by remixing the colours of your palette. All the greens go well together because they have the same sources.

◄ **14** Now work on the foreground foliage again, dampening the paper so that you can work wet-on-wet. Don't be frightened of dropping in pure colour, such as Hooker's green dark, shown here, to create exciting combinations.

► **15** To create the shimmering reflections of low evening light, our artist used a clean, wet brush to scrub off colour, then dabbed the area with kitchen paper.

Stand back and assess your painting, then refine any areas which you think need work.

▶ **16** Now comes the exciting moment when you can remove the masking fluid – but first make sure that the painting is completely dry or you will smudge it. Use a hair dryer if necessary to accelerate drying.

Rub off the masking fluid with clean fingers, then erase any unwanted pencil lines. The eraser may lighten the surrounding paint colour, but you may wish to use this to your advantage.

▲ **17** Mix various warm purple washes of ultramarine and burnt sienna with clean water, then use your 12mm flat to block in the colours of the trunk on the right, starting with the lighter areas. Make bold use of your brush, changing the angle to create different lines. Work into dry areas, then work wet-in-wet. Our artist used the edge of her brush to put in the shadow on the side of the trunk, blending it with a little water.

▲ **18** Use burnt sienna to add shadows to the islands and the branches of the bushes on them. Add ultramarine to the mix for areas of deep shadow. The contrast with the light areas creates the impression of bright sunlight.

◀ **19** Now work on the trunks of the trees on the left, using a watered-down mix of the same colours. For fine lines you can use the flat edge of the brush. Leave plenty of white showing through, but blend the paint at the ends of the trunks where the masking fluid creates hard lines. Work quickly, moving the brush to and fro, wet-on-dry to blend the colour.

◄ 20 To paint the wispy foliage in the foreground, use your No. 4 brush and a mix of ultramarine and cadmium red with olive green ink. Rest the side of your hand on a dry area of the paper to steady it while you add the foliage with swift, flowing movements.

Now charge your brush with burnt sienna to define the tree trunks on the left and touch in shady leaves. Change to the 12mm flat to paint the unmasked grass in the foreground with olive green ink and cadmium yellow.

► 21 While the paint is still wet, add burnt sienna and yellow highlights to the grass. Load your brush with cadmium red and add touches of pure colour to the grasses. Let it blend into the wet burnt sienna.

Add any final details you wish, but be careful not to overwork things. If in doubt, leave the painting for a while so you can be more objective about it.

▼ 22 Finish by scratching in fine lines of grass with the end of your brush or a craft knife, working from the bottom up with swift movements.

See how much variety has been created with just a few colours. Some washes have been enriched when dry by going over them with another wash; others are marbled by adding pools of colour to the wet paint, letting them blend on the paper. The ink adds more depth.

INTRODUCING GOUACHE

Gouache – opaque watercolour – has great versatility. You can paint from dark to light with it and cover up mistakes, it's excellent on tinted paper and it can be used for semi-transparent washes.

◀ You can buy gouache paints in a variety of forms to suit yourself – tubes, pots or pans, which all come in a number of different sizes.

▼ Watercolours are usually done on white paper, which is left blank for white areas or highlights, but with gouache, where you use white paint, you have the option of using some of the wonderful tinted papers available.

Put simply, gouache is watercolour paint with white pigment added. As with pure (transparent) water-colour, finely ground pigments are mixed with distilled water and bound with gum arabic. The difference is that chalk is added. This creates the opacity for which gouache is famous. (Adding white to transparent watercolour makes what is known as body colour – it's opaque and similar to gouache, but slightly more subtle in effect.)

Along with this opaque quality, the white pigment gives gouache substantial covering power. The two combined produce effects quite different from those of transparent watercolour.

When it is used opaque (or thick), gouache produces an effect similar to acrylics or matt oils, but it dries much faster, so you can work quickly. And you can dilute the paint to create the delicate washes so typical of watercolour. In a nutshell, gouache offers the best of both worlds.

This medium is also known for its rich, deep colours. The reflectivity of the white pigment gives the hue great vibrancy, resulting in strong, energetic colours.

Although never highly fashionable, gouache has always had its admirers.

CREATING TEXTURE

You can use just about anything you can get your hands on to create interesting textural effects with gouache. Try different objects to see what you can achieve.

use a sponge

or crumpled paper

or even a toothbrush

COMPARING WATERCOLOUR WITH GOUACHE

watercolour

gouache

Although the subject of these paintings is identical, you can see the opacity of gouache in the sky behind the yacht. This area is much more transparent in the watercolour. Our artist also used the opacity of gouache to add the white foamy water last – an area he had to mask out on the watercolour.

Famous Old Masters, including Rubens, van Dyck and Dürer, used it. And, in more recent times, Picasso, Burne-Jones, Egon Schiele and Henry Moore have all seen the appeal of gouache.

Gouache in practice

Gouache is probably one of the most versatile and 'user-friendly' mediums available to the beginner. If you've had some experience with watercolour, then most of the basic techniques will already be familiar to you. Watered down, gouache creates thin, delicate, semi-transparent washes which you can blend wet-in-wet on the paper, or build up by laying one flat wash of colour over another.

FOUR WAYS WITH GOUACHE

Gouache is extremely versatile, especially when it comes to texture, for instance. Here the same paint has been used in four different ways to create some interesting effects.

impasto

scumbled

a wash

opaque paint (with white added)

◄ Here the dense, flat quality of gouache serves to concentrate attention on the emotional intensity of the artist's subject.

GOUACHE ON TINTED PAPER

There's a long tradition of using tinted paper with gouache. Applying the opaque paint in thin washes allows the paper colour to show through in places, adding warmth or coolness to your work.

Since gouache is opaque, it has excellent covering power, enabling you to work from dark to light if you wish. Many artists commonly paint on coloured paper or on white paper tinted with watercolour or acrylic. Obviously if you ladle the paint on, gouache will cover up everything. But used fairly thinly, it allows the mid-toned ground to show through underneath.

Beige, yellow ochre, pale green and even light grey are suitable mid-tone colours to use. There are many more options available. Don't just pick a paper colour at random – choose one to suit the mood or colour composition of your painting. If you're working on a dull winter landscape, for instance, try using a light grey paper. Allow the paint to build up in some areas, but let the paper show through in others.

◀ **The set-up** These small, bright flowers are challenging to capture in the opaque colours of gouache. The hand-painted glazed jug has a smooth, round surface which contrasts with the asymmetrical flowers. The background is a piece of natural hessian, not unlike the beige tinted paper our artist chose.

YOU WILL NEED

☐ A 35.5 x 51cm sheet of stretched beige-tinted 210gsm NOT watercolour paper

☐ A 2B pencil

☐ Three round sable/synthetic brushes – Nos.4, 5 and 12

☐ Two jars of water

☐ One or two palettes

☐ Thirteen gouache colours – primary yellow, spectrum yellow, golden yellow, lemon yellow, yellow ochre, permanent light green, Winsor green, scarlet lake, cadmium red, cobalt blue pale, permanent white, cool grey No.5 and warm grey No.5

▼ **1** Use the 2B pencil to draw the jug and mass of flowers on the paper. Roughly indicate the line separating foreground from background.

Make a loose wash with permanent white and paint in the jug with the No. 12 brush. While this is wet, add some warm grey No. 5 mixed with a little cobalt blue pale to darken the bottom and side.

◀ **2** Mix some permanent light green and Winsor green, and form the stems rising from the jug with the No. 12 brush. Map out the foreground in yellow ochre. Add a little white to yellow ochre for variety. Allow the colour of the paper to show through here and there.

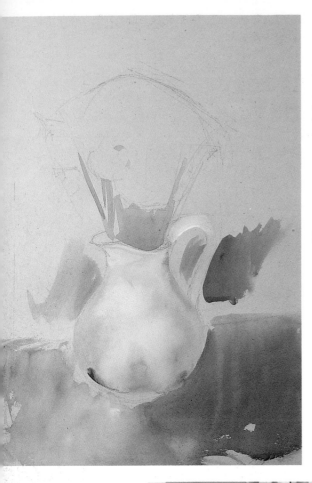

◀ **3** Add a little warm grey No. 5 to some yellow ochre to darken it. Continue working on the foreground and background with the same brush, interplaying light and dark areas.

▶ **4** Mix Winsor green with a touch of warm grey No. 5, and create more green tones on the stems with the No. 12 brush.

Use the same brush to block in the general area of the flowers with a mix of primary yellow and golden yellow. The colour isn't painted on uniformly – our artist has made some dark, impasto-like marks and allowed areas of the paper to show through for variety.

Mix cobalt blue pale, warm grey No. 5 and dilute white and darken part of the handle.

◀ **5** Still with the same mix, darken the base of the jug. Use some dilute white to highlight the side of the jug, blending it with the No. 12 brush. Let the paint flow freely; you can add detail later on. Don't panic if the paint runs – it's easy to correct at this stage of the painting.

▶ **6** Return to the background. Mix yellow ochre with warm grey No. 5, and paint in some areas at random. Add white to the mix to lighten it and apply to other areas to vary the background tone. Paint around the bunch of flowers – don't be afraid to redefine the shape if you wish. For the shadow areas on the right side of the jug, use a mix of yellow ochre, white and cobalt blue.

Darken the rim of the jug with a little Winsor green mixed with cobalt blue pale and cool grey No. 5. Vary the greens within the flower stems with a mix of Winsor green and permanent light green. Now adjust the tones of the jug as needs be. Leave to dry.

◀ **7** Add another layer of paint to the inside of the jug near the handle, using a strong mix of Winsor green. This is important because the stalks of the jonquils must appear to go into the jug, not sit on top of it. If the paint runs, simply blend it into the jug with a wet No. 12 brush.

Mix primary yellow with a touch of cadmium red and apply a few blobs to the flower area for tonal contrast.

▲ **8** Assess the tones of the jug once more. Then turn your attention to the foreground. Use the No. 12 brush to darken the shadow behind the jug with yellow ochre and a touch of cobalt blue pale.

Your aim is to achieve a sense of reflective colour from the jug, both in the background and foreground tones. As the layers of paint build up, the jug and flowers begin to sit convincingly in their space on the table. Use white to redefine the front lip of the jug with the No. 5 brush.

◀ **9** Continue adding white paint to the lip of the jug. Lighten the side of the jug with your No. 12 brush and a loose blob of white, and blend again.

Then blend the colours beneath the lip and around the jug handle with your No. 12 brush dipped in a little water.

▲ **10** Add a dark reflection near the handle with cobalt blue pale mixed with warm grey No. 5. Then soften the edges with the No. 2 brush, and continue to blend the colours on the jug. Don't overwork this area – you'll end up with a very flat grey. Blend selectively around its sides, leaving white in the middle. Our artist then blended the colours which ran down the paper. Lighten the foreground beneath the jug using white, yellow ochre and warm grey No. 5.

▲ **11** With the No. 5 brush lighten some of the flower petals with primary yellow mixed with white. Flick these on using quick brushstrokes, keeping the painting's surface lively and interesting. Mix a little scarlet lake and golden yellow, and paint in the trumpet-shaped centres of the jonquils.

◄ **12** To suggest roundness and depth, tidy up the stems using the same brush and three colours: Winsor green and cobalt blue pale; permanent light green; and Winsor green and lemon yellow. Then, using your thumb, merge the colours around the jug handle where the reflected light on the ceramic meets the colour of the background.

▲ **13** Mix cadmium red with spectrum yellow to intensify the colour in the flower centres. Add more detail to the stems and the leaf tips appearing through the blossom with the three green mixes from step 12. Use your No. 5 brush.

Wash your brush, then add thick blobs of primary yellow mixed loosely with white to the bunch to break up the uniformity of the flower mass and suggest individuals showing through.

◄ **14** Now that you've nearly finished, move your easel to the flat position or lay the painting on a table to prevent the paint from running. Use your No. 12 brush to build up the layers of grey on the jug. Apply warm grey No. 5 mixed with a little white. Add cobalt blue pale and Winsor green to this mix for the shadows underneath the jug.

Tip

A plateful of good advice
Why spend a lot of money on shop-bought palettes for watercolours when an ordinary white ceramic plate works equally well, if not better? It's cheap, offers a large working area and is easy to clean under warm running water.

◄ **15** For the jug's pattern, our artist used small strips of folded paper as a tool, instead of a brush. Practise applying the paint on a piece of scrap paper before working directly on to the painting.

Dip the folded corners into cobalt blue, and print the paint on. Use the paper straight and curved to help you capture the pattern, but don't copy it slavishly.

► **16** Mix some permanent light green and primary yellow, and apply this with the paper strips to make extra fine lines along the stems. Again, resist the temptation to make too many stems, or the painting will look overworked.

Some blobs of paint may accidentally appear. Don't worry – these give your painting spontaneity.

▲ **17** Add pure white highlights to the jug and sharpen the blue pattern, using your No. 4 brush. Mix cobalt blue pale and a little cadmium red for the darkest area underneath the jug.

The finished painting has been left fairly simple.

Our artist overpainted many different yellows to give an overall impression of a vase of flowers without labouring unnecessarily over each one. And parts of the tinted paper show through in areas to add warmth and pull together the whole image.

—

CHAPTER SEVEN

OIL PAINTING

TOOLS AND TECHNIQUES

BRISTLE BRUSHES FOR OIL

Brushes – the artist's main tool for applying oil paint – are available in an enormous range of shapes, sizes and materials. Choosing the right one for the job is vital for good results.

◀ Energetic brushstrokes give life and texture to this painting. Long horizontal strokes and short stabs of colour in the foreground foliage create a great feeling of vigour and growth.

The smoother, less defined strokes in the background aim for impression rather than detail, pushing the hills and trees back, suggesting space and distance.

'BANKS OF THE RIVER TAME, DELPH, LATE SUMMER' BY JOHN McCOMBS, 1991, 11⅜ X 16¼IN

▼ This detail of the stream shows how the broad horizontal strokes used to depict water also convey a feeling of calm and serenity.

Every type of brush is suited to one or more tasks and each leaves a different kind of mark. Since they vary greatly in cost as well as versatility, you must choose your basic kit carefully.

When you are selecting brushes, don't feel daunted by the large choice available. You don't need a huge variety – start with three or four that satisfy your initial needs. One artist may use a dozen or more, but another may be perfectly happy with just a few selected brushes. It all depends on the techniques and the effects you want to achieve. So experiment to get a feel for what suits you, and gradually add to your collection of brushes as the need arises.

Types of brushes

Oil painting brushes are made from either bristles or soft hairs (or synthetic substitutes for them). Each has a specific function. Bristle brushes are good for establishing the initial stages of composition and laying in large amounts of colour. Their stiff bristles make them ideal for impasto work. Soft hair brushes are useful for smoother lines and precise details, and are often used for smaller paintings. Restrict yourself to bristle brushes when you are starting out. They encourage you to work loosely, which is valuable in the early stages of composition.

Bristle brushes

Stiff and hard-wearing, each strand of a bristle brush has split ends that hold large quantities of paint. It's a useful brush for making bold, decisive strokes; bigger sizes are good for covering broad areas with thick colour. It's also ideal for larger paintings, but its point is too stiff for details.

Traditionally, bristle brushes are made of hog's hair, which is particularly suitable for oil painting since the strength and flexibility of the bristles are good for the thick, heavy texture of the paint. Look for ones that have plenty of spring and keep their shape when you make a

stroke on your hand with them. Avoid synthetic substitutes, which are usually made of nylon and rapidly lose their shape.

Bristle brushes are available in some interesting shapes, but the four most useful ones are flats, brights, rounds and filberts.

Flats are extremely versatile brushes and essential for any basic collection. They have flat ends and long bristles that hold a lot of fluid paint. This makes them ideal for applying broad, rectangular strokes and areas of thick, bold colour, as well as for short dabs of colour. You can use the side of the brush for thin lines and sharp details. Flats are especially suitable for working up to a clean edge and blending areas of colour. Bear in mind that, since the bristles are quite elastic, they won't pick up stiff paint.

Tip

Which size?
Choose your brush sizes according to the scale of your work and the degree of detail you wish to achieve. For example, use a range of larger brushes for broad colour on large canvases.

As a general rule, start with larger brushes than you think you'll need. Working on a larger scale helps you define the composition on your paintings and avoid focusing too soon on lots of details.

The brushes in the picture have been chosen because they make a good, all-purpose range of strokes and marks

No.12 Flat   No.5 Flat   No.2 Flat   No.8 Round   No.4 Round   No.2 Round

Flats – Nos.12, 5 & 2
Flat brushes are good for laying in large areas of colour. The side is good for narrow lines, while the flat of the brush can be used for blocks of colour. Flats are good for blending paint and moving it around the canvas.

Rounds – Nos. 8, 4 & 2
These are good general-purpose brushes. They can be used for laying in broad areas of colour and for scumbling, and the tip of small sizes can be used for fine line work and small dabs of colour.

Brights (sometimes called short flats) are the same shape as flats but with shorter, stiffer bristles that dig deeper into the paint and leave strongly textured, chunky marks. You'll find them useful if you want to apply stiff, thick paint to create impasto effects. Because of their shorter bristles brights are easier to control, making them better for moving in on details following a more generalized underpainting.

Rounds are exceptionally versatile brushes, indispensable in your basic kit. They have long, thin bristles that curve inwards at the ends. With heavily diluted paint, round brushes make soft, thin strokes that are ideal for establishing basic composition in the initial stage of a painting. Alternatively, by loading the brush with a lot of paint, you can make long, bold marks and lay in large areas of colour. Rounds are good for the technique of glazing, and also for delicate lines and outlines.

Filberts are similar to flats – they have a flat ferrule but curve inwards at the end. They are available in two versions. Filberts with long, springy bristles hold a lot of paint and make soft, tapered strokes. The other type, with short bristles, hold less paint and are easier to control – ideal for applying small dabs of colour. Tastes differ, but filberts are generally considered useful but not essential brushes.

Brush sizes

Each type of brush is made in a range of sizes, with each manufacturer offering their own range and numbering system. There are usually 12 sizes

▲ **Decorators' brushes – 12mm and 25mm**
Decorators' brushes are cheap, hard wearing and very useful. Because they have many bristles, you can load the brush heavily with paint to cover the entire canvas with a single wash. Or you can use them to block in large areas of for a bold underpainting.

Filberts – Nos. 12, 8 (short) & 2 (long)
Filberts produce a wide range of marks. The shape of the tip helps you avoid the blocky, rectangular marks sometimes left by a flat brush. The long-bristled brushes can be used to produce fluid lines. Because they are easy to control, the short-bristled ones are good for building up an impasto effect, and making short dabs of colour. The smaller sizes are good for detail.

No.12 Filbert | No.8 Filbert (short) | No.2 Filbert (long) | No.8 Bright | No.2 Bright | No.4 Synthetic (round)

Brights – Nos. 8 & 2
Because of the shortness of their bristles, brights are good for building up patches of pure colour in a controlled way.

Synthetic – No. 4 round
This brush is good for laying in an area of thin colour, and for details and fine lines.

in each series, with No. 12 the largest and No. 00, 0 or 1 the smallest. However, one manufacturer's No. 6, say, may not be the same size as another's.

Beginner's selection

When you start oil painting, bristle brushes are generally more useful than soft ones. Not surprisingly, better quality bristle brushes are more expensive than synthetic substitutes. However, their springiness, versatility and long life make the extra expense worthwhile.

It's far better to buy only three or four really good bristle brushes than a huge selection of poor-quality ones. Choose brushes with hairs that look neat and don't splay out from the ferrule (the metal or plastic case that holds the bristles together). A good selection to start with is a No. 8 round, a No. 5 flat and a No. 2 filbert or bright. You can experiment with other styles and sizes later on, as required.

For small-scale or detailed work, you will need a soft brush. Pure sable ones are extremely expensive and unnecessary for the beginner. Moderately priced synthetic soft-hair brushes provide an adequate alternative. A good size to go for is a No. 4 or 5 round brush. You may also find 12mm or 25mm decorators' brushes useful for laying in large areas of colour.

► A medium-sized No. 5 flat is large enough to make broad strokes to describe the bark of this Scots pine, yet small enough to make short dabs of colour for the foliage. The flat edge makes thin, angular lines for the branches.

► A large No. 8 round brush is ideal for laying in large areas of colour. Its flexible bristles allow you to make soft strokes, which, when the brush is angled, create texture for the thick, dense leaves on this cypress.

▲ A smaller brush such as a No.2 round, filbert or bright produces finer, more delicate lines – used here for the small needles on the outer branches of the Norway spruce. The body of the brush, used at an angle, lays in more colour for the denser foliage in the middle.

CHECKING UP ON OILS

To get the best out of your paints, it helps to know what their special qualities are and how to exploit both their advantages and their disadvantages.

Easy to work with and readily available, oil paints are extremely versatile, allowing you to create a wide range of superb effects. You can use them straight from the tube to make exciting, thickly textured impasto works in a single day, or dilute them with a medium to create layers of scumbles and glazes (which take rather longer). Opaque and transparent oil paints are available to increase your options further.

What are oil paints?

Generally, identical pigments – made from earth materials, minerals, plant extracts and synthetic chemicals – are used in oils, acrylic and watercolours. The difference comes in the binder (or medium) that holds the pigment together and sticks it to the support. Linseed oil, the binding agent used in most of today's oil paints, gives an unparalleled richness of colour.

► Colour selection is an individual matter, but you need both warm and cool colours for versatility. This all-purpose basic palette has a warm and a cool blue, and the same for red and yellow. An earthy green (oxide of chromium) and a sharp green (viridian) produce a wide range of colours for landscapes. White, black and two warm earth colours are also invaluable.

▼ Many artists arrange the paints on their palette from warm to cool colours (or vice versa). Always put your paints in the same order so you automatically know where to dip your brush.

The trays (dippers) can contain turps, linseed oil or a medium. Use a separate, larger container of white spirit for cleaning brushes.

viridian

oxide of chromium

French ultramarine

cerulean blue

alizarin crimson

cadmium red

lemon yellow

cadmium yellow

burnt umber

raw sienna

lamp black

titanium white

AN ALL-ROUND LANDSCAPE PALETTE

If you know you want to paint particular subjects, then choose your palette accordingly. For example, an all-round landscape palette has earthy colours – yellow ochre and Vandyke brown – along with natural-looking greens (viridian and sap green) for foliage. Use warm and cool blues, white and cadmium yellow on their own or mix them to create other colours. Here, from left to right, are: viridian, sap green, cobalt blue, cerulean blue, cadmium yellow, yellow ochre, Vandyke brown, ivory black.

Some art scholars reckon that artists in Germany in the 12th century were already mixing their pigments with linseed oil. But it was the 15th century Flemish master, Jan van Eyck, who really made oil paints popular.

A special character

Oil paints dry very slowly (unlike watercolour, acrylic and gouache, which are water-based). Depending on the thickness of the paint, oils stay wet and workable for quite a long time, allowing you to try again – or use a different technique – if you aren't getting just the effect you want.

This means that, unlike watercolour work, you don't have the pressure of getting the painting right first time. All you need do is simply wipe the paint off or add another layer over the first one. You can even scrape off thick paint with a knife and put it back on the palette – something unique to oils. And if the paint is thin, you can wipe it off with a rag soaked in white spirit. Finally, you can blend colours together and work wet-in-wet for a long while.

▼ The colours in the foreground (the figures) are sharp and pure. The artist has used oils in a completely traditional way, building up subtle skin tones with many glazes. To knock them back, background colours are mixed with white and complementaries.

The modern equivalent palette colours shown here, reading from top to bottom, are: lamp black, Prussian blue, purple madder, alizarin crimson, Venetian red, chrome yellow deep, burnt umber, raw sienna and sap green.

'FAMILY OF DARIUS BEFORE ALEXANDER THE GREAT' BY PAOLO VERONESE, OIL ON CANVAS, 93 X 187IN

It must be said, though, that working quickly with oils can be frustrating. For instance, the colours could blend together if you add a second glaze too quickly over a wet first layer. There's nothing for it but to wait until it dries – unless you wish to exploit or harness the effect in some way.

Using oils

Good quality paints have a class or star system to rate their permanence. Class AA (or three star) colours are permanent and very stable, while class C are fugitive (they fade quickly). Some colours contain hazardous materials, so don't get the paint on your fingers.

You thin oil paint with turpentine and/or linseed oil – don't use white spirit because it isn't entirely compatible with oil paints. You can wash your brushes in white spirit, then use soap and warm water or washing-up liquid, and rinse under the tap. Use a cotton rag soaked in white spirit to wipe paint off your hands. Some people are allergic to turps and white spirit. Other products are available, but they're expensive.

▶ Viridian is a cool, sharp green. Here it is used unmixed and also diluted with white to set up a bold contrast with the warm red. In much of the painting the colour is scumbled so the texture of the canvas shows through, but there are also many areas of thick impasto.

The equivalent modern palette colours, shown from top to bottom, are: cobalt blue, cerulean blue, cadmium red, yellow ochre, chrome orange, cadmium yellow, viridian and permanent green.

'YOUNG GIRLS IN THE GARDEN AT MONTMARTRE'
BY PIERRE-AUGUSTE RENOIR, OIL ON CANVAS,
21¼ X 25½IN

◀ Van Gogh's particular genius was to see – and use – colours in a heightened way. He used many straight from the tube, often enhancing the natural colour of his subject and thereby intensifying its impact. The blues here are used in pure form or mixed with white. Predominant in the sunflowers is Naples yellow, its chalky opacity contrasting well with the transparent viridian.

Modern palette equivalents, from top to bottom, are: cobalt blue, cerulean blue, Prussian blue, viridian, yellow ochre, Naples yellow, alizarin crimson.

'SUNFLOWERS' BY VINCENT VAN GOGH,
1887, OIL ON CANVAS, 17 X 24IN
(METROPOLITAN MUSEUM OF ART)

◀ The mostly dark background does much to bring this colourful dancer forward in the picture. The reds sparkle against the black of the skirt and the green-grey of the floor, and a thin scumble of opaque white suggests the crunchy texture of the lace veil. Modern palette equivalents, from top to bottom, are: lamp black, Payne's gray, cobalt blue, sap green, alizarin crimson, cadmium red, permanent rose, yellow ochre and raw sienna.

'LOLA DE VALENCE' BY EDOUARD MANET, OIL ON CANVAS, 123 X 92CM (MUSÉE D'ORSAY, PARIS)

Check in your local art shop for suitable alternatives. Whether you're allergic to turps or white spirit or not, work in a well ventilated room.

There are several mediums for use with oil. They can alter the paint in many ways – thin it down, thicken it, make it matt or glossy, speed up or slow down the drying time and increase the flow or transparency of the paint.

It takes a while to get used to all these different mediums, and not even professional artists know exactly what they all do. Many artists use 'fast-drying'

▼ Hot, intense colours glow in this painting – they aren't dirtied or knocked back by mixing with earth colours or complementaries, and you can see raw canvas between dabs of pure colour. Optical colour mixing occurs in the viewer's eyes, making for a shimmering surface.

Modern palette equivalents, top to bottom: ultramarine, cobalt blue, rose madder, deep yellow, golden ochre, transparent golden ochre, Prussian green and olive green.

'HOUSES OF PARLIAMENT' BY ANDRÉ DERAIN, 1905-6, OIL ON CANVAS, 31⅛ X 38⅜IN
(© ADAGP, PARIS AND DACS, LONDON 1994)

▲ The artist here has chosen his reds with great care. The warm reds – oranges and dusky pinks – are concentrated in the centre, around the light source (the lamp), but the cooler reds start to appear as you move away towards the edges (particularly in the bottom right corner).

Modern palette equivalents, from top to bottom, are: viridian, ultramarine, cadmium yellow, cadmium red, rose madder and ivory black.

'INTÉRIEUR WITH MME VUILLARD' BY EDOUARD VUILLARD, 1893-95

► Cool blue-grey neutrals contrast with the bright yellows of the daffodils and the warm, earthy, sienna-based colour on the windowsill.

Great delicacy of touch is evident here, both in the very thin layers of paint used in the background and on the windowsill and in the more generous application of paint on the daffodil heads and sprays of honesty.

Palette colours, from top to bottom, are: aureolin yellow, lemon yellow, yellow ochre, cerulean blue, ultramarine, cadmium red, alizarin crimson and burnt sienna.

'SPRING DAFFODILS, MOUSEHOLE' BY KEN HOWARD, OIL ON CANVAS, 24 X 20IN alkyd mediums such as Wingel or Liquin from Winsor & Newton to speed up the paint's drying time and extend its flow. Manufacturers don't all use the same names, so ask for more information in an art shop.

Supports, brushes, palettes

Canvas is the most popular support for oils, but hardboard, millboard and cardboard are all suitable surfaces. You should treat all supports before you begin painting (unless you buy them ready prepared). If oil paint is applied to an absorbent support, the surface soaks it up, which may rot the support.

Brushes come in a wide range of shapes, sizes and materials. In general, brushes for oils are made of synthetic fibres and bristle hair – both are hard wearing. Their long handles mean you can work at a distance from the easel and see what you're doing.

Your palette should be smooth, flat and non-absorbent. A ceramic plate, a sheet of coated hardboard or plate glass, plastic, melamine or Formica is fine. You can also buy pads of non-absorbent, disposable paper palettes.

▼ A range of earthy colours in this landscape are offset by a number of cool greys – in the trees on the horizon, the distant hills, the rooftops and the car in the foreground. The road is a soft grey, made from mixing complementary colours; patches of the toned ground show through to warm the whole scene. The season is early spring – cool, but with the promise of returning warmth.

'STONESWOOD, DELPH, EARLY SPRING' BY JOHN McCOMBS, OIL ON CANVAS, 14⅛ X 13¼IN

Palette colours, top to bottom: chrome yellow, yellow ochre, chrome orange, flesh tint, alizarin crimson, burnt sienna, Vandyke brown, sap green, Prussian blue.

J. McCombs 90.

STRETCHING YOUR OWN CANVAS

Although it takes a bit of practice to get right, learning how to stretch your own canvases gives you a great sense of achievement – and in the long run, it can save you some money as well.

Linen or cotton canvas, stretched over a wooden frame, is the most popular support available for oil painting. It holds the paint well and gives you a sympathetic surface to work on – taut, but with just the right amount of spring. Ready-stretched canvases are available from most art shops, and these save time, but they are expensive – it's much cheaper to stretch your own. Often the commercially prepared ones come in a standard range of sizes only, so if you stretch your own you can assemble unusual formats to suit yourself.

The only tricky part in the process is to achieve the right amount of tension. As a guide to what to aim for, the canvas should be stretched taut, but not as tight as a drum. If you strike it gently with the end of a brush, or even a pencil, the brush should bounce back very lightly.

The stretcher frame itself imposes a certain amount of strain on the canvas, especially so on the edges where the material is stretched over the wood. The staples or tacks used for securing the canvas should be attached fairly close together to distribute the tension evenly across the stretcher. Keeping the tension at the corners slightly less taut than along the lengths also helps; if the canvas does sag a little over time, less strain is put on it when it's readjusted. But choosing the right equipment, and assembling the stretcher properly, goes a long way towards alleviating problems of incorrect tension.

Follow the steps here and your first attempts at stretching canvas should work, but don't be too disheartened if they don't – you'll soon improve your technique with practice.

▼ The reverse side of the stretched canvas shows the wedges in the top and left corners. These can be tapped in with a hammer if further tightening is needed.

Materials and equipment

To assemble a stretcher frame you need a length of canvas at least 10cm longer and wider than the final size of your stretcher frame. (You can buy canvas by the metre from most art shops.) Pinking shears are best for cutting the canvas. You can use scissors but pinking shears prevent the edges of the canvas fraying, and you don't have to turn the edges under for neatness.

The wooden stretcher pieces – you need four – come in various lengths and thicknesses and have pre-mitred corners with slot-and-tenon joints that fit together easily. The inner edges are bevelled to reduce strain on the taut canvas and prevent the disfiguring ridge that may occur along the canvas edge. Along with the four stretcher pieces, you need eight small wooden or plastic wedges or 'keys' for each canvas you stretch. These fit into the slots on the inside of each corner of the assembled stretcher; if the canvas sags later on – often due to humidity changes – these can be driven in further (keyed out) to make the canvas taut again.

You can use your fingers to stretch the canvas across the frame, but canvas-stretching pliers do a much better job on large canvases and are a lot less tiring. Likewise, a heavy-duty staple gun and non-rusting staples, with a depth of at least 1cm, make light work of attaching the canvas to the stretcher frame. A hammer and non-rusting tin-tacks offer a cheaper alternative.

You also need a ruler or tape measure and a pencil; a mallet to tap the stretcher pieces together; a hammer for tapping home the wedges, and a T-square to check the frame is square (or you can simply use a length of string to check the diagonal measurements are the same).

◄▼ Assemble all your equipment before you begin since you don't want to be forced to rush off at a crucial point to search for something . . . and don't forget your ruler or tape measure.

1. Unprimed canvas
2. Stretcher pieces
3. Staple gun and staples
4. Canvas-stretching pliers
5. Mallet
6. String
7. Hammer
8. Wedges (keys)
9. T-square

CHOOSING YOUR CANVAS

Painters can work on a number of materials. **Linen** (flax) is by far the best (and most expensive) canvas for painting. It comes in different qualities from very fine to coarse with a distinctive dark colour and irregular weave. The denser the weave, the better the canvas. It's cheaper to buy it unprimed (**A**, **B** and **C**) and prime it yourself with special artists' primer for oils, but you can save time and buy it ready-primed. (**G** is primed coarse linen, **H** is primed superfine linen.) If linen is too expensive, **cotton duck**, which is thick, heavy cotton with an even weave, is the next best thing. It comes in different weights, from heavy to light (**D**, **E**, **F**). And you can also get it ready-primed (**I**). Avoid cheap cotton which isn't worth the outlay. **Sacking** and **hessian** can also be used.

Assembling the stretcher frame

▶ **1** Slot the stretcher pieces together, checking that all the bevelled edges are on top. This way the surface of each stretcher piece slopes slightly away from the canvas and prevents a ridge forming along the edge.

▼ **2** Tap the corners together gently with a wooden mallet or a piece of wood for a close fit.

▲ **3** Use a square (shown) or T-square to check that all the angles of the assembled frame make right angles. It's important to get the angles correct right from the start, since you can't alter them once the canvas has been stretched.

◀ **4** Double-check that the corners are true right angles by measuring the diagonals with a length of string; they should be of equal length. If the frame is out of true, correct it by gently tapping the corners with the mallet.

Stretching the canvas

◄ **1** Lay the frame bevel-side down on a piece of canvas, aligning the vertical and horizontal weave with the sides of the frame. Cut the canvas to fit the frame, allowing a margin of about 10cm all round for stapling. Use a metal rule and pencil to draw guidelines on the canvas if necessary. If you use pinking shears to cut the canvas then you only need to allow a margin of about 5cm all round since you don't need to fold the edges under when securing it.

► **2** Keeping the frame horizontal and centred on the canvas, push one long side firmly against a vertical surface, such as a wall, to hold it in position. Fold the canvas over the opposite long side, using canvas-straining pliers to grip the fabric firmly; lowering your wrist as the canvas passes over the back of the frame helps to achieve the right tension.

◄ **3** Insert a staple in the edge (not the back) half-way along the stretcher piece to secure the canvas frame. Turn the frame around, pull the canvas firmly, and secure a staple opposite the first one. Repeat this on the remaining sides so that one staple holds the canvas to the centre of each stretcher piece.

► **4** Now add two more staples to each of the four stretcher pieces – one either side of the centre staples, following the numbered sequence shown in the diagram. Pull the canvas taut with one hand and staple with the other, evenly spacing staples at 5cm intervals. Continue adding pairs of staples to each side, working towards the corners and stopping when you are about 5cm from the corners.

Stapling the canvas to the frame

Tip

A tight stretch?

If the canvas is to be primed ready for oil painting, be careful not to overstretch it since the canvas contracts slightly when size and primer are applied, which may well lead to warping. Acrylic primer, however, does not shrink the cloth as much, so the canvas can be stretched more tightly.

▶**1** Finish the corners off neatly – if they are too bulky you'll find it difficult to frame the picture. First pull the canvas tightly across one corner of the stretcher as shown.

▼**2** Now tuck in the flaps on either side smoothly and neatly, and fix with staples. Take care not to staple across the mitre join, since this will make it impossible to tighten the canvas later on. Then fix the diagonally opposite corner, followed by the remaining two.

▲**3** Finish with some stapling along the back of the stretcher for extra hold, folding under the cut edges of the canvas if you haven't used pinking shears. Insert two wedges in the slots provided in each inner corner of the frame; for correct fit, the longest edge of each wedge should lie alongside the frame, as shown.

◀**4** Tap the wedges home very lightly. If you hammer them in hard the frame will be forced apart slightly. Your canvas is now ready for sizing and priming before painting begins.

OIL – THE FLEXIBLE MEDIUM

There's something about the way oil paints mix on the palette and how they handle on the canvas that is enormously appealing.

Oil has a quite unjustified reputation for being difficult, but in many ways it is the most forgiving of all the painting media. Because it dries very slowly, it gives you plenty of time to think about your approach – and you have the valuable opportunity to rework the paint if you change your mind.

Oil painting is also less technique-led than, say, watercolour. This means that right from the start a would-be artist can produce pleasing images with a richness and depth of colour unmatched by any other medium.

In oil paints, the pigment is held in an oil-binding medium. This is usually linseed oil. The paint has a buttery consistency and is sup-

plied in metal tubes. You can use the paint directly from the tube but it is usually thinned with turpentine, or a mixture of turpentine and linseed oil.

The choice of whether or not to thin the paint depends on the effect you're after. You can build it up carefully in a succession of thin layers or apply it directly as thick dabs of creamy, textured colour. The resulting picture surface is either smooth and glossy or thickly encrusted with swirling paint which holds every detail of brush, rag or knife.

Various surfaces (known as supports) are suitable: these include hardboard, canvas boards, stretched canvas and paper.

▲ There are many finely worked details in this oil painting – note in particular the velvety qualities of the curtain and cushion, the coarse weave of the wicker chair and rug and the smoother surfaces of wall and patio.

'LUNCH TIME' BY ROSEMARY DAVIES, CANVAS, 42 X 46IN

Rag painting: vegetables in a bowl

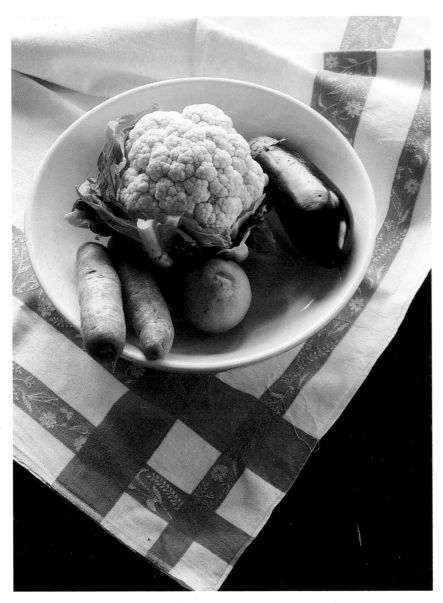

Whether you've used oil paints before or are starting out with them, this project – working with rags rather than brushes – is fun to do and encourages you to paint freely. It's a good discipline to use a limited palette to start with, and this helps to keep costs down as well.

Use a piece of good quality cartridge paper pinned to a board. If you haven't got an easel, prop the board against a chair. You want to be at a comfortable distance from your subject – about 1.5m. Position yourself so that you can look easily from the still life group to the paper. Leave enough room behind you so that you can step back from your painting from time to time.

Our artist chose a bowl of vegetables for this demonstration. You can either do the same or pick any interesting group of objects that appeals to you.

Keep to a still life to start with. This provides a subject for interpretation and makes a good picture – and there's no chance of it getting up and walking away.

◀ **The set-up** Note how the roughness of the cauliflower contrasts with the smoothness of the aubergine and the shiny glazed bowl.

The carrots and lemon bring warmth to the overall colour scheme, while the teacloth introduces a new texture and a dramatic design (it also reflects light up on to the bowl).

Cool, natural light from both sides illuminates the subject and creates interesting highlights.

▶ **1** Start with a simple underdrawing. Stand at a comfortable arm's length from the paper and use a piece of charcoal to sketch in basic forms and spaces. Remember your sketch is only an underdrawing, so don't get hung up on detail. Flick over it with a clean dry cloth to leave a 'ghost image' ready for painting.

▲ **2** Scrunch up a piece of clean cotton rag in your hand. (Cotton rag is more absorbent than synthetic material. But make sure that it has no loose fibres which will stick to the painting.)

Dip the rag into the turps and moisten the cloth. As a rough guide, just dampen the area of the rag that you want to use so that the turps doesn't run down your arm.

Use the rag to thin down some red paint on the palette. Don't do the whole lot in one go – just nick a little from the main blob and thin that by working in the turps. Make the paint fairly turpsy – the paper tends to absorb the turps as you work.

▲ **3** Use the rag to rub in the red for the carrots. Do the same with yellow for the lemons and Hooker's green for the cauliflower leaves. Use a new part of the rag for each area so you keep the colours clean.

◄ **4** For the cauliflower – which is mainly white – leave the paper to show through. Mix a little raw sienna with white to make a pale brown. Use this and a touch of cobalt blue to suggest the darks on the cauliflower.

Leave the aubergine – the darkest object – until more of the mid tones have been established. The table top is important, so rub that in with Payne's gray.

YOU WILL NEED

☐ Clean dry white cotton rags

☐ A 51 x 51cm sheet of white cartridge paper

☐ Wooden board

☐ Charcoal

☐ Spirits of turpentine (turps substitute is good enough for this exercise)

☐ Dipper (container) for the turps

☐ Small tubes of students' grade paints: white, cadmium red, cadmium yellow, cobalt blue, Payne's gray, Hooker's green, raw sienna

☐ Palettes and toilet roll cylinder

Tip

Clean turps
Pour only a little turps at a time. If you are using a shallow dish, for example, pour just enough to cover the bottom of the dish. Replace it with fresh turps before it starts to get muddy. This helps to keep colours clean and prevents unnecessary waste of turps.

▶**5** Screw up your eyes and look at the light and dark areas in your subject. Try to match these in your painting.

Lighten some Payne's gray with white and use it to paint in the mid tones on the inside of the bowl. Overpaint this with cobalt blue lightened with white. Paint in the grey shadow under the bowl to describe the rim.

Use cobalt blue for the aubergine and fill in the dark area with Payne's gray. Use the same grey for the shadow between the carrots.

Notice how the red from the carrot has been used to shade the lemon, while the lemon lends the vaguest hint of yellow to the carrot.

◀**6** Use your finger to build up a rich crunchy texture with white. (The light area on the cauliflower calls for a thicker ladling of paint – a turpsy rag tends to make it all a bit too thin.)

Don't worry about the white mixing with colours already on the paper – you don't want an unmodified white here anyway, and the mixing adds to the overall effect and texture.

▶**7** Look closely at the colours in your subject. Mix some of the same yellow as the lemon into the green of the cauliflower leaves. Tone the red in the carrots down by mixing in a touch of white. Leave a darker red to represent shade. A subtle smudge of warm pink brown on the aubergine turns this dark shape into a shiny, solid object. Make up this colour by mixing a little raw sienna, cadmium red and white.

Notice how the cloth forms a deep bank of shade behind the bowl.

▶ **8** Use the edge at the end of a flattened cardboard toilet roll cylinder (or any other thin piece of cardboard) to describe the florets on the cauliflower.

Pick up the red of the carrots and yellow from the lemon, but notice too how the artist has actually left an impression in the surface – removing paint at the same time as adding it.

Now stand back and have a look. The artist decided that the inside of the bowl was too dark, and used a Payne's gray with some white to lighten it.

Tip

▼ **9** A mere touch of outline serves to strengthen the composition. Use Payne's gray and cobalt blue to define parts of the oval rim and to suggest the stalkiness of the cauliflower leaves.

See how the colours are really working within the bowl now. Yellow from the cauliflower leaves is reflected at the back and red from the carrots at the front.

Mixing on palette
When mixing colours on a palette (above) it's important to keep them clean. Don't mix patches of colour too close together – keep them separate. Once you have mixed a new colour, keep a little of it on one side without adding any others to it. You may want to use it again later and it's next to impossible to mix exactly the same colour again

►10 Use a pale cobalt blue for the stripes on the tea cloth. Don't attempt to describe intricate designs. Here the artist puts in flecks of white to suggest detail on the stripes.

A few carefully observed highlights help to make the surface of the lemon really sing and lend form to the aubergine and the inside of the bowl.

SOLVE IT

Chop and change

The beauty with oil is that you can make changes at any stage. After leaving the painting for a couple of hours, the artist decided to simplify the foreground by removing a stripe on the tea cloth with a clean piece of rag and some white to cover the blue.

▼11 Your painting is finished when you are happy with the result. Here the artist removes one stripe to simplify the picture. But the area of cloth wasn't just left a blank white. Instead the artist used pale greys and greens to break up the cloth, making the whole surface of the painting more exciting to look at.

SCUMBLING WITH OIL PAINT

The word scumbling is rather strange, but the technique itself couldn't be simpler – it's a straightforward way of introducing texture and broken colour effects into your paintings.

To achieve a *textural* scumbling you drag thick paint lightly across the picture surface so that patches of the underlying colour show through the scumbled paint.

You can do this thick scumbling with a brush or painting knife, and it works on any toothy surface – including canvas, oil paper and paint itself. The paint must be as thick as possible, not diluted with turpentine. Good-quality paints are best because they contain less oil and have a stiffer consistency.

The alternative means of scumbling is effectively the reverse of a glaze – it is a film of paint that can be thin or creamy as long as it's also opaque or semi-opaque. With a semi-opaque scumble you modify rather than obliterate the colour beneath.

Another way of avoiding a complete cover like this is to apply the scumble with a dry brush, so you allow flecks or larger areas of the underlying colour to show through.

In the demonstration overleaf we show you textural scumbling with a brush and a painting knife.

▼ In this charming painting of a lavender field in France, the artist has achieved an exciting surface texture by scumbling paint on with fingers, brushes and painting knives.

'LAVENDER IN PROVENCE' BY MADGE BRIGHT, OIL ON CANVAS, 25 X 36IN

SCUMBLING WITH A PAINTING KNIFE AND WITH A BRUSH

1 A knife produces thick wedges of uneven paint that contrast with the thinner undercolour. Scoop up some paint on the underside of the knife and scrape it lightly across the surface, with the edge of the blade tilted.

2 For more regular texture, load a large flat bristle brush with undiluted paint and drag this lightly across the canvas. Hold the brush very close to the canvas, painting with the flattened side of the bristle head.

YOU WILL NEED

- [ ] 32 x 42cm piece of primed canvas
- [ ] Masking tape
- [ ] Turps; palette
- [ ] Sticks of charcoal
- [ ] One round No.0 brush and three flats – Nos. 12, 10, 4
- [ ] One 5cm flat brush
- [ ] One painting knife
- [ ] Nine oil colours: burnt sienna, cadmium red, carmine alizarin, olive green, terra rosa, Naples yellow, French ultramarine, cadmium yellow, white (see palette below)
- [ ] Two alkyd or acrylic colours: phthalo blue and burnt sienna

Strolling ducks

Scumbling works best on a textured surface, so use primed canvas or cotton duck for this painting. Buy a ready-to-use stretched canvas or simply use a length of primed canvas and stick it down on a rigid board with masking tape.

The initial drawing is crucial, so take time getting it right. You'll find it helpful to make a few quick sketches of the subject first, then copy one onto the canvas. Keep the drawing as simple as possible – too much drawn detail is a waste of time because it will get covered up as soon as you start to paint.

▲ 1 Use charcoal for the initial drawing, giving the ducks a single, confident outline. For the background, a few accurate lines are enough to establish the position of the bridge and buildings.

◄ 2 By making a textured underpainting in neutral acrylic or alkyd paint you lessen the drying time and can scumble over it in oil paint almost immediately without smudging the painted outline. For the outline, use a No.0 round brush and a mixture of phthalo blue and burnt sienna – this produces a very dark tone which is less stark than black.

► **3** While the outline is drying, squeeze out your oil colours on to the palette – burnt sienna, carmine alizarin, terra rosa, Naples yellow, French ultramarine, olive green, cadmium yellow, cadmium red and white.

Using the No. 12 flat brush, apply a loose wash mixture of terra rosa, carmine alizarin and burnt sienna across the ground and sky. Don't worry about drips and runs – these quickly become integrated into the picture.

◄ **4** For the river, use the 5cm flat brush to apply a thin wash of French ultramarine in short, vertical strokes. Paint over the outline of the ducks, but leave a few patches of white on the lightest parts of the birds.

Tip

Wait a while

If you are scumbling one colour over another, you may find it easier to wait until the first colour is slightly tacky, otherwise the colours may smudge into each other. The scumble is applied so lightly that the texture of the canvas itself almost drags the paint off the brush.

In fact, you might find it pays to wait to do your scumbling until the paint is dry to the touch. In this case, you need to exercise a little patience before continuing with the picture.

◄ **5** The blue and reddish brown washes look more natural if you allow them to overlap in places. Paint the shadows cast by the ducks and those on the ducks themselves in a darker tone of the blue wash colour.

► **6** For the pale background areas, mix a little white and Naples yellow with the blue and brownish red already used in the painting. Bring the ducks to life by painting the light tones in pale blue with your No. 10 flat brush.

▼ **7** Paint the black duck with the No. 4 flat brush. Real black would be too dominant, so use a mixture of olive green, French ultramarine and a little carmine alizarin.

◄ **8** It's almost time to start adding texture – time to start scumbling the ducks! But first you need to re-establish the duck outlines, which have become lost under washes of colour. Do this with your No. 0 brush and the acrylic or alkyd paint.

◄9 For the first layer of scumbled colour, dip the No. 10 brush into thick white paint – don't add any turps – and drag the loaded brush lightly across the canvas inside the outlines of the ducks. The pressure should be light enough to allow patches of undercolour to show through the thick paint.

▲10 For the beaks and feet, mix a bright orange from cadmium yellow and cadmium red and apply this with your No. 4 flat brush.

Tip

Keep it dry
When you are scumbling in this textural way, keep your paint thick but dry – use very little turps (preferably none at all, in fact).
Another point to bear in mind when you start is that scumbling works best on a textured surface.
Don't forget to use your fingers, either – they're great tools for scumbling.

◄11 Lighten the shadows underneath the ducks with a light scumble of white and French ultramarine. For the shadows on the feet, use the dark tone – olive green, French ultramarine and a little alizarin carmine – painting them in with the No. 0 brush.

228

DID YOU KNOW?

Cloisonné

Our artist has outlined her ducks in a fairly dark line. This is known as cloisonné, and is a technique taken from a style of jewellery in which outlines created by thin wire are filled in with brightly coloured enamel. The dark outlines highlight the bright colours inside. The French artist Paul Gauguin did many paintings in this style.

▲ **12** You can create the illusion of distance by applying a pale blue scumble across the entire background area. Do this with the No. 10 brush, held flat against the canvas, and apply the stiff colour in short vertical strokes to indicate the geometric, upright buildings.

◄ **13** Lighten the very pale background areas a bit more by cross-scumbling – pulling the brush horizontally across the previous vertical strokes. Your scumble should be light enough to allow the shapes of the buildings to show through.

► **14** Redefine the light background tones and highlights in white using your No. 4 flat brush.

▲ **15** The painting is almost complete, and it's time to stand back and take a critical look at the picture so far. Notice how the white ducks have become too similar in tone and texture to the background. They need to be brightened and strengthened.

▶ **16** A painting knife is useful here (see page 224). Use it to scumble a thick layer of white on to the ducks. Use the direction of the strokes to describe the curved forms of the birds.

► **17** Take care not to scumble a complete layer of white all over the ducks. Retain some shadows on the birds by allowing a few areas of darker underpainting to show through. These dark patches, and the shaded parts of the necks and abdomens, make the birds look solid and real.

▼ **18** In the finished picture the scumbled areas of white on the ducks – with the darker colours showing through – give zest and life to what could otherwise have been areas of dead colour. The bright beaks and feet contrast well with the white, while the gentle blues and earth colours of the background give a sense of hazy distance.

CHAPTER EIGHT

—

ACRYLIC PAINTING

TOOLS AND TECHNIQUES

CHOOSING ACRYLIC PAINTS

Today the range of acrylic paints is simply vast. With information about the most recent developments, you can use the right paint for the right job, saving yourself time, money and a lot of hard work.

Paint manufacturers are constantly developing and changing their acrylic paints. This is tremendously exciting – but keeping informed about current products is not easy. Even experienced professionals may miss out on new possibilities because they are unfamiliar with recent developments.

Liquid acrylics are a typical example. Fairly new products, they slightly resemble brilliant liquid watercolours or inks (which tend to be fugitive – fading when exposed to light). Because they all look similar they may often be grouped together – wrongly, since most liquid acrylics are permanent, not fugitive. If artists don't know about them, they're limiting their creative possibilities.

What is acrylic?

Acrylic paint is simply pigment dispersed in a film of transparent liquid plastic (technically speaking, an emulsion consisting of plastic acrylic resin and water). You can dilute acrylic paint with water, but remember that it is completely insoluble once dry.

In its liquid form the emulsion has a milky appearance, but after the water evaporates it is transparent. You can test this with one of the acrylic mediums – just brush some undiluted gloss or matt medium (an emulsion without any pigment) on to a tinted support. You'll see that it's rich and creamy straight out of the bottle, but completely transparent when dry.

Types of paint

Most paint manufacturers have at least one range of acrylic paint in their catalogue – and some have several. The main differences between one range and another are the consistency and the number of colours.

You can apply acrylics thickly for impasto and thinly for washes and staining techniques. Thick, textured impasto requires a stiff paint which can retain the strong mark of the brush or painting knife. Thinner, more fluid paint is best for washes. Adding proprietary mediums to thicken or thin the paint is one way to increase the paint's versatility.

Some manufacturers, however, produce several ranges of paint with different consistencies to save you the time and trouble of mixing. Here we look at three of the largest acrylic paint manufacturers. Their products are widely available in most art shops.

DID YOU KNOW?

What are alkyds?
Often confused with acrylics, alkyds are fast-drying oil paints (but not as fast as acrylic paints) that do not mix with water. Use them on their own, or combine them with oil paints. To modify the way alkyds behave and to quicken their drying time, use alkyd mediums such as Winsor & Newton's Wingel or Liquin.

▼ Here the artist's use of opaque acrylic is bold and loose. The scumbled water and the sky give a dramatic sense of depth, helping your eye to travel from the opaque water to the bright red building and into the city-scape and beyond.

'ST PAUL'S FROM THE SOUTH BANK' BY TERRY McKIVRAGAN, ACRYLIC ON HARDBOARD, 36¼ X 44IN

Winsor & Newton

Winsor & Newton Artists' Acrylic Colour is a range of 75 paints available in 20ml, 60ml, 120ml and 200ml tubes. This also includes six pearlescent and six metallic colours and an iridescent white. The consistency is similar to Liquitex Tube Colour paints. Though it holds a brush mark well, you may like to add gel medium for heavy impasto work.

Galeria, ideal for artists who work on a large scale, flows smoothly and freely but retains the mark of the brush. It's marketed as an economy paint, but the quality is excellent. There are 25 colours in 500ml tubs.

The six mixing primaries of the Galeria range are particularly interesting. You can mix many colours with the cadmium yellow pale hue, cadmium yellow deep hue, permanent rose, vermilion hue, ultramarine and cerulean blue hue. **Winsor & Newton Designers' Liquid Acrylic Colour** is a range of 36 colours supplied in bottles with dropper caps. Water resistant when dry, they have good lightfastness. Use them for all sorts of wash and line techniques, including airbrushing and technical pen work.

Liquitex

In the 1950s Liquitex produced the first commercially available acrylic paints. Now the range has 98 colours, including iridescent, interference and fluorescent ones. Most are lightfast, even in outdoor applications. Only the fluorescent colours are fugitive.

Liquitex Jar Colour is smoother and more fluid than the Tube Colour, making it ideal for watercolour techniques, covering large areas of flat colour and even airbrushing. Seventy-five colours are available in 60g jars, and some come in 230g, 450g and 910g sizes. In addition, you can buy titanium white and Mars black in 4.5 litre containers.

Liquitex BASICS, aimed specifically at the beginner, is quite a recent addition to the range of acrylic paints. With 24 colours to choose from, it's much cheaper than the Tube or Jar Colour, and the quality is excellent.

Liquitex Interference Colour consists of six shimmering colours – orange, red, blue, green, violet and gold. The pigment contains mica flakes thinly coated with titanium which creates complex optical effects. The green Interference paint applied to white paper, for example, refracts red, its complementary colour, and vice versa. But on black or dark paper the colours become iridescent. And you can mix them all with mediums and other colours. Interference Colour is useful for capturing the iridescent qualities on some bird plumages, for instance.

Liquitex Fluorescent Colour appears to glow even when mixed with other acrylic paints. Don't use it for paintings you want to keep because it's fugitive.

Liquitex Tube Colour, available in 22ml, 59ml, 138ml and 207ml tubes, has a soft, buttery consistency and handles very much like oil paint. It retains the mark of the knife or brush yet remains flexible when dry. The complete range isn't available in all tube sizes. Mars and ivory black come in large 237ml tubes.

Daler-Rowney

Daler-Rowney offers a range of 55 colours in two consistencies – Cryla and Cryla Flow.

Cryla has a creamy consistency and is good for impasto work. There are 38ml and 120ml tubes and a limited selection of colours in 2 litre tubs.

Cryla Flow is thinner and more suitable for washes, staining techniques and large-scale work. It's available in 60ml tubes, plus a 120ml tube of white. Some colours come in 2 litre tubs.

Rowney System 3 Acrylic is a range of 24 colours in 500ml nozzle-cap pots. A quality product at an economical price, it is compatible with Daler-Rowney acrylic mediums and is ideal for school and craft work and for large-scale projects such as murals.

PAINTING REFLECTIONS IN GLASS

Glass objects come in many attractive shapes and lend grace to any still-life. But conveying the transparency of glass, with all its reflections and highlights, is quite a challenge.

The secret of painting glass lies in resisting the temptation to put in too much detail: the more decisively and simply you paint glass, the more transparent it looks. Bear in mind that faithfully copying every detail you see doesn't work – too much detail destroys the illusion of a smooth, light-reflecting surface. Fewer details in fact say more. A few telling highlights and reflections are all you need for a convincing illusion of glass.

Looking at your subject through half-closed eyes cuts out weaker details and throws up the stronger tonal contrasts, helping you see the reflections as an abstract pattern of shapes and colours. (Note how some of these shapes have hard edges and some soft.) Compare one tone with another as you work – if, say, you are painting a glass half-filled with wine, check whether the rim highlight is brighter or duller than that on the stem. Is the colour of the wine cooler on the surface than in the bowl of the glass?

Only when the basic tones and colours are correct should you add small touches of highlight to give the glass sparkle. Remember too that glass reflects the colours of surrounding objects – both dark and light tones. Paint only the brightest highlights with pure white, modifying the others with a hint of the local colour of each object reflected in the shiny surface.

◀**1** Lightly draw the bottles, the ribbon and the main folds in the cloth with charcoal, dusting off the excess with a rag so that it doesn't sully the paint.

Mix a thin wash of cadmium yellow knocked back with some cobalt blue, and go over the charcoal lines with the tip of the No. 5 flat brush.

◀**The set-up** These two elegant perfume bottles make an ideal subject for the study of reflections in glass. The lavender water they contain links them with the pink and green backcloth and adds further interest to the reflections. The sweep of green satin ribbon not only provides a link between the two bottles, but its soft highlights also contrast interestingly with the sharper, brighter highlights in the glass.

Tip

Keep it simple
If you include glass objects in your still life, as in this demonstration, try not to have too much overhead light, which causes a confusion of shadows, reflections and highlights. Choose, instead, a strong sidelight, which emphasises three-dimensional form while creating relatively simple shadows and highlights.

YOU WILL NEED

☐ A 30.5 x 40.5cm stretched canvas or canvas board

☐ Three brushes: a No. 1 and a No. 5 flat and a No. 3 round

☐ Easel

☐ Charcoal stick and a clean rag

☐ Nine acrylic colours: titanium white, cadmium yellow, permanent magenta, alizarin crimson, cobalt blue, cerulean, chromium oxide green, permanent green light and Mars black

▶ **2** Use the same brush to block in the dark areas of the background in a mix of chromium oxide green and cobalt blue, adding cadmium yellow for the lighter parts. Assess the tones in the green ribbon, then use chromium oxide green/cerulean to block in the dark areas on it with the Nos. 1 and 5 brushes.

◀ **3** Mix cerulean, titanium white and a little chromium oxide green and block in the lighter parts of the ribbon.

Suggest the pattern of leaves on the cloth using the background green, softened with titanium white or cadmium yellow. Don't go into too much detail – concentrate on how the greens change in tone, becoming lighter or darker as the pattern follows the contours of the cloth.

Tip

Weave your colour
As you paint, think of yourself as a weaver, twining threads of colour through your picture. Repeating touches of similar colour from one area to another all over the picture encourages the eye to explore the composition, while at the same time giving it harmony and unity.

▶ **4** Mix permanent magenta and a little white and use the No. 5 flat brush to start painting the lavender water in the large bottle. Add a drop of cerulean to the mix where the tone is slightly darker on the right of the bottle.

Assess the composition in terms of broad areas of colour at first – once these are blocked in you can break them down with shadows and highlights.

5 The hue of the lavender water reflected in the glass appears cooler. Paint broad tonal areas in blocks – magenta/white for mid tones, magenta/cerulean for dark. For the dark patch at the back use cobalt blue/magenta/chromium oxide green. Use magenta/white for the water in the other bottle, adding cerulean for the darker surface and cobalt blue for the violet tones.

6 Before adding any further detail to the reflections, establish the pink flower pattern on the backcloth, using the No. 5 flat brush. Again, don't worry about detail at this stage – get the main shapes right, so the pattern follows the curves and folds in the cloth. The basic mix is alizarin crimson and white, darkened with a little magenta and cerulean for the areas in shadow, plus touches of cadmium yellow.

7 Paint the large rose near the top of the backcloth with curved strokes of the fairly dry No. 5 flat brush, using a partially blended mix of magenta and alizarin crimson, broken with white for the light parts.

8 Now paint the cork stopper on the larger bottle with the No. 3 brush. The basic mix is cadmium yellow, alizarin crimson and a touch of cobalt blue – a warm brown. Add more blue for the shadows. So the stopper isn't too dominant, add touches of cadmium yellow, broken with hints of alizarin crimson and cobalt blue among the flowers on the backcloth (see Tip, opposite).

9 Block in the darks and mid tones on the silver stopper of the small bottle with mixes of chromium oxide green, Mars black and cobalt blue. Use the No. 1 brush to enrich the colour of the ribbon with thicker paint. Apply chromium oxide green/cerulean, with more blue where the ribbon turns into shadow. For the cool highlights, add permanent green light and a touch of white; for the warm reflections, add cadmium yellow. Blend the edges where the light and dark tones meet to suggest the soft sheen of satin.

10 Now polish up the finer details of pattern and texture. Finish the green velvet backdrop, using the No. 5 flat brush and a warm green mixed from cadmium yellow and chromium oxide green, overlaid with drybrush strokes of cerulean and cobalt blue to enliven the shadows. Loosely brush in some pure white between the flowers on the fabric. Then mix a soft grey from cobalt blue, white and a touch of Mars black and put in the fabric's shadows and its folds and creases.

11 Introduce some dark reflections to the lavender water in the large bottle with the No. 5 brush. The corners of the bottle reflect the green velvet drapery: put this in with cobalt blue/magenta/ chromium oxide green. For the warm reddish reflections in the glass above the water use white/magenta.

For the brightest highlights use the No. 1 brush to skim pure white over the wet surface so it blends with the undercolour in places. Add a soft highlight on the cork stopper, blending it gently.

In the finished picture you will see how the glass bottles have been treated quite simply with broad strokes and blocks of colour. The key is to assess the tones correctly, then apply the colours decisively.

THE PATTERNS OF NATURE

The patterns and symmetries observable in nature can make the subject of highly decorative yet realistic paintings.

The natural world is full of patterns – everything from a snowflake to a tree has some regularity of structure. Though in day-to-day life we take such symmetries for granted, artists are constantly on the lookout for that element of design which runs through or governs a subject. Repeated symmetrical shapes not only help to organise the composition, they are pleasing to the eye on their own account.

Some painters, indeed, take the process a step further, seeking to make pattern itself the focus of their work. Using the natural subject (whether still life, landscape or animal) as a reference, they exaggerate its decorative, pattern-making aspects, giving these overwhelming prominence in the picture space. Two-thirds of our artist's painting of a peacock, for example, is devoted to the splendid colours, textures and shapes of its feathers. It's an inventive piece of cropping which deliberately focuses on the pattern inherent in the exotic plumage.

▲**The set-up** A good selection of reference photographs proved essential for this composition. Our artist combined the close-up of the head with the picture dominated by the bird's tail fan to create the best composition out of both images.

◀**1** Lay out the four base colours – titanium white, burnt umber, yellow ochre and ultramarine – on the paper palette. Use water and the decorators' brush to mix these colours roughly, making sure you retain some streaks of pure paint. Dip the sponge in the mixture and dab over the entire upper third of the board, creating a marbled cloud. This provides an interesting textured background for the main image, without distracting the eye with unnecessary detail.

YOU WILL NEED

- ☐ An A3 board primed for acrylics

- ☐ Paper palettes and a sponge

- ☐ Six brushes: a large decorators' brush, a No. 10 flat and Nos. 10, 6, 4 and 3 round hogs

- ☐ Seven acrylic colours: titanium white, yellow ochre, burnt umber, ultramarine blue, phthalo blue, phthalo green and burnt sienna

▶ **2** Load the No. 10 flat brush with the base mixture and start work on the underlying structure of the feathers. Stroke long arcs of paint radiating out from the base of the peacock's tail, set right of centre where the background colour meets the unpainted board. Try to use single strokes of the brush, turning the board on its side if necessary for ease and fluidity of movement.

◀ **3** Add more burnt umber and ultramarine blue to the base mixture to darken it. Load the No. 10 flat brush with paint and, with the board on its side, scrub in hoop-like lines across the lines painted in the previous step. Allow these sweeping strokes to fade out towards the right side of the composition to help give the impression of recession.

▲ Our artist's palettes – one for his base mixture, one for his green and blue glazes.

▶ **4** Load the No. 10 round brush with pure white as the base colour for the 'eyes' of the peacock feathers. Dab these in at intervals over the grid created in the previous steps. Remember that the lower section of the painting constitutes the foreground – so make sure the white blotches are large here and decrease in size as they get nearer to the head of the bird.

◄5 Load the No. 4 round brush with a mixture of ultramarine and burnt umber, and stroke in the downward-slanting, fishbone-like stems of the feathers. Allow these strokes to overlap, giving depth by suggesting feathers underneath.

Load the No. 6 round brush with ultramarine and thickly underscore each 'eye' on the feathers.

►6 Stand back from the picture, and let the paint dry for a few minutes. You have now put in the 'scaffolding' of the composition; the rest of the painting process largely involves building up the textures and colours of the plumage and, of course, painting in the body of the bird itself.

◄7 Load the No. 4 round brush with well-thinned white and stroke in the long quills of the feathers radiating from the back of the peacock. Make these marks slightly scrubby or fluffy, varying the pressure you exert on the brush as you paint.

Intensify the white on each 'eye' of the feathers, using pure, unthinned paint.

►8 Now begin to develop the detail on the feathers, constantly referring to the reference photographs. Load the No. 4 round brush with ultramarine, and paint in the blue rings at the centre of each peacock 'eye'. Vary the dilution of the paint, making those rings farthest away fainter than those closest to you. This helps to suggest depth.

▶ **9** Thin some yellow ochre with water. Load the No. 4 round brush with this and paint the rings around the blue centres of each 'eye'. Follow the process adopted in the previous step – that is, make sure some of the rings are fainter than others to imply that the feathers lie at varying depths in relation to the picture surface.

◀ **10** Darken the shadowy areas between the peacock plumes, using the No. 4 round brush and a strong mix of ultramarine and burnt umber.

If you stand back from the picture now, you can see how the patterning process (which concentrates on the design) goes hand-in-hand with the normal painterly process of creating an illusion of three-dimensional depth.

▶ **11** Draw the outline of the peacock's head with the No. 4 round brush loaded with ultramarine. Use pure ultramarine for the left of the bird's neck, and a mixture of ultramarine and burnt umber in the shadow under the head and on the right.

◀ **12** Now lay in the white patterns on the peacock's head, using the No. 4 round brush and pure titanium white. Touch in the beak, the spots on the top of the head and the lines around the bird's eye.

Scrub dilute white into the front portion of the neck, where the light strikes the iridescent feathers.

◄ **13** Continue to develop the feathers on the peacock's body, using the No. 4 round brush loaded with mixes based on ultramarine. Mottle the rear of the bird with white and ultramarine mixed with burnt umber. Outline and highlight the peacock's eye with pure white.

► **14** Use the No. 3 brush and pure titanium white to highlight the quills of the feathers running between the 'eyes'. Constantly vary the thickness and intensity of the lines. Use white to detail the 'eyes' themselves with strokes radiating from their centres. Leave the picture to dry.

Tip

Reference only
Reference photographs are there to help you create an original painting of your own – so don't feel you have to copy their cropping and composition slavishly. Our artist's use of photos for this demonstration is a good case in point; he reversed one image and adapted parts of another until he had found exactly the composition he wanted.

◄ **15** Concentrate now on capturing the iridescence of the feathers. Use the decorators' brush to lay a glaze of phthalo green over the whole plumage. Put a ring of light green near the circumference of each 'eye' and add further shadows with ultramarine/burnt umber.

► **16** Leave the picture to dry again so you can apply another glaze. Mix a turquoise from phthalo green and blue and, once again using the decorators' brush, lay a thin glaze over the entire plumage. Notice how the bird's plumage now seems to shimmer and glow.

▶ **17** Work on the markings of the 'eyes' a little more, using the No. 4 round and more green. Intensify the blue in the centres if necessary with pure ultramarine. Finally, use one of your finer round brushes to spread dilute phthalo blue over the tips of the peacock 'eyes'.

Tip

The real peacock
Inevitably, some of the resplendent colours of the peacock's feathers will look duller in photographs than in real life. To ensure that you capture the full richness of

these colours, try to find a real peacock feather which you can compare with the acrylics you apply as the painting progresses. Here, the painted feather is well able to withstand comparison with the real thing.

▼ **18** The painting is now finished. Note how the final glazes of green and blue add depth and brilliance to the feathers – the acrylic colours are perfect for capturing the deep sheen and jewel-like colours of the bird's exotic plumage.

The artist has made the viewer aware that the natural subject has both a decorative surface and a living depth. By closing in on the bird's plumage he emphasises its striking pattern, yet his painting techniques help to show recession.

A PLAY OF LIGHT AND DARK

To simplify apparently complicated subject matter, try ignoring superfluous detail and limiting yourself to a small selection of colours which tone well together.

The amazing amount of detail in a close-up study of a forest can be daunting. To depict this sort of subject in a realistic way – capturing every leaf on every tree – is a time-consuming and, some would say, thankless task.

The artist here made a deliberate decision to simplify his Australian forest scene by concentrating only on the features that struck him as most important. In particular, he was interested in the play of lights and darks. Note, for example, the striking horizontal highlights on the tree trunks and how well these work with the diagonal stretches of sunlight on the path. With simplification in mind, he also limited himself to seven colours, building up a series of glazes for a picture with depth and subtlety.

▼**1** Begin by covering your support with phthalo green using the 2.5cm decorator's brush. This gives a dark-toned ground from which the highlights will jump out. Our artist then transferred his initial pencil drawing on to the support using a sheet of yellow Transtrace, which shows up well on a toned ground.

◀ **The set-up** Working from a photograph – rather than from life – can be a distinct advantage when you want to simplify a painting. Photos cannot register all that the human eye can take in – lots of details, as here, are lost in deep shadows and burnt-out highlights. This can be a great help when you are trying to be selective, and don't want to over-complicate your painting.

Using this photograph, our artist made a pencil drawing of the forest on a sheet of cartridge paper, bringing out the separate trunks and branches and outlining the main highlights.

◀**2** Start the painting by plotting a few of the brightest highlights, using a mix of cadmium yellow and titanium white. Then turn to some of the darker vegetation, applying a glaze of phthalo green/raw sienna with the No. 3 brush.

YOU WILL NEED

☐ A 45 x 33cm piece of illustration board

☐ An acrylic palette

☐ An HB pencil and sheet of cartridge paper

☐ A sheet of yellow Transtrace – to transfer your drawing from paper to board

☐ Several jars of water

☐ Three brushes: a 2.5cm decorator's brush; Nos. 2 and 3 round

☐ Seven acrylic colours: titanium white, cadmium yellow, raw sienna, phthalo blue, phthalo green, burnt umber, Mars black

▶ **3** Carry on working up the lights, using both neat titanium white and your mix of cadmium yellow and titanium white. The neat titanium white marks may appear a little crude at this stage, but they will be modified by a number of glazes as the painting progresses.

◀ **4** For the patches of sky showing through the dense foliage at the top of the picture, apply a mix of phthalo blue and titanium white. This creates an opaque colour that stands out from the green.

▲ **5** Establish the path at the bottom of the picture with a thin glaze of raw sienna. Apply this over both the green ground and the highlights. Then scrub in some of the darker areas with a mix of burnt umber and Mars black.

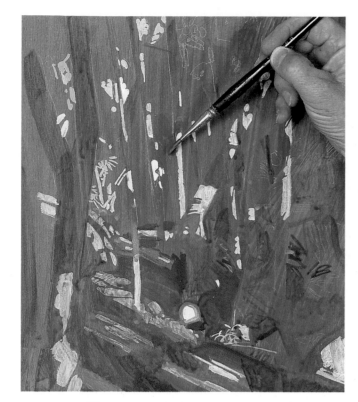

◄6 The green ground that still shows now looks too stark and needs to be modified with subtle glazes. Apply a mix of cadmium yellow/phthalo green with the No. 3 brush for the lighter vegetation. For the mid tones use glazes of phthalo green and phthalo blue.

►7 Now you need to re-emphasise the brightest highlights on the path with titanium white and traces of cadmium yellow and raw sienna. Don't view this merely as correcting mistakes, but as building up layers to give the painting depth and subtlety.

▼8 Now return to your phthalo blue/titanium white mix to continue building up the sky. Only small fragments of sky show through the dense network of branches and leaves, so work quite meticulously, applying small dabs of paint with the No. 2 brush. Gradually add more phthalo blue to your mix to achieve a deep colour suitable for the Australian sky.

▼9 The painting is now virtually complete. The murky depths of the forest have been rendered well, but as a final touch you need to put in some of the brightest highlights.

►10 Add more white to the titanium white/cadmium yellow mix and carefully overlay this on some of the highlights on the trees and path – especially those in the foreground. Set against the yellow base colour, the new paint will appear almost white.

►11 In the final picture, it is evident how carefully the artist has thought out the composition. Note how the diagonal shafts of sunlight encourage the viewer's eye to travel up the path towards the sky. The sky itself occupies a triangle at the top left of the painting that echoes the triangular shape of the path at the bottom of the picture.

The painting's success, of course, also relies on the startling highlights. The yellows used for these are not particularly hot or deep, but they are warm enough and light enough to jump out from the cool, dark background.

WORKING WITH ONLY ONE BRUSH

Choosing to paint your whole picture with just one brush might seem at best restricting, at worst perverse. But it is a discipline that can actually free up your painting style.

For many artists, the essence of painting is to observe carefully and render faithfully. Others find it more challenging to interpret the world and produce an original and personal view. For many who want to take the latter path, often the problem is how to put your distinctive stamp on your paintings.

One way is to limit your equipment. You may, for instance, want to reduce the colours you use – Paul Gauguin's Tahitian paintings, even if you ignored the subject, would be recognisable from the palette alone. Alternatively, you may want to limit your brushes – the later work of Post-Impressionist Paul Signac is readily identifiable from the uniform brushstrokes.

In this demonstration, our artist chose to restrict herself to one large brush – a No. 10. This

liberated her painting style, forcing her to work in bold, confident strokes. Prevented from meticulously registering detail, she was able to concentrate on the overall effects of shape, colour and tone. The expressive possibilities of the brushstroke became as important as the subject it described.

Every time our artist felt she was tightening up, she would step back, review the painting and attempt to work backwards. Strong lines were softened by lightly brushing colour back and forth over them. Dabs of unmixed colour – cadmium red, yellow ochre and titanium white – were applied to add to the vibrancy of the picture. These colours are neither entirely arbitrary, nor entirely naturalistic – instead, they can be seen as an imaginative exaggeration of existing colour.

YOU WILL NEED

☐ A 66 x 44.5cm support (our artist used thick, primed card)

☐ An easel

☐ A No. 10 hog filbert brush

☐ A palette for acrylics

☐ Two jars of water

☐ Ten acrylic colours: titanium white, yellow ochre, cadmium red, ultramarine, Hooker's green, pale olive green, transparent brown, burnt sienna, raw umber and Payne's gray

The set-up The choice of a pub as subject matter seemed particularly appropriate for our artist's style of painting. The interior of a thriving pub – with low lighting, smoke-filled air and customers constantly moving – seems to demand a loose, imprecise rendition.

The artist used photos and sketches as reference material.

▲ The artist's palettes, showing the generally muted colours she mixed for the demonstration here.

◀ **1** Start by establishing the tonal range of the painting. Lay in a base colour of cadmium red with touches of transparent brown and yellow ochre. Then broadly mark out the dark areas – the figures and the window frame – with raw umber and burnt sienna, and the highlights with a mix of yellow ochre and titanium white.

► **2** Continue to apply dry mixes of yellow ochre and white to build up the light tones, especially on the surface of the table, around the drinkers, and on the side of the window frame on the left. Use Payne's gray to describe the curved backs of the chairs.

At this early stage you can use unmixed colour in a rather playful way. Dab pure cadmium red near the chair backs and above on the window frame. Also apply small strokes of yellow ochre and then titanium white over the window on the right. As the painting progresses, some of these unmixed colours may appear a little too obtrusive, in which case they can be modified by glazing and scumbling other colours over them.

▲ **3** Continue working with unmixed colour, reinforcing the backs of the chairs with Payne's gray. Also use Payne's gray to beef up the figure on the right so that she is almost in silhouette. Apply more dabs of cadmium red around the chair backs.

► **4** Add more yellow ochre over the glass in the top right of the picture. Also use more Payne's gray to model the arm of the middle figure and to strengthen the shadow tones under the table.

Having established the warm, dark colours, it's time to give an impression of the cool exterior light. Start by scumbling a dry mix of Hooker's green, ultramarine and white over the window.

◄ **5** Continue to lighten the tone in the window with the blue/green mix and with unmixed titanium white. Note that the colours are applied lightly and unevenly so the underlying red still shows through. Apply a strong stroke of white adjacent to the window frame on the left.

▼ **6** Build up the shadow tone on the central figure's back with a mix of transparent brown and burnt sienna. Also use a mix of yellow ochre and white over the face of the figure on the left.

Scumble on a pale blue tint between the two figures to obtain a strong tonal contrast. Note how painting in the negative shape of the window light allows you to refine the figures' outlines. In keeping with the loose style of the picture, however, make sure you are not too precise.

◄ **7** Apply a dark mix of ultramarine with touches of Hooker's green, Payne's gray and white to continue to build up the shadows on the back of the central figure. Also use this mix to begin on the bottle on the table and to give the impression of the light from the window falling under the table.

▶ **8** Use yellow ochre to put in two tabletops in the bottom right corner – these help guide the eye into the centre of the picture. Paint two chairs next to them with Payne's gray, adding highlights with a mix of white and touches of your blue mix.

Note how the foreground is kept dark and not many forms are discernible so the eye is compelled to travel upwards into the scene.

◀9 Scumble a mix of pale olive green, ultramarine and white over the central figure's back. Note that the light skims across his right shoulder and arm, so leave this area yellow. Use a mix of yellow ochre, white and touches of cadmium red to put in the faces of the two figures on the left. For the central figure's hair, use transparent brown with touches of white, yellow ochre and cadmium red.

Continue working up the bottle with Hooker's green, adding white to render the neck. Add a small stripe of purple (made from cadmium red, ultramarine and Payne's gray) along the left edge of the bottle with the side of the brush. Also begin on the white wine glass by using a mix of yellow ochre with touches of cadmium red and white.

▶10 Now you are ready to put in the final details. Aim in particular to enliven the picture with eye-catching highlights. Use white and yellow ochre where the light skims across the chair backs. With the side of your brush, put in some small strokes of white on the wine glass. Also use white to strengthen the light in the window and the shafts of light falling behind the table. As a final touch, add a couple more glasses on the table with a mix of ultramarine and Payne's gray.

In the final painting, note how we are drawn towards the light, from the dark foreground to the table and the figures, and ultimately to the window. We not only contemplate the picture itself, but are encouraged to imagine the view that the drinkers see through the window.

—

CHAPTER NINE

WORKING WITH PASTELS

A GUIDE TO PASTELS

Choosing from the huge range of pastels available can be as confusing as a cryptic crossword! Our guide to pastels outlines the main varieties – and the differences between them.

When you try to learn more about the pastels available, it can seem as if the manufacturers are out to confuse you! You may be stumped immediately by the long list of names – soft pastels, hard pastels, chalk pastels, pastel chalks, Conté crayons, pastel pencils, pastel crayons and square pastels – and by what they all do.

To simplify matters for you, we've split up the wide range of pastels available into three groups – those that are either **round** or **square** in cross-section, and **pastel pencils**. We have chosen this classification because the different shapes are suited to particular ways of drawing, and so determine, to an extent, the way you use them.

Hard and soft

Another determining factor is that of hardness and softness. Pastels are made with powder pigment and a binder. The higher the binder content, the harder the pastel. Hard and soft pastels are different in the way they feel in use, and in the effects they create.

With soft pastels (like those used in most of the demonstrations shown in this section), the colour crumbles off smoothly and easily, covering the paper rapidly. It sinks into many of the tiny pits of toothy pastel paper, leaving a film of dust to blow away. With the same amount of pressure on a hard pastel, you'll find it has a slightly scratchy feel and covers the paper less readily. It catches the tooth of the paper, sinking less into the pits to leave a quite grainy effect.

Some manufacturers grade their pastels as hard, medium or soft. However, one manufacturer's 'hard' can be the same as another's 'medium', for instance, so it's best to try them out for yourself on the pads of paper provided in art shops.

Round pastels

These tend to be the softest, and are widely known as artists' soft pastels. Traditionally, they were made by the artists themselves. They come in different widths and range from soft to very

▲ Using just one coloured chalk with very careful handling, the artist has created a wide range of tones, producing a convincing three-dimensional image. Notice the contrast between the clear skin and textured hair.

'ROSALIND' BY E.R. HUGHES, RED CHALK ON BOARD, 9¾ X 7¾IN, COURTESY OF PETER NAHUM AT THE LEICESTER GALLERIES, LONDON crumbly. Their softness makes them less suited to linear work. You can use a sharpened tip for details, but it wears down quite quickly.

This type of pastel really comes into its own when used for broad areas of brilliant colour. You can work with the side of the pastel, laying wide bands of colour, or use shorter, broken bits in a similar way but on a smaller scale. Using the tip gives you more control when working details. The softness of the round variety makes them ideal for blending and smudging with your fingers or a soft cloth or torchon.

◀▼ The chalks used by Michelangelo and Leonardo da Vinci were the ancestors of the square pastel. The square shape makes for a versatile drawing tool – you can use the tip, the flat of the tip, the side or a side corner for a wide range of marks. Square pastels come in a range of bright colours, as well as some earth colours, black, white and several greys.

The clean-hand alternative to hard and soft pastels is the pastel pencil. Use pencils with other pastels to add detail, or by themselves for loose drawings and sketches.

Square pastels

Often known as chalks, chalk pastels or Conté crayons, these are generally, though not always, harder than round pastels. They feel chalkier and cover the paper less rapidly.

This variety of pastel is a traditional drawing tool. It's the modern-day equivalent of materials used by Leonardo da Vinci, Michelangelo and Raphael in their famous drawings. In fact, they are available in the same earth tones, evocatively named by one manufacturer as burnt sienna, burnt umber, bistre and sanguine. You can also buy them in black, grey, white and a variety of bright colours, including greens and blues.

These are excellent for drawings and sketches in line and tone, and are often used to add detail to soft pastel drawings. They can be sharpened to a fine point for line drawing, and you can hatch and smudge with them to create blended tones. The chalky pastel line is soft and expressive, with a powdery texture, velvety smooth finish and great intensity of colour.

Pastel pencils

These are, quite literally, pastels in pencil form. They tend to be harder than round pastels, making them good for complex line work, detail and shading. They are non-waxy and can be blended and softened with water. In use they have a slightly scratchy, chalky feel, very different from the smooth flowing feel of coloured pencils.

Pastel pencils have the intensity of colour associated with soft pastels and are a marvellously expressive medium. They're excellent for direct, bold sketches or for dense, detailed drawings with subtle nuances of tone rendered with careful shading and broken colour. They can be used with round or square pastels, but you'll find yourself in trouble if you try to combine them with coloured pencils. The waxy surface created by coloured pencils resists the pastel pencil, causing it to slip and slide.

Papers

Traditional pastel paper, available from art shops, is a soft, fibrous paper that helps the adhesion of the pigment. It comes in different colours and grades. The fine grade is for line work; the coarser grade for broad, free strokes. The coloured sheets provide a good toned ground, rather like using a preliminary colour wash in painting. Your colour choice should enhance the subject of the picture.

You can also buy some specialist papers with coatings to add different textures. Marble dust and velour paper are two examples. (For more on pastel papers, see page 264.)

Storing and sharpening

Pastel pencils are easy to store – just tie them up with an elastic band and place them point up in a jam jar. Round and square pastels are a bit more of a problem. Storing them together in a tin, for example, is a bad idea, since dust comes off the pastels quite easily, which can cause the colours to contaminate each other. The best way to store them is

according to colour. Keep your greens and blues separate from your reds and oranges, and so on. Store them in a shallow plastic box or wooden tray filled with dry rice. Any pastel dust comes off on the rice, rather than on the other pastels.

With all varieties of pastel, it's a good idea to avoid pencil sharpeners for sharpening, since they tend to blunt the blade. Use sandpaper (glasspaper) or a craft knife.

▼Artists' soft pastels – round in shape – can't be beaten in terms of colour intensity. The crumbly colour is almost pure pigment. With so many different ranges, sizes and tempting colours to choose from, you may find you spend a lot more money than you bargained for. Try them out first, since they vary in softness.

Portrait in sanguine pencil

▲ **The set-up** The artist asked the model to shift her position until he found a pose he liked – a three-quarter view, with her head tilted. It's worth spending time finding a pose you find interesting.

In this demonstration our artist used just one classic pastel colour – sanguine – with a touch of white for subtle highlights. He picked a warm beige paper – again a traditional choice for this type of drawing.

▲ **1** Use the sanguine pastel pencil to establish the basic inverted triangle of the face – measure from the side of each eye to the chin. Use light marks at first so you're not committed to them. Re-check your proportions until you're sure they're correct, then sketch in the main outlines of the face. Focus on the eyes, blocking in the lights and darks.

▲ **2** Work up the eye and eyebrow to your left, then soften the marks around the eye to your right by smudging them with your finger. Apply loose lines to block in areas of dark tone on the face – on the turn of the cheek and under the nose, lower lip and chin. Use widely spaced but regular lines to indicate the dark tones on the forehead.

▶ **3** Soften the areas of dark tone around the face by blending the lines with your finger. Pastel pencils are fairly soft and powdery – excellent for smudging and blending.

▶ **4** Sketch in the hair. This is a very distinctive feature so try and avoid the temptation to treat it as a flat, superficial pattern. Notice how, with just a few lines, the artist gives the hair a sense of shape and volume.

◄ 5 Work on the face as you did before, smudging lines for areas of tone to make it look three-dimensional. Once you're satisfied with the face, start to add detail to the hair. Use less or more pressure on the pastel pencil to make light and dark lines which follow the form of the hair. These tones, especially the dark ones, help to give the hair volume.

YOU WILL NEED

☐ An A3 sheet of warm beige Artemedia art & pastel paper

☐ Conté à Paris sanguine drawing pencil

☐ White square pastel

▼ 6 Add more dark tones to the face to build up its rounded quality, then, using your white square pastel, put on a few subtle highlights where the light catches the model's forehead, nose and eye.

Lightly sketch in the model's shoulder and T-shirt, smudging in a few tones where appropriate. Don't work up this area too much, so the emphasis remains on the face.

► 7 This traditional monochrome approach creates a charming result in the final drawing. The sanguine line has a natural and seductive appeal, with the few touches of white highlight finishing it off wonderfully.

Study of hands

YOU WILL NEED

☐ An A3 sheet of taupe Artemedia art & pastel paper

☐ One umber (32) Conté pastel pencil

☐ White square pastel

▶**1** Draw the broad outlines of the two hands lightly with the umber pencil, seeing them as a single form. Measure and re-check all the time between one point and another.

▲**2** Begin to suggest details such as the fingernails, the ring and the lines on the hands. Screw up your eyes so you can see the planes of light and dark on your subject. Then scribble on the dark tones and smudge them with your finger. As the drawing progresses you can use darker, more emphatic lines.

▲**3** Continue to work up the details on the hands, using the white square pastel to add highlights.

▶**4** Hands are amazingly complex subjects and many people find them difficult to draw. The trick is never to make assumptions about what you're looking at, but draw only what you see, starting by simplifying the forms.

The choice of materials here is perfect for the subject. The simplicity of the umber line and white highlights complement the familiar subject. This is an excellent choice of drawing tools for the beginner, since they force you to concentrate on the broad forms.

SOFT PASTELS, PURE COLOUR

Artists' pastels provide colour in its most intense form, and in a range from soft, powdery pinks to deep velvety purples.

▼ The great attraction of pastels is the freshness and immediacy of their colours – evidence that they are almost pure pigment. Beautifully blended colours give soft flesh tones, complex webs of textured colour bring the background alive, while fine linear strokes depict folds in the clothing of mother and child.

'MATERNAL KISS' BY MARY CASSATT, 1896, PASTEL ON PAPER, 22 X 18¼IN PHILADELPHIA ART GALLERY, BEQUEST OF ANNE HINCHMAN

► Almost every imaginable colour is available in pastels – this is because you can't mix different colours with each other as you do with water-colour and oil paints.

These are artists' pastels, which are very much more expensive than the students' range, but you can buy them one at a time and build up your collection gradually.

▼ For the beginner a box of 24 pastel sticks provides plenty of scope.

Pastels are pigment powders bound together in stick form with gum or resin. Soft pastels are made with relatively little binder, which is why they have a light, crumbly texture – and why the colours are so pure.

As a sketching and drawing medium, pastels are extremely versatile. By using the broad end of the stick, you can create a wide line of coarse crumbly texture. Or you can work with the edge of the stick to make a mark as fine and delicate as one drawn with a pencil. You can even draw a line of thicks and thins by varying the pressure, or by turning and chang-ing the angle of the pastel stick as you draw.

Soft pastels are available in a vast range of colours and tones, and large expanses present no problem – with the stick laid on its side, you can rapidly fill them in with layer upon layer of rich velvety colour.

Colour mixing

With pastels, the manufacturer does the mix-ing for you, which is why they come in such a wide range of colours and tones. One manu-facturer makes 60 basic colours, with three to ten darker and paler versions of each one.

Such a choice can be bewildering and is cer-tainly personal. Some artists use an enormous selection of colours and tones, while others are happy with a limited choice.

The basic kit

One of the great advantages of pastels is that you don't need a lot of equipment. Your basic requirements are the pastels themselves and a sheet of paper.

You do need a drawing board or other rigid support for your paper. Whether you also use an easel or not depends on whether you prefer to work horizontally or vertically. Easels have one main plus point – pastels create a lot of dust which can fall straight to the ground when the drawing is worked on vertically.

One final thing you need is fixative, avail-able from art shops. This fixes pastel to paper and does away with the risk of smudging. Don't overuse as it can darken the picture.

Pastel paper

Pastels are a dry medium, so the paper surface must be textured enough to hold the pigment particles in place. Pastel papers have a surface with a definite key ('tooth'), which is designed to capture and hold the tiny particles of colour. These papers allow you to build up sev-eral layers of pastel to a dense, matt finish.

White chrysanthemums in a vase

This picture demonstrates neatly that you don't need a vast repertoire of pastel drawing techniques to create an attractive result. The image is made up of a few basic marks, which are well worth practising before you start.

Setting up

To carry out this project, you can either copy our bunch of flowers or set up a subject of your own at home. Our artist chose a glass vase to draw because of the way the light reflects on it, creating interesting patterns. But if you want to make life easier for yourself, you could use an opaque vase. (This means you don't have to worry about drawing in the bottom of the flower stems.) Make sure your still life is well lit. And check that you can see it properly. You also need enough light to work in.

The colour of the paper should contribute something to the final image. The artist here went for green, which holds the whole picture together behind the foliage and flowers. A white background would look too stark.

Before you start drawing, stand well back from the vase. Half-close your eyes and look for its overall shape and form. Look out for the lights and darks, too. Now come in a bit closer. Have your pastels to hand and look for the colours for the petals, leaves and so on.

Pin the paper to the drawing board. It's now worth spending a few moments working out where you're going to position the image in the paper area. You don't want the vase slipping off the bottom of the page, for instance. If it makes you feel more comfortable, draw in an outline with charcoal or Conté crayon.

Once you start, keep studying the flowers intently. Try not to concentrate too much on individual areas, though. Instead look at how the whole picture is building up.

YOU WILL NEED

☐ 75 x 55cm mid green pastel paper

☐ Box of 24 pastels including white, lemon, lizard green, olive green, pale cool grey, Hooker's green, green grey, yellow green, dark cool grey, burnt umber, yellow ochre

☐ Spray fixative

▲ **The set-up**

◀**1** Draw circles for the flower centres with white pastel. Follow with some simple petal outlines, then fill them in loosely. If you're working on a horizontal surface, blow away any excess dust.

(To avoid smudging your drawing, roll up your sleeves before starting and try not to rest your hand on the paper.)

▲ **2** Continue drawing petal shapes and filling them in until you've completed the first flower. There's no need to make every petal exactly the same size and shape.

THE FIVE BASIC MARKS USED IN THIS PROJECT

1   2   3   4   5

These are the basic pastel marks used in the picture of chrysanthemums. Bear in mind that new pastels have flat round ends, but these soon wear down with use to a blunt shape.

1 Hold pastel at an angle and scribble, using edge of end
2 Hold vertically and draw straight line with blunt end
3 Hold a new pastel at an angle and draw a straight line using the edge of the end
4 Scribble tightly, using the edge of the end
5 Take wrapper off and draw with side

▲**3** Draw in some more flowerheads, but don't feel you need to reproduce every single one exactly – remember you're not doing a botanical drawing. Quick marks can often trigger the whole image and be effective and lively.

▶**4** When you've drawn in all the flowerheads, spray the picture with fixative, following the maker's recommendations.

▲**5** Look closely at the centre of the chrysanthemums for lights and darks. Now go across the drawing, putting them in with blobs of lemon yellow and cadmium yellow.

Add a blob of lizard green at the very heart of each flower. Notice how the drawing now feels as if it's coming together, with the green paper playing its part.

▶**6** Stand well back and half-close your eyes. Look for lights and darks in among the stems and leaves. Then, using olive green, roughly draw in some of the leaves and stems and part of the vase. Start to fill in the darker background shapes between the leaves with the olive green.

◀ **7** Continue drawing in all the lighter parts of the glass vase using a pale cool grey.

▼ **8** With Hooker's green, draw in some patches of the green stems and leaves in the vase.

▶ **9** Still using Hooker's green, indicate some of the chrysanthemum leaves (but don't try to put in every one!). Now continue the background around the stems with green grey.

◀ **10** Add emphasis to the stems with yellow green. Put in some of the darker patches of water with a dark cool grey. Now use the green-grey to continue the background among the petals.

With burnt umber, add darker touches to the background showing through the vase. Then using the same pastel on its side, lightly put in all the background above the table top, carefully filling in among all the outside petals. Move the pastel in different directions to build up a web of colour with varying lights and darks. Don't worry about the texture of the paper showing through – this all adds to the effect.

▶ **11** Block in the table top with yellow ochre. Again use the side of the pastel, but this time apply more pressure so you end up with solid colour.

▲ **12** To represent the grain of the wood, draw in a few lines with burnt umber. Finish off the bottom of the vase by adding white highlights and green-grey shadows.

▲ **13** Spray the finished picture with fixative, following the manufacturer's instructions.

IMPACT WITH PASTELS

Pastels are not only suitable for delicate subjects – they can achieve as bold and striking an effect as any other medium. Choosing a suitable support and being adventurous with your choice of colours is all you need to bring life to your work.

The type of paper you decide to use with pastels can make a huge difference to the impact of the finished picture. With fairly smooth paper the pastel colour simply slides off, but with the toothed papers designed specially for pastel drawings, you can build up rich layers of colour. For this exercise, our artist chose a Frisk pastel board (formerly known as Rembrandt paper) which has a lovely velvety, toothed surface, which feels rather like very fine-grade sandpaper. These papers are available in 14 subtle colours – choose one which will enhance the tones of your subject.

Using black

Some artists feel that the use of black in a painting is taboo. It doesn't exist in nature, it can dirty your colours and it is easy to misuse, so many artists suggest that beginners avoid it. However, when well used its effect can be stunning. In this example our artist used plenty of black pastel: the yellow centres of the pansies really twinkle out of the velvety rich blacks and luscious blues. You might like to try using black pastels in your drawing too, but bear in mind that it is a strong colour, so be careful not to overdo it.

▶ The high-tooth surface of Frisk pastel board was developed specially for use with soft pastels. It comes in four sizes: 65 x 50cm (full), 50 x 32.5cm (half), 32.5 x 25cm (quarter) and 40 x 30cm (art). Here are just a few of the 14 Frisk colours available (from top to bottom): yellow ochre, raw sienna, light oxide red, permanent red deep, gold ochre, caput mortem red, green grey and raw umber.

▶ You can build up very strong layers of colour on the high tooth provided by specialist pastel papers. This, added to the fact that pastels provide some of the purest pigments available, goes some way to explaining how this artist has managed to build up such a wonderfully vibrant image, with all the richness and sheen of velvet.

'POINSETTIAS IN BLUE POT' BY MAUREEN JORDAN, PASTELS ON GREEN PAPER, 16 X 13IN

Terracotta pot of pansies

◀ **The set-up** Our artist worked directly from life, but then rearranged some of the flowers and invented a different setting to suit the composition she wanted. She decided to set the pots by the edge of a pond to add depth and provide a range of textures for the picture.

▶ **1** Using scarlet, St Michael green, light green and ultramarine hard pastels, lightly position the flowers, leaves and pots. Alter the composition to suit your taste, but take care not to overwork the pastels or to apply too much pressure at this stage, since Frisk paper can only take so much pastel before it clogs.

▼ Our artist used a selection of pastels from different ranges. For ease, we've listed Rembrandt equivalents, but just use whatever pastels you already have.

◀ **2** Use the black pastel to draw in the dark area of the pond behind the pots. This acts as a base into which you can blend other colours later, so continue to use light pressure to avoid clogging. Make quick, scratchy marks to feel your way into the drawing.

◄ 3 Start building up the picture loosely, indicating the approximate colours of each area so you can see how they work together. The shape of the pastels encourages boldness and freedom of expression.

With bold, loose strokes, draw over the foreground with the side of the deep yellow pastel. Use orange 3 and Saturn red on the pots and ultramarine deep 5 on the pansies.

▼ 4 Loosely build up the foliage – use chrome green deep 3, chrome green light 3, permanent green light 3, phthalo blue 3 and 5 and black for the foliage on the right. Now use the same combination on the left, but this time replace the black with olive green.

Vary the texture of the marks you make by using lines as well as blocks of colour. Scribble marks with quick, almost nervy, movements of your hand to indicate the tangle of foliage.

◄ 5 Use smudges of black for the centre of the pansies and cobalt blue ultramarine 5 and 7 to block in the petals of the pansies at the front. Use ultramarine deep 3 and 5 to draw the pansies in the middle and back. Gradually build up the picture, keeping an eye on the overall effect.

Use just a little colour on the pots – the Frisk paper provides most of the colour. Add flashes of red-violet light 5 among the flowers for added colour.

◄ 6 At this stage you should have the general shape and colours of the complete picture more or less blocked in. Now work on the darks, and leave the highlights until last.

A few pansies at the back can be really rich and dark. Develop them with dark colours to make them recede – black, blue-violet and Prussian blue.

With permanent green deep, add some marks to indicate the mould on the sides of the pots. Put some blue into the shadows beside the pots to show reflected colour and to enliven the area.

Tip

▶ **7** Now work back into the foliage, filling in to cover up the colour of the support. If you don't eliminate the little spaces between the leaves, you'll get a dotty effect which will distract from the flowers. Use several greens to build up the foliage, including the hard pastels to achieve a variety of textures.

▼ **8** Now more of the pansies should be starting to emerge from the foliage. Keep the foliage on the left quite light, with more of the background showing through than in the darker areas. Keep your marks quite scribbly to suggest leaves. A range of dark, medium and light greens and some burnt sienna 3 suggest the dappled light.

▶ **9** Using the side of the pastel sticks, deepen the shadow of the pots on the right with more black and phthalo blue 5. Use horizontal strokes to indicate the flatness of the stone. Mix some dark greens and raw umber 5 into this shadow to make a good, rich colour.

Now add some raw umber 5 and olive green 3 to the shadows behind the pansies. Blend these colours together with the tip of your finger for a soft-focus effect. Use a scrubbing motion and apply very little pressure. This makes a slightly different texture which contrasts with the smooth, dappled shadows and lively pansies.

◄**10** When you are satisfied that the blues, blacks and blue-violets of the pansies are all in place, use the light yellow to dot in the centres of the flowers. Don't worry about getting the dot exactly in the middle – it looks more natural if it is slightly off-centre.

►**11** Use the light green hard pastel to work on the grasses in the foreground. These help to enliven an otherwise plain area and bring it forward. Now use St Michael green hard pastel to add depth. The harder pastels produce a sharp edge which is ideal for the fine grasses.

◄**12** Assess the picture and fill in any areas of the pansies that need strengthening. Look at the shadows and foliage, and use your ultramarine deep pastels to broaden the tonal range of the work. Now add two touches of pure white over the yellow dot on each pansy as a highlight.

Notice how the flashes of red-violet light 5 and black help to bring out the rich blues of the flowers.

▶ **13** Add highlights to a few pansies at the front with cobalt blue ultramarine 7. Until now you should have been using fairly light pressure, but now apply more pressure in small areas, leaving a thick coating of pastel on the pansy petals to create rich colour.

▼ **14** Add more reds, browns, greens and yellows to the pots and paving. Make any other final adjustments and then fix your picture with a spray fixative.

The final picture demonstrates dramatically how dark colours can strengthen a composition and help to enhance the brighter colours by contrast.

Soft Pastels: Optical Mixing

Soft pastels are perfect for optical mixing. They're chunky and crumbly, allowing for speedy progress, with bright, brilliant colours that complement the vibrant effects of this technique.

In optical colour mixing, instead of blending together two colours to make a third, you place small flecks or dots of two or three colours close together. From a certain distance they blend optically (in the eye) to create the effect of a third colour. Being made of many individual marks, the hue you achieve has great vigour and energy.

You can create an infinite variety of colour combinations like this. To make orange you use dabs of red and yellow. More yellow lightens it, more red darkens it. Introducing a different red or yellow dramatically adjusts the shade of orange. And you can modify it more by adding another colour, maybe brown, to knock it back.

How you space the marks on the support also controls the shade – the denser the marks, the darker the shade. And changing the size and nature of your pastel marks creates a sense of distance and perspective. Small strokes close together give a clear image with a sharp outline – useful for showing the focal point. Larger, looser strokes make a less defined shape – perfect for background areas, which should recede.

Paper colour is vital with optical mixing, since some of it always shows through to affect the final drawing. White or light-toned paper lends an overall brightness; strong colours dominate the final image. Unless you're sure what you want the paper to do, stick to a mid tone.

Successful optical mixing depends on spacing colours well from the start. Think how many colours you'll use; as you lay in the first, leave enough room for those to come. If you run out of space you can overlay marks, but do this with care, or you'll lose the benefits of the tinted paper and your picture will be unbalanced.

YOU WILL NEED

☐ A3 sheet of cool grey Artemedia pastel paper

☐ Drawing board and pins

☐ Stick of brown Conté crayon

☐ Spray fixative

☐ Twenty-three soft pastels – our artist used Rowney Artist's Soft Pastels (for colours see pages 276 and 277)

◀ **The set-up** Our artist worked from a few sketches (see inset) of a hat and jacket abandoned on a chair on a warm sunny patio.

He chose to work on the less textured 'wrong' side of the paper to produce a smoother finish. Most pastel techniques involve building up colours over each other, for which you need the toothy side. But optical mixing requires no overlaying, so you have the choice of using both sides.

◀ **1** Lightly sketch the main outlines with your brown Conté crayon. Dot in the darkest tones on the jacket, hat and chair with indigo dark, adding flecks of indigo medium and crimson lake medium. Keep your marks small for the jacket, hat and chair for clearly defined edges. Use indigo dark for the deepest shadows on the pots and ground. Loosely indicate the trellis with Vandyke brown, leaving the edges fuzzy so it isn't dominant.

Your palette

Vandyke brown

Cadmium
orange medium

Cadmium
orange pale

Cadmium
tangerine

Naples yellow

Cadmium
yellow

Indigo dark

Indigo medium

Crimson lake
medium

Crimson lake
pale

Rose madder
pale

◀ **2** Now start on the foliage behind the trellis, using larger, looser flecks to help it recede. For this, use cadmium orange very pale, adding flecks of olive green dark, grass green, olive green medium, sap green and coeruleum blue. Keep the colours sparsely scattered, with patches of paper showing through.

▼ **3** It's important to stand back and take a good look at your progress from time to time so you get an overall view of your drawing. Think about the colours you intend to use so you can leave enough paper space for them.

Dot in the terracotta flower pots with Indian red, burnt umber pale and cadmium orange medium.

▼ **4** Use widely spaced blue-green flecks to add the light tone on the chair's back and legs, with indigo dark and Hooker's green for the darker shadows.

Apply cadmium orange very pale to the ground – use loose, horizontal strokes to give an impression of flatness.

Tightening up your marks, use cadmium orange pale and very pale for the hat. For deeper shadow tones, use Vandyke brown.

▶ **5** Indicate the geranium flowers by laying bold strokes of crimson lake medium, cadmium orange medium, rose madder pale and crimson lake pale side by side. Notice how these bright colours put a little more emphasis on the background, bringing out the colours of the foliage.

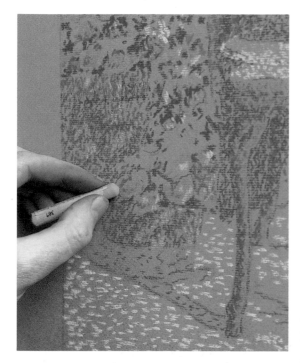

◀ **6** Put in the chair cushion with cadmium orange pale and dots of blue green and crimson lake pale, using Hooker's green to work into the initial indigo for the dark tone on the edge of the cushion.

The sunlight on the terracotta flower pots makes a much lighter area of tone – put this in with dabs of Naples yellow and cadmium orange medium. Work up the leaves of the potted geraniums with flecks of blue green, grass green, Indian red and crimson lake pale, using coeruleum blue for the light areas.

▶ **7** Develop the lighter tones of the jacket with indigo medium, cobalt blue, cerulean blue and blue grey. Lightly strengthen the trellis with loose strokes of burnt umber pale, adding dots of cadmium yellow to the background foliage to the left of the chair. Here, our artist corrected the position of the hat by softening the outline with flecks of cadmium orange pale.

Indian red

Cerulean blue

Cadmium orange very pale

Blue grey

Olive green dark

Olive green medium

Hooker's green

Cobalt blue

Blue green

Grass green

Sap green

Burnt umber pale

▶ **8** It's important to keep an overall sense of harmony by repeatedly stepping back and assessing your work as a whole.

The shadows cast by the chair and terracotta pots are an important element in this composition – develop these with cobalt blue and Hooker's green, with the occasional dab of rose madder pale and crimson lake pale. Our artist used gentle, feathery strokes of cerulean blue to soften the edges of the shadows and integrate them with the other colours on the ground (see inset below).

▶ **9** Notice how the cool grey paper is still clearly visible between the pastel marks. It acts as a unifying element, drawing together all the colours and shapes in the composition.

▲**10** Add touches of coeruleum blue to the pale areas on the chair legs so they stand out from the surroundings.

Strengthen the light tones on the ground with more horizontal flecks of cadmium orange very pale, then add touches of crimson lake pale and coeruleum blue to the ground. Since these colours are used all over the picture, they give an overall harmony.

Now make adjustments as necessary. Add touches of cadmium tangerine to the terracotta pots and define the shadows around the pots and leaves; indicate the pattern on the chair back; darken the bottom of the jacket, using indigo dark just below the chair seat and adding indigo medium and cobalt blue at the bottom of the jacket.

Spray the complete work with a light coating of fixative to stop it from smudging.

◀**11** Optical mixing is perfect for this subject. The many touches of colour add a shimmering quality to the surface, making it dance and vibrate. All the colours play together and unite to form the picture – quite similar to the way the eye sees things in life.

Hazy summer afternoon sunlight is successfully created by the fuzzy outlines and the many dots and dabs.

PASTEL DUST BACKGROUNDS

Save up those tiny pieces of pastel that break off your sticks as you draw – they are worth their weight in gold.

Soft pastels are so crumbly that small pieces often break off as you draw – and the pieces are invariably too small to grasp comfortably for drawing. But don't throw them away – crush them up with a mortar and pestle or a hammer, and use the pastel dust to create exciting, unusual backgrounds for your drawings.

Simply wet your sheet of paper and sprinkle the powder on it, then spread the pigment around with a wet paintbrush, finally blotting off excess water with a piece of kitchen towel. The colours settle unevenly to leave an irregular background, to which the different colours and visible brushstrokes give added zest.

You can create a background using any colours you like. Whether the effects you go for are bright and colourful or muted, two-tone or multi-coloured, the possibilities are virtually endless, and the results unique each time. Go for colours that complement those of your subject. This enhances the composition and makes the background an important element within the picture as a whole.

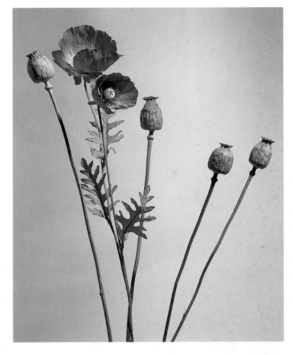

◀ **The set-up** These poppies make a pleasing subject, with the soft, bright silk petals contrasting texturally and tonally with the dried seed heads. Our artist chose a mixture of greens and greys, spiked with blue, red and yellow for her background – they contrast well with the simple yet attractive subject.

CREATING YOUR BACKGROUND

▲ Crush the pastel pieces using a mortar and pestle or a hammer. Don't grind them down too hard, since the small gritty bits tend to leave streaks which create some exciting effects.

▲ Lay your paper flat and apply acrylic matt medium solution in broad brushstrokes (this makes the picture more permanent). Tip the pastel dust on the wet paper and brush it over the surface.

▲ Colours dry a lot lighter than they look at this stage, but if you do find the colours too strong, blot off the excess pigment with kitchen paper. This technique creates a weathered look.

▲ Blot off more colour from areas which will fall behind the subject so you don't loose it in the background. Leave to dry. (Or try blocking out these areas with masking fluid before you start.)

YOU WILL NEED

- [ ] A 56 x 38cm sheet of stretched 296gsm Bockingford watercolour paper
- [ ] Mortar & pestle or hammer and wooden tray
- [ ] A solution of ½ teaspoon acrylic matt medium to ½ pint of water
- [ ] 5cm sable/synthetic flat brush
- [ ] Kitchen roll
- [ ] Easel
- [ ] Pastel pieces for crushing
- [ ] Spray fixative
- [ ] Six Conté pastels: beige light, burnt umber, chrome green medium and dark, carmine medium, purple dark
- [ ] Eleven Schminke or Rembrandt pastels: lemon yellow light, Naples yellow light, yellow ochre, chrome green light, sap green medium, grey light, white, mauve medium, alizarin medium and light, indigo dark (if you don't have these colours, try to match them with the ones you already have)

▶ 2 Now for the leaves. Use the flattened side of the tip of each pastel to block them in. Apply chrome green light for the lighter tones and chrome green medium for the mid tones. Work over the darkest lower leaves with chrome green dark.

▼ 3 Work up the dried seed head to the left. Run the tip of your burnt umber along the left of the stem over the existing line. Twist your stick to create an undulating line for distinct areas of light and shade. Use burnt umber for the seed head shadows – under it, on its left side and around the top. Then touch in a little colour on head and stem with mauve medium.

▶ 4 Switch your attention to the dried seed heads to the right. Work on them in the same way as before, drawing into the stems and heads with burnt umber. Use indigo dark to flick in the darkest areas on all three seed heads, merging the colours slightly with your finger to give them roundness. Return to the burnt umber to draw into the flower stems.

◀ 1 Outline the poppies on the prepared paper with beige light, and draw the frilly petals with carmine medium. Apply heavy pressure on a sharp edge of the stick for intense colour, rotating it as it wears down. Put in the centre of the lower flower with burnt umber.

Use the flat side of a small piece of Naples yellow light for the dried seed heads, and apply sweeping, continuous strokes for the stems. (Our artist drew the tallest dried poppy lightly at this stage, but didn't return to it until later.)

5 Use indigo dark to indicate the darker tones around the centre of the lower flower and the sepals (the leafy parts directly beneath the petals) of the higher one. Make jagged movements with alizarin light on the petals, dragging the colour into the darker outlines to give them a crumpled look. Add a little carmine medium to darken the pinks, then blend the colours together. Leave some background areas within the petals to work as a mid tone.

Our artist took advantage of the indigo on her finger to merge it with a touch of purple dark on the lower flower to create a bluish shadow.

6 A touch of alizarin medium beneath the centre of the lower flower gives depth. Add some white highlights to the same flower. Work around its centre with yellow ochre, and edge some petals on both flowers with purple dark. Touch in Naples yellow light to the pale areas of the upper flower to bring them out.

Now the flowers are almost complete. Stand back and look at the picture to judge the overall balance of harmony and tone.

7 Introduce light tones to the leaves and stems with lemon yellow light and sap green medium. Edge some leaves with chrome green medium and burnt umber, and use burnt umber to darken the flower stems too.

282

Tip

Dust buster
Clean air dusters, available
from photographic suppliers,
are an excellent way of

blowing pastel dust from your
drawings without the danger
of choking. The pressurised
container contains
compressed air which is
released from the steel
nozzle when you press down
on the trigger.

◀ **8** At this point, our artist
decided to feature the missing
dried seed head. She worked
over its remaining ghost image
subtly with lemon yellow light,
raising its position slightly at the
same time. Merge some grey
light into the yellow on the
darker side.

Add a lighter tone to both
seed head and stem with
Naples yellow light, blending it
with the side of your finger,
then work on the stem with
burnt umber as before.

▶ **9** Make the final
adjustments to your picture. Our
artist gave the background a few
streaks of beige light to add
more interest and to disguise the
positioning lines she began with.
Spray your drawing with a coat
of fixative.

In the finished painting, the
beautiful subjects emerge out of
an exciting, abstract
background. The background
textures and colours contrast
with the delicate petals and
complement the dried seed
heads, and provide an
entertaining backdrop to offset
the flowers.

Glossary

Abstract art Art in which the accurate or realistic depiction of objects is unimportant or entirely discarded. Abstract art is concerned with formal qualities, such as composition, line, and colour.

Acrylic paint Paint in which the pigment is bound with a synthetic, acrylic binding medium. Acrylic paints are diluted with water but, unlike watercolour, the paint film is insoluble once dry.

Advancing colours Colours that appear to be closer to the viewer. Warm colours and dark tones seem to advance while cool colours and pale tones appear to recede. These qualities can be exploited in aerial perspective.

Aerial perspective The use of colour, tone and texture to create an illusion of space in a painting. As objects recede towards the horizon they appear paler and bluer, and their edges become less defined. This is because they are viewed through a veil of atmospheric particles.

Alkyds Alkyds are fast-drying oil paints and mediums. The binder is a synthetic resin derived from a combination of alcohol and acid. Alkyd mediums can be used with oil paint to reduce its drying time.

Alla prima Direct painting in which the picture is completed in a single session.

Binder or **binding medium** A liquid medium that is combined with a pigment to form a paint. Linseed oil is the most common binding medium for oil paint, gum arabic is the binding medium for watercolour.

Bleed The effect achieved when a wash of watercolour, or other thin medium, runs into an area of wet colour. Creates a softly blurred and blended mix of colour.

Blending Merging adjacent colours so that the transition between the colours is imperceptible.

Blocking-in The first stage of a painting in which the main forms of the composition are laid down as approximate areas of colour and tone.

Body colour Describes pure transparent watercolour that has been rendered opaque by adding Chinese white to the mix. Sometimes also used to describe gouache.

Broken colour (1) A pure colour (primary or secondary) to which a third colour has been added. The result is a muted, greyed, or knocked back colour. (2) Paint applied as small dabs or dashes, or scumbles so that when viewed from a distance it creates an optical mix.

Chiaroscuro The use of light and dark in a painting or drawing. Applied especially to the work of painters, such as Rembrandt and Caravaggio, who used strong contrasts of light and dark.

Cold pressed Watercolour paper with a medium-textured surface achieved by pressing the paper between cold rollers in the manufacturing process.

Complementary colours Colours that are opposites on the colour wheel. The three primaries are complemented by a secondary: red by green; blue by orange; yellow by violet. The complementary pairs have a special relationship. When placed side by side they enhance each other, so that red appears redder alongside green than if it stands on its own. A colour can be knocked back by adding a touch of its complementary pair.

Composition The organisation of colour, tone, and form within a picture area.

Cool colours The cool colours are blue, violet, and green, with blue the coldest. Cool colours appear to recede.

Cross-hatching Tone created by layers of parallel, criss-crossing lines.

Dilutent A liquid, such as turpentine (oil paint) or water (watercolour or acrylic), which is used to dilute paint. It evaporates completely and does not become part of the final paint film.

Dry brush In this technique, a brush with very little paint on it is dragged across the support to create areas of broken colour or texture.

Earth colours Pigments derived from naturally occurring clays, rock or earths – the ochres and umbers, for example.

Ferrule The metal collar of a brush that secures the bristles to the handle.

Figurative art Art that depicts recognisable subjects, such as the human figure or landscape, in a realistic way.

Fixative A transparent liquid that is applied to works executed in mediums, such as pastel and charcoal, which do not have good adhering qualities. The fixative helps to attach the particles to the support and protects the fragile surface.

Flow improver A medium that is added to a paint to reduce surface tension so as to create even washes of colour.

Fugitive Pigments that fade on exposure to light.

Glazing The application of a thin, transparent film of colour over another colour.

Golden section A proportion that has been used by artists in composition for centuries. It is based on a division of a line so that the ratio between the shorter section and the longer section is the same as that between the longer section and the whole. This can be expressed as the 0.618:1 or approximately 5:8.

Gouache An opaque form of watercolour, sometimes described as body colour.

Graphite A type of carbon used in the manufacture of lead pencils.

Ground A substance applied to any support to isolate it from the paint film and to provide a pleasant surface on which to paint.

Gum arabic A watersoluble gum derived from a species of acacia tree. It is used as a binder in watercolour and gouache paint. It can also be added to watercolour to enhance colour and texture.

Hatching A system of parallel lines used to create tone.

H.P. (Hot Pressed) Watercolour paper that has a smooth surface created by pressing between hot rollers during the manufacturing process.

Hue The colour of a colour – its redness or blueness.

Impasto Paint applied thickly so that it retains the mark of the brush or knife.

Impressionism A movement that originated in France in the 1870s. Artists such as Monet, Renoir, and Pissarro were concerned with capturing the fleeting effects of light. They worked out of doors and used pure colour applied as unblended dabs and dashes.

Lean Oil paint that has very little or no added oil.

Linear perspective A method of creating the illusion of depth and three dimensions on a flat surface through the use of converging lines and vanishing points.

Local colour The actual colour of the surface of an object unmodified by light, shade, or distance.

Mahl stick A cane used to steady the arm when painting fine detail. One end is covered with a soft pad to prevent the tip from damaging the support.

Mask (1) Tape, paper, or fluid used to isolate an area of a painting while paint is applied. (2) A card frame that is used as an aid to composition. It can be dropped over a sketch to isolate a section so that the artist can decide which area to use and what format the final image should be.

Masking fluid A liquid rubber solution that is painted onto a support to protect that area from subsequent paint applications. It can be removed when the paint is dry.

Masking tape A low-tack tape that can be applied to a support to mask an area. Especially useful for creating crisp, straight lines. It can be peeled off when paint is dry.

Medium (1) The material used for a painting or drawing, such as watercolour, acrylic or pencil. (2) A substance that is added to paint to modify the way it behaves.

Mixed media A work executed in more than one medium.

Monochrome A drawing or painting made in a single colour.

Negative space The spaces between and around the main elements of a subject. Observation of the negative spaces can be a useful aid to accurate drawing – they are also an important aspect of composition.

NOT Another term for cold pressed watercolour paper applied because it has 'not' been hot pressed.

Optical colour mixing Creating new colours by placing separate patches of colour side by side on the canvas so that they blend in the eye of the observer.

Painting knife A knife with a thin, flexible steel blade available in a range of shapes and sizes, and a cranked handle. The knife is used to apply paint to the support.

Palette (1) A tray or dish in which paint is mixed. (2) A selection of colours.

Palette knife A knife with a straight steel blade used for mixing oil paint or acrylic on a palette.

Photorealism A painting style that imitates the detail and sharp definition of photography.

Picture plane The imaginary vertical plane that separates the viewer from the world of the picture. The picture plane is an important concept in linear perspective.

Pigment The colouring substance in paint. May be derived from natural materials, such as earths and minerals, or from synthetic sources.

Planes The flat surfaces of an object. These are revealed by light and can be seen in terms of light and dark or tone.

Plein air A French term meaning 'open air' used to describe pictures painted out of doors.

Primary colours Colours that cannot be created by mixing other colours. For painters the primaries are red, yellow and blue.

Priming Applying a ground to a support.

Resist A technique that involves two materials that do not mix. For example, if wax crayon or oil pastel is applied under watercolour, the crayon or pastel will 'resist' or repel the watercolour to create an interesting effect.

Retarder A medium that slows the drying time of paint. Most often used with acrylic paint that dries very fast.

Rough A watercolour paper with a noticeably textured surface. Handmade paper has a rough surface.

Scumbling An oil or acrylic painting technique in which a thin, broken layer of opaque paint is applied over an existing colour. The underlying paint shows through the top layer creating an optical colour mixing effect.

Secondary colours Colours created by mixing two primaries. Red and yellow gives orange; blue and yellow gives green; blue and red gives violet. Each secondary colour forms a complementary pair with a primary colour.

Size A gelatinous solution, such as rabbit skin glue, which was traditionally used to seal a canvas for oil painting.

Sketch A quick, spontaneous drawing.

Spattering A watercolour technique in which texture is created by flicking colour from a brush onto the support.

Stippling Dabbing the tip of the brush onto the support to create dots of colour. Stippling can also be created with a special stippling brush that has short, stiff bristles that have been cut to create a flat end. The brush is held upright and tapped onto the support to create a stipple effect.

Support Any surface used for painting or drawing.

Tertiary colours A range of intermediate colours created by mixing a primary colour with an equal quantity of one of the secondaries. For example, by mixing blue with green you can create a bluish-green and a greenish-blue.

Thumbnail sketch A small, simple sketch, generally used to explore aspects of composition, such as tone.

Tone The lightness or darkness of a colour.

Tooth The texture of a paper that affects its ability to hold the particles of a medium, such as pastel or charcoal. Very smooth paper has no tooth and is not suitable for work in pastel.

Underdrawing A preliminary drawing for a painting, executed on the support. Can be made in a drawing medium or in paint.

Underpainting The preliminary blocking-in of the main forms, colours, and tonal masses.

Vanishing point In linear perspective the point at which parallel lines appear to meet at the horizon.

Warm colours The warm colours are red, orange, and yellow, with red being the hottest. Warm colours appear to advance.

Wash In watercolour painting diluted colour applied thinly to the support to create a transparent film.

Watermark A design that is impressed into paper during the manufacturing process. It can be seen when the paper is held up to the light. The watermark helps identify the right side of the paper because the design is right-reading on the right side.

Wet in wet A watercolour technique that involves applying paint to a wet support to create soft edges and blended colours.

Wet on dry In watercolour, applying paint to a dry support, or over paint that has been allowed to dry. This technique creates crisp edges.

Index

Acknowledgments

Artists
1 Stan Smith, 2 Eaglemoss/Nigel
Robertson, 3 Maureen Jordan, 6 Madge
Bright, 7–8 Stan Smith, 9(t) Ian Howes, (b)
Ian Sidaway, 11(bc,bl) Terry Evans, (br)
Stan Smith, 12 Stan Smith, 13–16 John
Crawford-Fraser, 17–34 Stan Smith, 35–38
Lynette Hemmant, 39 William Coldstream/
Tate Gallery, 40–41 Stan Smith, 42 Tod
Ramos, 43 Caroline Mills, 45, 46(b) Donald
Hamilton-Fraser, 46(tr) Ian Sidaway, 47
Bridgeman Art Library/Baltimore Museum
of Art, Maryland, 48 Donald Hamilton-
Fraser, 49(t) Ian Sidaway, (b) Caroline Mills,
51 Artothek/Kunsthalle, Hamburg, 52(t)
Bridgeman Art Library, 53(r) Fred Cuming,
54 Whitford and Hughes/ Bridgeman Art
Library, 55 Sarah Spackman, 56 John Ward
CBE, 58(t,c) Stan Smith, (b) Tate Gallery,
61–62 Patricia Monahan, 63(t) Hulton-
Getty, (b) Minneapolis Society of Fine Arts,
Minnesota/Bridgeman Art Library, 64,65
Bridgeman Art Library, 66(t) Llewellyn
Alexander, (b) City Museum Art Gallery,
Stoke/Bridgeman Art Library, 67 Fred
Cuming/Brian Sinfield, 68 Bridgeman Art
Library, 69(t) Tom Coates/Geoff Fletcher,
(b) Bridgeman Art Library, 70(t) Whitney
Museum of American Art, (b) Paul
Neuland, 71(t) Linda Blackstone Gallery,
(b) Bridgeman Art Library, 72(t) Alison
Musker, (b) New Grafton Gallery, 73, 74
Albany Wiseman, 75 Tom Coates, 76(t)
Carolyn Piets, (b) Kate Simunek, 77(t)
Bridgeman Art Library, (b) Kate Simunek,
78(t) Graham Painter, (b) Bridgeman Art
Library, 79 The Image Bank, 80(t) Andy

Wood, (b) Bridgeman Art Library, 81(t)
Rosalie Bullock, (b) Bridgeman Art
Library/Bristol Museum and Art Gallery, 82
Five Women Artists Plus, 83 Ronald
Maddox, 84(t) City of Edinburgh Museum
and Art Galleries/ Bridgeman Art Library,
(b) Chris Beetles, London, 85(t,bl) Kate
Simunek, (br) Ruth Stage, 86(t,b) Kate
Simunek, (c) Godfrey Tonks, 87(l) Kate
Simunek, (tr) Bridgeman Art Library, (cr)
Greta Fenton, (b) Giraudon, 88(l) Kate
Simunek, (tr) Jacqueline Hines, (cr) Guy
Billings, (b) National Gallery, London,
89–91 Albany Wiseman, 92(t) Albany
Wiseman, (b) Artothek, 93–95 Albany
Wiseman, 96 Stan Smith, 97–99 Albany
Wiseman, 100 Bridgeman Art Library,
101–104 Dennis Gilbert, 105 Albany
Wiseman, 106 Stan Smith, 108–110 Albany
Wiseman, 111 Bridgeman Art Library, 112
John Harvey, 113–116 Ian Sidaway, 117–122
Stan Smith, 123–126 Albany Wiseman,
127(t) Malvina Cheek, (c,b) Stan Smith,
128–129 Susan Pontefract, 130 Humphrey
Bangham, 131 Albany Wiseman, 133 Albany
Wiseman, 134 Steve Shott, 136–138 Tig
Sutton, 139 Ian Sidaway, 140 Sarah
Donaldson, 141 Joe Ferenczy, 142–144
Pippa Howes, 148(t) Ian Sidaway, (b) Sarah
Cawkwell, 149 John Ward CBE, 150(t) Anne
Wright, (b) Sue Smith, 151(t) John Raynes,
(b) Gordon Bennett, 152(tl) Stan Smith,
(tr) John Tookey, (b) Dennis Gilbert, 153
Gillian Burrows, 154(t) Jennifer J. Tuffs, 155
Albany Wiseman, 156–158 John Raynes,
159 Louise Hill, 161 Albany Wiseman, 164
V&A Museum/Bridgeman Art Library,

165 Chris Beetles/Bridgeman Art Library,
166–168 Ian Sidaway, 169–174 Penelope
Anstice, 175 CCA Galleries, 176–180 Ronald
Maddox, 181 Roger Sampson, 182–188
Louise Hill, 190(b) Museo Picasso,
Barcelona/ Bridgeman Art Library, 191(t)
V&A Museum, (b) Carolyn Moran, 192
Duncan Campbell Fine Art, 193–198 Stan
Smith, 199 Stan Smith, 201 John McCombs,
202–204 Ian Sidaway, 206–207(t)
Bridgeman Art Library, 207(b)
Metropolitan Museum of Art, New York/
Bridgeman Art Library, 208 John McCombs,
209(t) Musée d'Orsay/Bridgeman Art
Library, (b) Bridgeman Art Library, 210
Bridgeman Art Library, (b) Ken Howard,
216(br) Ian Sidaway, 217 Rosemary Davies,
218–222 Stan Smith, 223–230 Madge Bright,
231 Debra Manifold, 233 Terry McKivragen,
237–240 Ted Gould, 241–246 Richard
Smith, 247–250 John Raynes, 251 Debra
Manifold, 255 Ian Sidaway, 256 Derek
Daniels, 257 Peter Nahum, 262 John
Raynes, 263 Philadelphia Museum of Art,
264 Jeremy Hopley, 265–268 Ian Sidaway,
269–274 Maureen Jordan, 275–278 Derek
Daniels, 279–282 Diana Constance.

Attributions to each fine art painting are as
supplied by the copyright holders.

Photographers
Julian Busselle, Michael Busselle, Mark
Gatehouse, Jeremy Hapley, Ian Howes,
Graham Rae, Nigel Robertson.

040-831-1